Strike Songs of the Depression

Strike Songs
of the Depression

by
Timothy P. Lynch

University Press of Mississippi
Jackson

www.upress.state.ms.us

Copyright © 2001 by University Press of Mississippi
All rights reserved
Manufactured in the United States of America

09 08 07 06 05 04 03 02 01   4 3 2 1
⊗
Library of Congress Cataloging-in-Publication Date
Lynch, Timothy P.
    Strike songs of the depression / Timothy P. Lynch.
       p. cm.—(American made music series)
    Includes bibliographical references and index.
    ISBN 1-57806-344-2 (cloth : alk. paper)
     1. Protest songs—United States—History and criticism. 2. Working class—United
States—Songs and music—History and criticism. 3. Depressions—1929—United
States—Songs and music—History and criticism. I. Title. II. Series.

ML3780 .L96 2001
782.42'1593'0973—dc21   00-053403

British Library Cataloging-in-Publication Data available

To Peg and Abby

Contents

Preface

Folklorist and labor historian Archie Green once wrote: "Ultimately, we read history books as a guide to our future rather than a map of past terrain." There is much wisdom in his words. Without historical understanding, we suffer from a kind of social and cultural amnesia, not knowing the relationship of the past to the present, making our steps into the future even more uncertain than they might otherwise be.

But what this story of striking millhands, miners, and autoworkers means to the labor movement today is difficult to say. Amid the contemporary world of work fashioned by globalization, deindustrialization, and corporate restructuring, the struggles of workers during the Depression appear remote. More and more, workers are "on the job" while being "on line," as the computer keyboard and mouse become the new tools for millions of workers in a technologically driven economy. This seems far removed from the thrashing of looms, clang of the tipple, and din of the assembly line that characterized the workplace for those I write about.

Yet other realities of working people today tie them to workers who toiled during the Depression. As the United States begins the new millennium, less than 15 percent of the nonagricultural workforce are union members, the approximate level of the early 1930s before workers enjoyed collective bargaining rights. Many workers today find that they must work longer hours in order to make ends meet, just as workers did during the Depression. Moreover, the rift between the rich and the poor continues to widen, much as it had during the 1930s.

To what degree song can promote economic justice today is hard to guess. But I am encouraged by the words of the irrepressible Pete Seeger, who in an interview published in 1998 in *WorkingUSA* said: "I look forward to a whole new generation of people . . . who are going to show us that songs can sometimes do what speeches cannot do." I hope he is right.

My interest in the Great Depression and the labor movement was first kindled by my parents' experiences. Born during the first part of the twentieth century, they were both adults during the Depression. Even before the stock market crashed, both were working to help support their families. Getting by, making do, and appreciating what one has were the hard lessons they learned during that difficult time.

World War II brought economic relief, but it also meant military service for millions of Americans, my father among them. Material want was replaced by sacrifices of a higher order. After the war my parents married and began a family. It was during the construction boom of the postwar period that my father entered the building trades as a union carpenter. A soft-spoken man, few things raise his dander as those who criticize unions. He knows that his ability to provide for his family was inextricably tied to union representation. For that reason, it was a proud moment for him in December 1999 when he received his pin for fifty years membership in the union.

Like the children of so many working-class families, there was little time for my parents' formal education. Largely because of what they themselves had to do without during their youth, my parents committed themselves to providing the best education possible for their three children. For me, that meant attending Jesuit schools, St. Ignatius College Prep in Chicago and Xavier University in Cincinnati. As an undergraduate at Xavier, I first came to appreciate the importance and excitement of historical research. Roger Fortin's enthusiasm for American history was contagious. His example as a teacher and scholar enlivened my own desire to study history.

It was as a graduate student at Xavier that I was first encouraged to examine the Depression through labor songs and songs of protest. Richard Gruber, the director of my master's program, provided me with both the intellectual challenge and guidance I needed. He also instilled in me the confidence for continuing my graduate studies.

I benefited from a number of outstanding teachers and scholars as a doctoral candidate at Miami University. Mary Kupiec Cayton, Jeffrey Kimball, Michael O'Brien, Carl Pletsch, and Allan Winkler did much to nurture me intellectually. I am particularly grateful to Curtis Ellison, Elliott Gorn, and Jack Kirby who served on my dissertation committee, providing valuable comments and criticisms. Mary Frederickson, my doctoral adviser, promoted my efforts in ways I will never be able to adequately acknowledge. Her perceptive insights, thoughtful suggestions, and unwavering support guided me through my dissertation. Her friendship and genuine concern were always present.

As my manuscript traveled the road from dissertation to book, it again profited from many individuals. Archie Green's careful reading, pointed commentary, and friendly assistance were heartily welcomed. David Evans, who serves as general editor of the American Made Music series, similarly provided sound advice and helpful suggestions. Robert Burchfield's careful copyediting and Robert Swanson's thorough indexing improved my work substantially. At the University Press of Mississippi, Craig Gill, Anne Stascavage, Walter Biggins, Shane Gong, Katie Baxter and John Langston brought their skills to bear as my manuscript went to press. Thanks are also due to Thomas Featherstone, Mike Smith, and Mary Wallace at Wayne State University's Walter P. Reuther Library for their assistance. I am grateful as well to David Macleod, editor of the *Michigan Historical Review*, for granting me permission to reprint my chapter on the Flint strike, which first appeared in that journal.

I am also appreciative for the assistance I have received from the College of Mount St. Joseph where I teach. A sabbatical in the fall of 1997 and a reduced teaching load in the spring of 2000 afforded me the time necessary to research and write. Paul Jenkins, director of Library Resources at the Mount, not only provided valuable assistance, he shares my enthusiasm for labor songs and songs of protest. In addition, my colleagues in the humanities department have supported me in ways both subtle and profound.

My wife Peg's encouragement, patience, and love sustained me through it all. And our daughter Abby's curiosity and laughter have deepened my own sense of wonder. This book is dedicated to them.

Strike Songs of the Depression

"Their Sharpest Statement"

Beware that movement that generates its own songs.

—Ray Stannard Baker,
"The Revolutionary Strike"

The songs of the working people have always been their
sharpest statement, and the one statement that cannot
be destroyed. You can burn books, buy newspapers, you
can guard against handbills and pamphlets, but you
cannot prevent singing. . . .

Songs are the statements of a people. You can learn
more about people by listening to their songs than in any
other way, for into the songs go all the hopes and hurts,
the angers, fears, the wants and aspirations.

—John Steinbeck,
From preface to John Greenway,
American Folksongs of Protest

Autoworkers had already taken control of a key General Motors (GM) plant in
Flint, Michigan, when Maurice Sugar wrote "Sit Down" in 1937.[1] The song was
an immediate hit among the sit-down strikers in Flint. Sugar later recalled,
"They went for 'Sit Down' in a big way."[2] As an attorney for the United Auto
Workers (UAW), Sugar's greatest contribution to the organization effort in
Flint was providing legal counsel for the union, not composing music.
Nonetheless, from his years of labor activity, Sugar understood the
importance of maintaining strikers' morale and building worker solidarity.[3] "Sit
Down" promoted the power of collective action in fighting against low wages,
poor working conditions, and the intimidation and bad faith of bosses. With
driving force, "Sit Down" implored workers to join together for their common
benefit.

When they tie the can to a union man,
Sit down! Sit down!
When they give him the sack, they'll take him back.
Sit down! Sit down!

1

CHORUS:
Sit down, just take a seat,
Sit down, and rest your feet,
Sit down, you've got 'em beat.
Sit down! Sit down!
(Repeat after each verse)

When they smile and say, "No raise in pay,"
Sit down! Sit down!
When you want the boss to come across,
Sit down! Sit down!

When the speed-up comes, just twiddle your thumbs.
Sit down! Sit down!
When you want them to know they'd better go slow,
Sit down! Sit -2down!

When the boss won't talk, don't take a walk.
Sit down! Sit down!
When the boss sees that, he'll want a little chat.
Sit down! Sit down![4]

In addition to being sung by the sit-down strikers at GM, this rousing song energized a wave of sit-down strikes that followed in the wake of Flint. Indeed, "Sit Down" became something of the anthem for workers who employed this tactic. As emblematic as "Sit Down" became to this tumultuous period in American labor history, there were dozens of other songs written by striking workers during the years of the Great Depression. This is the concern of the study that follows, the songs that striking workers wrote and sang during the Depression, and the meaning of those songs and that singing.

The Great Depression brought unprecedented changes for American workers and organized labor. Following the "lean years" of the 1920s, the 1930s witnessed an unsurpassed level of militancy within the labor movement.[5] As the economy plummeted, employers cut wages and laid off workers while simultaneously attempting to wrest more work from those who remained employed. In mills, mines, and factories, workers organized and resisted, striking for higher wages, improved conditions, and the right to bargain collectively. And as workers walked the picket line or sat down on the shop floor, they could be heard singing.[6]

While striking workers sometimes sang such standard labor songs as "Solidarity Forever," more often they wrote their own songs. Changing the lyrics of traditional folk songs or popular tunes, workers retold the events of their own strikes, praised the bravery of their leaders, denounced their employers, promoted solidarity within their ranks, and beckoned others to their cause. The lyrics emboldened striking workers; the melodies sustained them and drew others to their ranks.

For the unions involved in Depression strikes, music served some very pragmatic ends. Not only did singing boost and preserve the morale of those who walked the picket lines, but the lyrics told the workers' side of the strike story. Concerts were used to raise much needed strike funds, and singing was sometimes employed as a strategic weapon, a diversionary tactic to distract company police. Moreover, singing filled empty hours for striking workers, helping them escape boredom and restlessness and stay focused.

Although song-making and singing had practical uses, perhaps the greatest benefit was psychological. Singing provided workers an opportunity to vent their frustrations and assert their strength. The songs workers wrote, sang, and heard instilled in them a sense of their own power. These poignant articulations of workers' complaints and aspirations allowed them to exercise a form of control over their situation. As the workers' most common form of performative expression, song brought workers together physically and emotionally. Although labor and strike songs were most often the creation of one individual, sometimes two, they communicated shared feelings, thoughts, and values. Songs helped build community and class consciousness among the workers. In this way, labor and strike songs advanced the workers' social and political agenda in a manner quite similar to the role songs played in the more recent Civil Rights and antiwar movements of the 1960s and 1970s.[7]

The spontaneity with which many of these songs were written rendered them rough hewn. But the fact that they were composed as events unfolded makes them particularly valuable documents of the labor unrest that engendered them. As historical sources, labor songs give voice to workers who might otherwise be deemed inarticulate. Songs captured the sorrows and desires, complaints and worries, concerns and anxieties of the strike participants. Workers described their oppression and articulated their claims for justice in songs. Songs resound with workers' thoughts and emotions, providing insights into worker consciousness during this tumultuous period in labor history. They are, as John Steinbeck has written, workers' "sharpest statement."[8]

.   .   .

Scholarly interest in labor songs and songs of protest has a long and varied history. In a 1991 article in the *Journal of Folklore Research*, folklorist Archie Green noted that as early as the late nineteenth century critical attention was being given to songs of labor.[9] These early collections and commentaries were followed by the groundbreaking work of George Korson. Korson's travels into the coalfields of Pennsylvania and the eastern United States resulted in several studies of mining songs and ballads, the first of which was published in 1927.[10] Following the course charted by Korson, other folklorists paid attention to songs of labor and songs of protest. An examination of the literature they produced would require a study in itself. Indeed, the bibliography and discography of songs of protest compiled by R. Serge Denisoff for the American Bibliographical Center numbers nearly seventy pages, and that was published in 1973. Nonetheless, a number of significant works deserve mention here.[11]

As important as Korson's work has been to the study of industrial folklore and the preservation of the songs that are a part of it, the fruits of his labor have their shortcomings. In an effort to maintain the folk purity of what he collected, Korson deliberately rejected much of the protest music that came out of the coalfields of the United States during the 1920s and 1930s. Believing these songs to be the compositions of union organizers who were "outsider[s]," and not of workers themselves, he chose not to include them in the collections of coal-mining music that he published. As a result, the songs of such radical bards as Aunt Molly Jackson from Kentucky did not find their way into the pages of Korson's compilations.[12]

John Greenway's *American Folksongs of Protest* (1953) served as an important corrective to Korson's lyrical myopia. In his volume, Greenway began with a chapter providing a "historical survey" of protest music in the United States. Six subsequent chapters arranged songs of protest by occupation or condition: "Negro Songs of Protest," "The Songs of Textile Workers," "The Songs of Miners," "The Migratory Workers," "Songs of the Farmers," and "A Labor Miscellany." Greenway's last chapter provided brief biographies of four minstrels who had written songs of complaint and protest: Ella May Wiggins, Aunt Molly Jackson, Woody Guthrie, and Joe Glazer. Although Greenway did much in this one work to advance the study of labor songs, he had, by his own admission, only sampled "the rich material that awaits further exploration."[13]

Among the songs found in Greenway's chapter entitled "The Migratory Workers" are some from the International Workers of the World (IWW). Better known simply as the Wobblies, their efforts to form "one big union" during the early twentieth century involved music and song to a level unsurpassed in the history of American labor. The Wobblies attempted to "fan the flames of discontent" through the use of their *Little Red Songbook*. Widely distributed among IWW members, the *Little Red Songbook* went through thirty-five separate editions featuring almost two hundred different songs. Within its pages were traditional labor songs, original compositions, and parodies of church hymns and contemporary tunes. Indeed, the most popular, and powerful, American labor song ever written, "Solidarity Forever," was composed by a Wobbly, Ralph Chaplin.[14] In *Rebel Voices: An I.W.W. Anthology* (1964), Joyce Kornbluh compiled the rich heritage of Wobbly songs, poems, stories, skits, cartoons, and more. This impressive collection not only provided scholars with a valuable resource on the IWW, but it also underscored the importance of song and artistic expression to workers and the American labor movement.[15]

A few years after *Rebel Voices* was released, Philip Foner published *American Labor Songs of the Nineteenth Century* (1975). Foner had spent years collecting songs and ballads he came across in the American labor press. As a result of his efforts, more than 550 songs fill the pages of this work. This massive collection dispelled any notion that singing in the labor movement began with the Wobblies. In fact, Foner included a number of songs from the Colonial and Revolutionary periods, suggesting the tradition of labor songs in America has very deep roots indeed.[16]

Until quite recently, interest in the labor songs found in the works of Korson, Greenway, Kornbluh, Foner, and others largely came from folklorists and songsters. Their concerns with labor songs centered primarily on such questions as transmission, textual variation, authorship, and the very definition of "folksong" and "folk." Green's *Only a Miner* (1972) exemplifies this approach. In it he investigated the relationship between folk culture and popular culture as evidenced in recorded coal-mining songs. More recently, Green has examined worker culture through work songs and labor lore in *Wobblies, Pile Butts, and Other Heroes* (1993).[17]

The interest of the American Left in labor songs and songs of protest has also received considerable scholarly attention. In *Great Day Coming* (1971), sociologist R. Serge Denisoff explored the use of folk music by the Left, especially the Communist Party.[18] A narrower focus was given to this subject by Robbie Lieberman in *"My Song Is My Weapon"* (1989), which examines People's Songs, a left-wing organization active during the late 1940s.[19] Folklorist Richard Reuss has probed into the origins of the Left's attention to folksong in "The Roots of American Left-Wing Interest in Folksong" (1971) and *American Folk Music and Left-wing Politics, 1927-1957* (2000), the latter published posthumously with the assistance of his wife, JoAnne C. Reuss.[20] In addition, Ronald Cohen and Dave Samuelson have chronicled the Left's use of song from the mid 1920s to the mid 1950s in *Songs for Political Action* (1996). Their book accompanies a set of ten compact discs, which contain songs of the Left from that period, the majority of them original recordings. A number of the songs from the three strikes examined here are included in this collection.[21]

Biographies of various individuals who wrote and sang labor and protest songs are too numerous to enumerate here. Two do bear mentioning, however, because of their importance to the miners' strike in Harlan County, Kentucky, discussed in chapter 2. The Garland clan, who figure prominently in that strike—Aunt Molly Jackson, her half-sister Sarah Ogan Gunning, and half-brother Jim Garland—have received recent attention. Jim Garland, with the assistance of Julia Ardery, wrote his memoir, *Welcome the Traveler Home* (1983). Aunt Molly Jackson's story was told by Shelly Romalis in *Pistol Packin' Mama* (1999). Romalis also devotes a chapter in this biography to Sarah. These two texts provide both personal accounts of the strike and new perspectives on the urban folk revival that followed.[22]

Despite the attention given to labor songs by folklorists and anthropologists, historians were initially cool toward these lyrical expressions of worker culture, reluctant as they were to accept them as legitimate historical sources.[23] The emergence of the new social history during the last three decades, however, has done much to change the disposition of historians toward such cultural expressions. In an effort to tell the story of America's past "from the bottom up," historians began to give greater consideration to these previously discounted sources. Giving voice to those once labeled "inarticulate" has encouraged historians to cast a larger net when choosing documentary materials for scrutiny.[24]

Scholars studying the history of slavery and African American culture were among the first to recognize the valuable contribution an examination of music and song could make to their field. Roger Abrahams's *Singing the Master* (1992), John Blassingame's *The Slave Community* (1972), Eugene Genovese's *Roll, Jordan, Roll* (1974), and Lawrence Levine's *Black Culture and Black Consciousness* (1977) are among the best examples of how such nontraditional sources as songs could fundamentally alter historical interpretation. These historians argued that enslaved blacks, and later free blacks, expressed anger and discontent through their spirituals, secular music, folktales, and humor. Although sharply limited by what actions they could take against their white oppressors, African Americans communicated their antagonism toward their conditions in these veiled ways.[25] The work of these scholars exploded the thesis advanced by Stanley Elkins and others, who concluded that slaves had lost their will to resist, becoming childlike, docile dependents of their masters.[26] Elkins's controversial theory could not stand up against the evidence teased from the folk culture of the slave community. The "closed system" of slavery had not destroyed the slaves' African culture and broken their spirit, as Elkins contended. Instead, their resistance had found new forms and expressions. Although it has taken quite some time, historians of the African American experience have come to appreciate what Frederick Douglass had understood more than 150 years ago. Describing slave songs, he wrote:

> They told a tale of woe which was then altogether beyond my feeble comprehension; they were tones loud, long, and deep; they breathed the prayer and complaint of souls boiling over with bitterest anguish. Every tone was a testimony against slavery, and a prayer to God for deliverance from chains. . . . If anyone wishes to be impressed with the soul-killing effects of slavery, let him go . . . analyze the sounds that shall pass through the chambers of his soul,— and if he is not thus impressed, it will only be because "there is no flesh in his obdurate heart."[27]

Labor historians, for their part, had likewise been disinclined to consider labor songs as a worthy subject for investigation. The parameters of labor history had long been established by John R. Commons and the Wisconsin School.[28] Trained to examine labor history as essentially the story of unions, labor leaders, and government policy, worker culture was given little notice. This began to change in the wake of E. P. Thompson's monumental study of the English working class. Class analysis for Thompson was not orthodox Marxism but an understanding of worker culture incorporated in customs, traditions, institutions, and ideology.[29] Inspired by Thompson's work, American labor historians such as Herbert Gutman began to reexamine the history of American workers through a similar lens. As a consequence, the study of American labor history has been fundamentally reoriented.[30]

The cultural meanings of gender and race relations, immigration patterns, religious practices, material culture, consumer habits, leisure activities, and much more offer new insights into the world of work and the lives of workers.

As a consequence, the study of labor history embraces sources previously neglected. Just as the examination of folklore has substantially altered historians' understanding of slavery and African American history, this new focus on worker culture has changed the questions labor historians ask and the resources they muster to answer those questions.[31]

As the landscape of labor history changed, the lines that had previously delineated one academic discipline from another blurred. The interests of folklorists, sociologists, cultural anthropologists, and others are no longer remote from those of the labor historian. In the area of labor songs and songs of protest, much of the most important writing has thus far been done outside the mansion of history, as the work of Green, Denisoff, Lieberman, and Reuss suggest. There have been, to be sure, some historians—Irving Bernstein, for example—who have included the texts of labor songs within the pages of their works on the American labor movement, underscoring their value.[32] But even then, labor songs have been treated by historians more as garnish than as substance, with no rigorous analysis or exegesis of the lyrics offered. In the early nineties, however, historian Clark Halker explored labor protest during the Gilded Age through an examination of labor "song-poems." *For Democracy, Workers, and God* (1991) has effectively shown how these song-poets instilled a sense of class consciousness among workers through a "ceaseless defense of labor's cause and caustic criticism of the rising order." Moreover, Halker has demonstrated how the study of labor songs can advance our knowledge of worker culture and enhance our understanding of labor history.[33]

This study is inspired and informed by the work of Green, Denisoff, Levine, Halker, and others who have recognized the value of labor songs to the study of American history in general and working-class culture in particular. It is predicated upon the assertion that these expressions of workers' hopes and fears, beliefs and values, complaints and aspirations are worthy of historical inquiry. The importance of the unions workers joined, the strategies labor leaders employed, and the policies the government enacted during these tumultuous years in labor history certainly cannot be discounted. But this study maintains that a critical examination of the songs workers wrote, sang, and heard can deepen our understanding of that period. In the lyrics of these songs, the lives of the workers are unveiled. As powerful statements of worker consciousness, songs reveal how workers perceived their situation and the nature of their oppression. They articulate the workers' claim to justice and their felt need for solidarity and collective action. In so doing, these songs express both the class and gender identity of the workers, providing a valuable lens through which to examine labor unrest during the Depression years.

The three chapters that follow explore the songs of three different strikes: the Gastonia, North Carolina, textile workers' strike (1929); the Harlan County, Kentucky, coal miners' strike (1931–32); and the Flint, Michigan, autoworkers' sit-down strike (1936–37). These three strikes were selected for specific reasons. First, all three generated dozens of songs written by strike participants. While undoubtedly many strike songs from Gastonia, Harlan, and Flint have been lost forever, never having been copied down or recorded, much of the musical legacy of these strikes was preserved. Independent journalists such as Margaret Larkin and the staff of the *Daily Worker* published a number of songs during the Gastonia strike. From Harlan County, the songs of Aunt Molly Jackson, Jim Garland, and Sarah Ogan Gunning were recorded by Alan Lomax for the Library of Congress several years after the strike. In Flint union leaders collected the songs of the sit-down strikers and reprinted many of them in the union's newspapers, the *Flint Auto Worker* and the *United Automobile Worker*. In addition to the large body of songs these strikes provide, a number of the songs, which were born of these struggles, became classics, finding their way into union songbooks for use in other strikes. Florence Reece's "Which Side Are You On?," inspired by "Bloody Harlan," and Maurice Sugar's "Sit Down," from the GM strike, are two such songs. These time-honored songs have been used, and undoubtedly will continue to be used, by workers and protesters in other situations.

Second, the music and its minstrels played an important part in all three strikes. Ella May's murder during the Gastonia strike made her a martyr for the cause. Other workers believed she had been singled out by the bosses because of the strike songs she wrote, and the Communist Party, active in the strike at Gastonia, was quick to capitalize on that sentiment for its potent propaganda. In addition to Reece's "Which Side Are You On?," the coal-mining strike in Harlan generated some of the most powerful protest music ever sung. Aunt Molly Jackson, Jim Garland, and Sarah Ogan Gunning combined their Appalachian folk idiom with strident verses of unionism and class consciousness to tell the story of that bitter struggle. They brought their music and their memories from Bloody Harlan with them when they migrated north to New York City. There they had contact with members of the Left, particularly musicians, influencing the likes of Pete Seeger, Woody Guthrie, and Lee Hays. During the GM strike, music played a central role in maintaining morale among both the workers inside the plants and those on the outside. With time on their hands, sit-down strikers composed dozens of songs about the strike, replacing the verses of popular songs with their own lyrics. Moreover, the union amplified music through speaker systems and sound cars to encourage strikers and their allies on the picket line. During a critical point in the strike, singing was also used as part of the diversionary tactics employed by UAW strategists to capture an important plant, gaining the advantage for the union.

Third, these three strikes represent three different industries: textiles, mining, and automobile manufacturing. Coal mining, especially, and textiles have long traditions of labor songs. Consequently, the songs that emerged from the mills of Gastonia and the coalfields of Harlan County represent only a small fraction of the rich heritage of singing that these two industries possess. The automotive industry, on the other hand, was a relatively new enterprise when the workers sat down at Flint. Its tradition of industrial music was just beginning. Closely tied to the heritage of singing in these three industries was the location of the three strikes. The study of these strikes allows for some comparison between the southern rural experience rich in its folk traditions and the northern urban experience with its more heterogeneous culture.

Fourth, despite the fact that these three strikes occurred within only eight years of one another, much happened during that time that profoundly affected the American labor movement. When the workers walked out of the mills in Gastonia on April 1, 1929, Herbert Hoover had been president for only a few weeks. Although signs of an economic downturn were already being felt in a number of sectors of the economy, the textile industry included, the stock market crash that heralded the Great Depression had not yet occurred. And even once it had, Hoover did little to mitigate the pain and suffering millions of Americans were experiencing. As a result, in November 1932, voters dumped Hoover for Democrat Franklin D. Roosevelt, who promised to remember the "forgotten man." FDR's New Deal jettisoned the economics of his predecessor and brought in an alphabet soup of programs and policies to combat the Depression and its causes.

Among the barrage of legislation that came during Roosevelt's First Hundred Days was the National Industrial Recovery Act, creating the National Recovery Administration. One of its provisions, Section 7(a), guaranteed workers the right to bargain collectively. With it the federal government had legitimized labor organizing and unions. Even after the Supreme Court ruled the law unconstitutional, protection for workers' collective bargaining rights was regained in 1935 with the passage of the Wagner Act. Thus, the strikes examined in this study offer a look at union organizing during these "turbulent years" both before and after federal protection for labor organizing had been established.[34] The ways in which changes in federal labor policy were reflected in the workers' consciousness will be examined using songs as a text.

Lastly, because many of these songs were written by women, this study will examine how gender affected the lyrics. Whether as striking workers themselves or as the wives, daughters, and sisters of strikers, women involved in the labor struggles at Gastonia, Harlan, and Flint viewed the events somewhat differently than their male counterparts. Specifically, their role within the family influenced their perceptions of the events that surrounded them. Unlike their husbands, brothers, and fathers, women lyricists drew an overt connection between the deprivation they saw their families experiencing and the fight for higher wages, improved working conditions, and collective bargaining rights.

Few periods in the history of the United States have been as important to American labor as the Depression years. Amid economic hard times, workers experienced profound and lasting changes. Militancy within the labor movement was strong, as workers flexed their collective muscle. A fundamental shift in federal labor policy encouraged unions, especially among industrial workers. As but one measure of this activity, membership in labor unions tripled, rising from approximately 3 million in 1930 to nearly 9 million by the decade's end.[35]

While labor leaders, corporate bosses, and government officials strategized, postured, and negotiated, workers were active as well. Fighting for higher wages, improved working conditions, and collective bargaining rights, they organized strike efforts, walked picket lines, and occupied factories. As they did, they wrote their own songs. And those songs, as spontaneous and varied as they often were, communicated their thoughts and feelings and the depth of their commitment in the struggle for justice.

Chapter 1

"Mill Mother's Lament":
Gastonia, North Carolina, 1929

[The music] was their own story, put in incredibly simple
terms. Every one had lived through this. There was no
piece of sentiment; it was the history of every one there
put into song.

—Mary Heaton Vorse, *Strike!*

As Ella May's coffin was lowered into the ground, Katie Barrett sang one of Ella May's best-loved songs, "Mill Mother's Lament."[1]

> We leave our homes in the morning,
> We kiss our children good bye
> While we slave for the bosses
> Our children scream and cry.

Ella May's five children stood by the grave site and heard the words their mother had composed. Possibly only the eldest, Myrtle, understood why her mother had died. Ella May's coworkers knew why she was killed, however. "The bosses hated Ella May because she made up songs, and was always at the speakings," many contended. "They aimed to git Ella May. They was after her."[2] There had, in fact, been an earlier attempt to poison her water supply.[3] Whether the shooting of Ella May was a deliberate act may never be proven, but what is certain is that Ella May's music, and that of the other strikers at Gastonia in 1929, tells a compelling and revealing story.

Explaining the failure of the Gastonia strike and others in the region to bring unionization to the Carolina Piedmont, labor historian Irving Bernstein writes, "The causes of this defeat are to be found in the millhand, in the mill owner, in the community, in the economic situation, and in the unions." With respect to the southern worker, Bernstein maintains that "his rural tradition, his ingrained individualism, his ignorance, his isolation, his restless mobility, his apathy, his poverty, and his suspicions of northerners joined to impede his capacity to act collectively." It was not "a yearning for organization" but unbearable conditions that served as "the explosive that touched off the textile worker."[4] Bernstein's assessment does well to identify those forces that have inhibited and discouraged organized labor in the South. Collective action on the part of labor has had a decidedly difficult time overcoming the economic conditions, attitudes, and values of the southern worker. This was certainly the case in Gastonia in 1929.[5]

What should not be lost in the wreckage of Gastonia, however, are those voices that promoted class consciousness and solidarity as the hope for struggling workers. By advocating unity and cooperation, workers advanced values, however tenuously, to cope with their changing economic conditions. Such values coexisted with the "ingrained individualism" of the southern worker and offered a solution to his or her problems. No longer self-sufficient pioneer farmers, the realities of industrial labor required collective action if wages were going to be raised and working conditions improved. Independence of action and self-reliance did little to benefit the worker struggling against the exigencies of the labor market. Although perhaps feebly and imperfectly, workers came to understand that such individualism had little benefit for industrial laborers. The move from farming community to company town inspired among many workers a parallel psychological journey from individualism to class consciousness.

It was in the songs of workers such as Ella May that the values of unity and collective action were articulated and attempted to gain currency. The rhetorical "we" in Ella May's "Mill Mother's Lament" invoked the shared experience of women who "slave for the bosses" as they struggled to provide and care for their families, an intersection of class and gender. But if they "stand together" and "have a union here," as she implored them in her last verse, their situation would improve.[6]

The songs strikers wrote and sang reveal not only how these workers came to understand their situation, they also served as the very means by which women and men verbalized and communicated that understanding. In so doing, songs helped create a shared identity of attitudes and values. By employing traditional, familiar melodies and religious hymns, songs expressed workers' thoughts and feelings in idioms deeply rooted in the culture. The use of traditional forms closely tied to the workers' religious fundamentalism and mountain culture helped legitimize the ideals being voiced by workers. As strike leader Fred Beal wrote, "home-made poets and lay-preachers . . . made something of a spiritual revival of the strike."[7]

Of course, striking millhands did not have a monopoly on invoking cultural forms and symbols to advance their cause. Company bosses and civil authorities effectively raised the specter of fundamentalist religion and American patriotism in discrediting the Communist-affiliated National Textile Workers Union (NTWU) and its strike effort. Indeed, a mob opposing the strike sang the hymn "Praise God from Whom All Blessings Flow" and shouted patriotic slogans as its members demolished the union's headquarters and its relief store.[8] By trumpeting efforts to combat the union and bust the strike as the work of the righteous and patriotic, mill owners justified their actions in the name of God and country. By characterizing the strike as the work of godless Communists hell-bent on destroying America, unionism could be depicted as an alien ideology not compatible with the cultural values of the region. Thus, the striking millhands and the mill owners each laid claim to and utilized cultural forms and symbols in their fight.

It was the violence of the angry mob that destroyed the union's facilities, however, not the cultural symbols the mob embraced. The mill owners' control over the company town, their ability to evict striking workers from company housing, and their influence on local government and the press were the most formidable weapons in their arsenal against unionism. But by justifying their actions as consistent with the values of the region, mill owners could cloak their efforts to combat unionism, "stand[ing] together," as culturally illegitimate.

The songs of the striking workers in Gastonia reveal that many workers recognized the importance of collective action as a means by which to improve their situation. They had become class conscious. By expressing discontent with their situation, relating the events of the strike, praising their leaders, building solidarity within their ranks, and beckoning others to their cause, the songs striking workers composed and sang advanced an ideology of class requisite for collective action. There was a "yearning for organization" among the millhands at Gastonia, even if it did find an ill-fated agent for its cause in the NTWU. The songs of the striking millhands suggest that class consciousness emanated from the workers themselves and their own understanding of their situation, not merely from outside organizers seeking to foment a workers' revolution among southern textile operatives. That those ideals of unity and solidarity were often expressed in the workers' own cultural idiom further suggests an effort to present ideas of industrial resistance as harmonious with the workers' own culture and values.

The union, for its part, recognized the latent class consciousness expressed in the songs strikers wrote and hoped to make potent propaganda of the lyrics. To that end, the lyrics of many of the songs appeared in the pages of the *Daily Worker* and other publications of the Communist Party. Moreover, when Ella May was murdered, the strike had a martyr who could be exploited for the party's own purposes.

As a strike tool, organizers keenly appreciated the value of singing and music. Union organizers not only encouraged homespun poets like Ella May, they taught striking workers songs that had long been part of the labor movement, like the old Wobbly favorite "Solidarity Forever." Singing quickly became a central activity at strike meetings, at rallies, and on the picket line. Music inspired striking workers, empowering them with the will to fight against extreme odds. In situations over which they had little control, song instilled in them strength and resolve. Accounts of the strike also describe how song filled empty hours for imprisoned strikers. As Vera Buch, a union activist, remembered, "[songs helped us] forget for a moment our bodily aches and discomforts, above all our anxiety."[9]

It is through the music, then, that the Gastonia strike of 1929 will be reexamined here. The songs of the Gastonia strike provide insights into the strike and workers that otherwise would be lost and forgotten. This perspective casts new light on those troubled times and the individuals involved, what they thought, and how they felt. The music was, as Mary Heaton Vorse suggested, "the history of every one there put into song."[10]

During the late nineteenth and early twentieth centuries, the South steadily industrialized. In the Carolina Piedmont, this change was marked by the appearance of scores of textile mills. The proximity of raw cotton and the availability of cheap labor combined to entice mill owners to locate their mills in the region. No longer would the Northeast dominate the textile industry. During the 1920s, the Carolina Piedmont eclipsed New England as the leading textile-producing region in the country.[11]

Yet, while much of the United States was experiencing general prosperity during the 1920s, the textile industry was suffering. Overproduction, foreign competition, dramatic swings in the price of raw cotton, market encroachments from other fibers, commission merchants' cuts, and changes in fashion were among the economic forces that wracked the industry. In an effort to cut costs, mill managers turned to night work and the stretch-out system (known in other industries as the speed-up system). The stretch-out increased productivity and lowered the per unit price of cloth by requiring a worker to operate more machinery without additional compensation. Widely implemented in northern and southern mills alike by the late 1920s, the stretch-out promised the mill owners more for their labor dollar. But such techniques only furthered the problem of overproduction in an unrationalized industry. Although textile workers in the Piedmont had previously struck in protest against long hours, low wages, and poor working conditions, it was to no avail. It seemed as though there was little they could do to combat such practices. Moreover, with southern agriculture impoverished, the mill owners enjoyed the benefits of a labor surplus.[12]

The mill owners' control over their employees was further strengthened by the fact that many workers and their families lived in mill villages. Originally designed to concentrate enough labor for the mill operation in a rural area, the mill village gave owners a hold on their workers' lives that went beyond the ten- to twelve-hour shift in the factory. The company store provided the worker's family with their basic necessities, extending credit when needed. Some mill villages had schools, recreational centers, and medical facilities. And come Sunday, the mill family prayed and sang in the mill village church. Mill villages created whole layers of dependency, so that striking workers could face unemployment from their jobs, eviction from their homes, and a loss of credit at the company store.[13]

The millhand's wages were meager. The pay workers received in cotton mills was only half as much as the all-manufacturing average. The average hourly rate in the mills in 1928 was less than thirty cents, with weekly earnings under thirteen dollars. Most workers labored six days a week, and each workday lasted ten to twelve hours. Conditions varied from mill to mill but generally were poor. Dust from the cotton fiber, filthy washroom facilities, dangerous machinery, and excessive heat in the summer and cold in the winter were among the discomforts and hazards plaguing the industry. Mill owners often employed entire families, with women and children comprising the bulk of the labor force, and women and children were assigned to the night shift as well as the day shift. There was some protective legislation, but it was seldom enforced.[14]

Mill workers were woefully unorganized, with unions virtually nonexistent in the southern mills. In 1929 the American Federation of Labor (AFL) affiliate, United Textile Workers (UTW), claimed only 30,000 members of 1.1 million in the industry, or less than 3 percent. Moreover, membership was exclusively in the North, much of it concentrated in hosiery mills. The UTW had conducted a strike against the Loray mill in Gastonia in 1919, but it ended in failure.[15]

These were the conditions of southern millhands just as a wave of strikes broke over the Carolina Piedmont during the late 1920s and early 1930s. The Gastonia strike of 1929 was one of the most dramatic of these southern mill strikes. Labor unrest was but a few weeks old at Elizabethton, Tennessee, where the first of these strikes took place, when workers walked off the job at the Loray mill in Gastonia.[16]

By the late 1920s, Gaston County was the leading textile-producing county in the region and ranked third in the nation. The county seat, Gastonia, prided itself as "the South's City of Spindles." The Loray mill was Gastonia's largest, accounting for almost a fifth of those spindles. A division of the Manville-Jenckes Corporation of Rhode Island, Loray produced cord-tire fabric. In 1927 the mill manager, G. A. Johnstone, had been instructed to save $500,000 a year. To this end, he introduced the stretch-out, extended piecework, replaced high-wage with low-wage labor, and made two 10 percent wage cuts. He also eliminated a number of jobs, reducing the number of employees from 3,500 to 2,200. Within one year, Johnstone was well on his way to achieving his goal, but animosity among the millhands was strong. When weave-room workers staged a brief walkout on March 5, 1928, tensions heightened. In an effort to mollify workers, Loray's owner replaced Johnstone with J. A. Baugh. Any good feelings resulting from this move were fleeting. It would not be long before labor troubles would erupt again.[17]

The Communist-controlled NTWU had been seeking to organize southern textile workers. They decided to focus their attention on Gastonia, specifically the Loray mill, and sent Fred E. Beal to Gastonia. Arriving in March 1929, Beal began building an organization. When management got wind of this, five pro-union workers lost their jobs. In protest, workers walked off the job on April 1. The night before, more than a thousand workers attended a meeting sponsored by the NTWU. The union had established a strong foothold. Two days after the strike began, the union sent a series of demands to Baugh, which contrasted sharply with the existing conditions at Loray:

> (1) elimination of piecework; (2) a minimum standard wage of $20 per week; (3) a forty hour, five-day week; (4) abolition of the stretch-out; (5) equal pay for equal work for women and children; (6) free baths and better toilets in the mill and screening in the houses; (7) 50 per cent reduction of rent and light charges; and (8) union recognition.[18]

Baugh quickly and flatly rejected these demands. Thus began the strike that Irving Bernstein has described as "a phenomenon without parallel in the chronicle of American labor."[19]

Once the strike broke out, workers expressed their frustration and discontent with their conditions in song. Not surprisingly, in an industry dominated by female labor, a majority of the songs written during the strike were composed by women and addressed the particular concerns of women. Many of these women carried the double burden of breadwinner and caregiver, as they fulfilled their roles as wives and mothers. Moreover, with child labor common in southern textile mills, many women worked alongside their own children.

Certainly, the most important songwriter of the Gastonia strike was Ella May. Born on a small farm in Sevierville, Tennessee, in 1900, Ella May's family moved to a logging camp near Andrews, North Carolina, when she was ten. The transient nature of the logging industry forced the family to move from camp to camp. In the camps, she and her mother did washing for the men during the day, and in the evening Ella May sang for the loggers. At the age of sixteen, Ella May married John Wiggins. After their first child was born, John Wiggins suffered a crushed leg in a logging accident. Left unemployed by his accident and with no opportunity for full-time work for Ella May in a logging camp, the family moved to the new cotton mills of North Carolina. A mill agent had come through the area, recruiting entire families to these new mills. There Ella May learned to spin yarn, never making more than nine dollars a week. John Wiggins helped out at first by doing odd jobs around the mill, but he became despondent and turned to drink. Finally, he deserted his wife and family.[20]

By this time Ella May had given birth to eight children, losing four, however, to various diseases. She dropped her married name, although accounts of her life do not always acknowledge this fact. She would have a ninth child by another man, Charles Shope. Ella May continued to work in American Spinning Number One in Bessemer City, North Carolina, relying on her eldest to care for the younger children while she worked. At union meetings she told of her difficult life in the mill.

> I never made more than nine dollars a week, and you can't do for a family on such money. I'm the mother of nine. Four died with the whooping cough. I was working nights, and I asked the super to put me on days, so's I could tend 'em when they had their bad spells. But he wouldn't. He's the sorriest man alive, I

reakon. So I had to quit, and then there wasn't no money for medicine, and they just died. I couldn't do for my children any more than you women on the money we git. That's why I come out for the union, and why we all got to stand for the union, so's we can do better for our children, and they won't have lives like we got."[21]

As Ella May's comments so powerfully express, the workers' struggle for higher wages, better working conditions, and union recognition was inextricably tied to the poverty and want their families experienced. Her music, too, connected the fight striking workers were waging with the deprivation mill families faced every day. Ella May's "song ballets," as she called them, emanated from such a bitter life. Although her songs reflect her own personal experiences, they spoke of and to many others like her. Again, it was the shared experience of "we" that she sang. "Mill Mother's Lament" poignantly described the anxiety and pain of mothers unable to provide for their children. In the song, mill work not only creates family disruption by separating mothers from their children, but this sacrifice fails to bring in enough money to raise a family. Indeed, "wages are too low" as measured against the ability to "buy for our children."

> We leave our homes in the morning,
> We kiss our children good bye
> While we slave for the bosses
> Our children scream and cry.
>
> And when we draw our money
> Our grocery bills to pay,
> Not a cent to pay for clothing,
> Not a cent to lay away.
>
> And on that very evening,
> Our little son will say:
> "I need some shoes, Mother,
> And so does sister May."
>
> How it grieves a heart of a mother,
> You everyone must know,
> But we can't buy for our children
> Our wages are too low.

But for these common concerns of mill mothers, "[t]he bosses do not care." In this way, striking and union organizing become an extension of the role of mother: protecting, nurturing, and caring for her children. Ella May's song, which was so popular with her coworkers, squarely stakes its claim to justice on the basis of motherhood, inextricably connecting class with gender. These lyrics most certainly struck a resonant chord of shared experience among mill women, tying their strike efforts to their heart-felt identity as mothers. Margaret Larkin, a journalist who spent considerable time in Gastonia during the strike, reported that "when Ella May sang, 'How it grieves the heart of a mother / You every one must know, . . . ' every woman in her audience did know, and responded to the common feeling." Moreover, by modeling her song on "Little Mary Phagan," Ella May drew upon the memories of many workers who were familiar with the 1913 murder of Mary Phagan at an Atlanta pencil factory. This connection, between the victimization of Mary Phagan at the hands of her boss, Leo Frank, and that of mill children by company bosses, would have conjured powerful images and emotions in the minds and hearts of the workers who heard Ella May's song.

> It is for our little children,
> That seem to us so dear,
> But for us nor them, dear workers,
> The bosses do not care.

> But understand, all workers,
> Our union they do fear;
> Let's stand together, workers,
> And have a union here.[22]

Ella May did more to promote the union than merely compose songs. She served as a secretary for the union and once traveled to Washington, D.C., with a delegation, lobbying for the workers' cause. At the Capitol, the delegation happened upon Senator Lee Slater Overman of North Carolina. When Overman questioned why Binnie Green, a fourteen-year-old striker with the delegation, was not in school, Ella May challenged the senator. How could mill children attend school? she questioned. "How can I send my children to school when I can't make enough to clothe them decently? When I go to the mill at night I have to lock them up at night by their lone selves. I can't have anyone to look after them. Last winter when two of them were sick with the flu I had to leave them at home in bed when I went to work. I can't get them enough good clothes to send them to Sunday School." Ella May's outburst was picked up by the press, bringing the strike national attention.[23]

Ella May also tried to organize black workers in Bessemer City, where she worked and lived. In this regard, her support of the NTWU's policy of racial equality was rare among the strikers. Mill management and the local press often attempted to discredit the union by playing upon the white millhands' fear of race-mixing. In her autobiography, *A Radical Life*, union organizer Vera Buch later maintained it was Ella May's "appeal to the black people, and especially her role in their organization, that incensed mill owners and like-minded people in the South. I am certain it was as an organizer of the Negroes that Mrs. Wiggins was killed." Though there is no hard evidence supporting Buch's claim, Ella May's efforts to bridge the racial divide did anger mill bosses, if not confuse the other strikers. But of Ella May's various contributions to the strike effort, music is her most enduring legacy.[24]

Another songwriter to emerge during the Gastonia strike was eleven-year-old millhand Odel Corley. Corley's "On Top of Old Loray," set to the tune of "On Top of Old Smoky," describes the poor working conditions in the cotton mills. The song gives both a picture of the deplorable conditions in the Loray mill and a call for the workers to strike. The song begins with a description of the physical structure of the mill and its ominous powers over life itself.

> Up in old Loray
> Six stories high,
> That's where they found us,
> Ready to die.

Other verses replace the false-hearted lover in the original song with the bosses and the betrayed woman with a spirited striker. The bosses will "starve you," "rob you," and "tell you more lies." They will also "take half you make" by claiming you "took it up / In coupon books." Coupon books were used as part of a credit system that kept the millhands in constant debt to the company store.

> The bosses will starve you,
> They'll tell you more lies
> Than there's crossties on the railroads.
> Or stars in the skies.

> The bosses will rob you,
> They will take half you make,
> And claim that you took it up
> In coupon books.

Not only will the mill owners "starve you," but Corley mentions other physical afflictions. Even at the tender age of eleven, she was aware of the aging effect of mill work. The crippling labor and the cotton dust "will carry you to your grave." But this song of sadness, anger, and betrayal is not without hope. At the same time Corley painted this dismal picture of mill life, and death, she called for the workers to strike. Just as the betrayed lover in the original departs to go "back to Old Smoky" to soothe the sting of a broken heart, so, too, Corley's song seeks renewal through physical separation: "Say 'Goodbye, old bosses, / We're going on strike.' "

> Up in old Loray,
> All covered with lint,
> That's where our shoulders
> Was crippled and bent.
>
> Up in old Loray,
> All covered with cotton,
> It will carry you to your grave
> And you soon will be rotten.
>
> REFRAIN:
> Go pull off your aprons,
> Come join our strike.
> Say "Goodbye, old bosses,
> We're going on strike."

Whether this remarkable creation was the product of "a militant feminist consciousness at an early age," as Stephen Wiley suggests, or simply the fervent outpourings of a young girl, it poignantly describes the wretched conditions experienced by southern millhands. By patterning her song on the mountain ballad "On Top of Old Smoky," Corley presented mill life through a tune with strong regional association to rural North Carolina.[25]

"Loray Workers," by young striker Christene Patton, also narrates the problems of the mill worker. It cites many of the same difficulties that Ella

May's "Mill Mother's Lament" relates: long hours (or in this song, long weeks), low wages, and bills that exceed one's income. The song goes on to suggest these conditions force parents to send their children to the mills, depriving them of any opportunity for an education and escape from the world of their parents. Thus a vicious circle is created, trapping another generation into mill work.

> We work from week end to week end and never lost a day.
> But when that awful pay day comes, we draw our little pay.
> Then we go home on pay day night and sit down in our chairs.
> The merchant raps upon the door, he's come to get his share.
> When all our little debts are paid and nothing left behind,
> We turn our pockets wrong side out, and not one cent we find.
> We get up early in the morning, we work all day real hard,
> To buy our little meat and bread, sugar, tea and lard.
> Our children they grow up, and have no time to go to school,
> Almost before they learn to walk, they learn to spin and spool.

Although the tune to which Patton's song was to be sung was not given when the song was printed in the *Daily Worker*, it might possibly be "Little Mary Phagan," the same song Ella May's "Mill Mother's Lament" modeled. It seems to work when put to "Little Mary Phagan," suggesting how other strikers might have been following the example of Ella May. If this is, in fact, the case, it reveals something of the process of folksong construction. Patton's song appeared in the *Daily Worker* with long individual lines, as shown here, not in four-line verse like "Mill Mother's Lament."[26]

Another song-poem printed in the *Daily Worker* during the strike was written by the union local's secretary, Will Truett. It contrasts the easy life of the bosses with the dismal lives of the mill children. While the bosses and the police enjoy springtime, the children labor "thru the long and loathsome day." It is the bosses who are "out on the playground," not the children. Here, "playground" is probably referring to the golf course at a local private country club. Whatever "Spring Time in Gastonia" lacks in literary merit, it more than compensates as a statement of class consciousness. Although the song-poem suggests an end to child labor, that was not one of the original demands submitted to Baugh at the beginning of the strike. Very possibly workers felt so pinched by bills, even with the added income their children provided, it may have seemed inconceivable not to have them laboring in the mills.

"Mill Mother's Lament"

It is spring time in Gastonia
It is spring time by the mill
It is spring time for the robin
And it's spring time for the bee

It is spring time for the bosses
In the playground on the hill
And its [*sic*] spring time for the police
But it's work time for those in the mill

Where the child is forced to labor
Thru the long and loathsome day
While the bosses out on the playground
May plot and plan and play

But once the workers organize, their troubles will be over; piecework will be eliminated, air inside the mill will be ventilated, and children will be free. By the time "Spring Time in Gastonia" appeared in the *Daily Worker*, most workers had already returned to their jobs. The failure of the workers to stick to the union and stay out on strike is implied in the fourth verse.

But the time is soon approaching
When the workers will realize
That their only hope for freedom
Is to fight and organize

Then we'll eliminate the piece work
And we'll ventilate the mill
And will free the child from labor
And be content on Loray Hill[27]

Although such poor conditions as described in these songs made the Loray millhands quick to strike, Fred Beal and the NTWU were ill-prepared for the walkout when it occurred. Having been in Gastonia only a few months, Beal was not ready for a showdown between the fledgling union and Loray mill owners. But when a group of workers arrived at union headquarters April 1, announcing they had been fired for having attended "the speakin' " on the previous Saturday, Beal knew the union could not hesitate in its response.[28]

The workers' initial reaction to the strike call was filled with celebration and exuberance, which manifested itself in song. As Beal recalled: "They marched around the side of the hall singing whatever songs came to their minds." Recognizing "the tremendous value of singing the right songs on a picket line," Beal typed up a number of copies of "Solidarity Forever." The workers were unfamiliar with this popular union song, so he explained that it should be sung to the tune of "Glory, Glory Hallelujah." It was only years later that he realized the irony of southerners singing to the tune of "John Brown's Body," which has the same melody as "Glory, Glory Hallelujah" (better known as "The Battle Hymn of the Republic"): "I . . . told them to sing it to the tune 'Glory, Glory Hallelujah.' It comes to me only now that it is also the tune of 'John Brown's Body' and was perhaps somewhat inappropriate for Southerners."[29] And so, in the very first hours of the strike, singing played a critical role. Union leader Beal turned to music to rally the workers behind the strike, and in the process, he introduced hundreds of southern textile workers to the anthem of labor, "Solidarity Forever."

> When the union's inspiration through the workers' blood shall run,
> There can be no power greater anywhere beneath the sun.
> Yet what force on earth is weaker than the feeble strength of one?
> But the union makes us strong.
>
> REFRAIN:
> Solidarity forever!
> Solidarity forever!
> Solidarity forever!
> For the union makes us strong.[30]

The strikers then marched from the union hall to the mill and formed a picket line. During the course of the day, enthusiasm waned. While estimates had the initial number of picketers between 150 and 200, their numbers dropped to approximately 35 as the day wore on due in large part to the fact that company bosses were writing down the names of those present. To stem the strikers' ebbing tide, the union organizers again employed the power of song. Beal gave a descriptive account of this in his autobiography, *Proletarian Journey*:

> Then [George] Pershing [another NTWU organizer] and I harangued the back-sliders and shamed a few of them back. We formed a solid group and began to

Striking workers at the Loray Mill. Courtesy of Walter P. Reuther Library, Wayne State University.

yell, "To hell with the bosses. Come on the line. Stick together and win this time."

"Sing," I cried "sing 'Solidarity.' "

As the song rang out, the workers on the sidelines began to draw nearer to our group. Their lips began to move; soon they were singing. Then we started to march again, two by two, two by two, the line growing longer and longer. The timid ones had been swayed by the militants; the revival spirit again gripped the crowd. From a window of one of the mills a worker shouted that the bosses had locked them in until quitting time but that they were coming out to join us. We answered with a cheer and sang louder, more sincerely than ever, "For the union makes us strong."

The strike was on.[31]

It would not take long for the lines to be drawn between the NTWU strikers and their opponents. On the second day of the strike, a scuffle took place on the picket line. That prompted Governor O. Max Gardner, himself a mill owner, to order a howitzer company of the National Guard to the scene. The strike was not only criticized by the company's management and civil authorities, but the AFL denounced it as well. When the *Gastonia Gazette* ran a full-

Woman struggling with National Guardsman. Courtesy of Walter P. Reuther Library, Wayne State University.

page advertisement "paid for by the citizens of Gaston county," it became clear the cards were stacked against the strikers. Indeed, the *Gazette* advertisement seemed to be a call to arms of the patriotic and God-fearing against those who professed foreign ideologies and atheism:

> Men and women of Gaston County, are you willing to permit men of the type of Beal and his associates to continue to preach the doctrines of Bolshevism anywhere in America and especially in Gaston county?
>
> Before the troops arrived yesterday the mob was rampant at and near the Loray Mill in all its seething hideousness, ready to kill, ready to destroy property. The troops arrived, men uniformed and armed, men true and loyal to their country, and all became quiet and the mob disappeared.
>
> Let every man and woman in Gaston county ask the question: Am I willing to allow the mob to control Gaston County? The mob whose leaders do not believe in God and who would destroy the Government?
>
> The strike at the Loray is something more than merely a few men striking for better wages. It was not inaugurated for that purpose. It was started simply for the purpose of overthrowing this Government and destroying property and to KILL, KILL, KILL.
>
> The time is at hand for every American to do his duty.[32]

A number of songs from the early days of the strike recognized that only the union and its leaders were on the side of the workers. "Union Boys," written by Loray striker Kermit Harden, was one such song. Sung to the tune "Sonny Boy," the song urged the workers to trust the union if they hoped to gain "high pay" and the "eight-hour day." Its call for "union boys" specifically addressed the male workers at Loray. Unlike Ella May's "Mill Mother's Lament" or Christene Patton's "Loray Workers," Harden's appeal was not based upon the disruption mill work rent on the family. It is male solidarity among a brotherhood of workers, not the shared experience of mill mothers, that undergirds "Union Boys." If "the workers all stand by us" and their leaders Beal and Pershing, the union would win the day against Manville-Jenckes and its managers. Male camaraderie among workers would prevail over those who would "squeal and squeal," "steal and steal," and "lie and cheat us." The song even acknowledged the *Gastonia Gazette* as "against us." With such a pitting of forces, loyalty of workers to the union and its leaders would prove essential.

> Crowd around me here, union boys,
> And lend me your ears, union boys.
> You've a way of knowing
> I've a way of showing
> What the union means, union boys.
>
> Beal was sent from Bedford and we know his worth
> He will make a heaven for us here on earth.
>
> We've all worked for low pay right here in Loray.
> Our union will stay, union boys.
>
> Manville Jencks [*sic*] betrays us, but the workers all stand by us,
> We still have the union, union boys.
> And when we get our high pay, we will never, never stray
> From our eight-hour day, union boys.
>
> T. A. Smith will squeal and squeal
> Painter he will steel and steel.
> With our union we will go, union boys.
>
> The Gazette is against us,
> Pershing is with us. Choose of the two, union boys.
> Smith will grow lonely, want us and us only.
> With our union we will go union boys.

So climb up on the ties, union boys.
Show up all their lies, union boys.
Jencks may lie and cheat us, but he'll never beat us
Until we've won our strike, union boys.[33]

The reliance of the workers on the union as their only friend and ally was also the theme of "We Need You Most of All," written by striker Russell Knight and printed in the *Daily Worker*. Again, solidarity among the workers was the key to victory, as strikers were beseeched to "stand up and fight" and "stick to it." Set to the tune of "I Love You Most of All," the song promised "a dawning" of "a brand new day." The line "Let's keep the darn mill standing" meant standing still. During the first days of the strike when the vast majority of workers walked off the job, the mill owners kept the lights on in the mill and the machinery running to give the illusion the strike had not stopped production. According to union organizers' accounts of the strike, this tactic fooled no one.

> The time has come for our freedom
> We must stand up and fight
> The strike is on boys stick to it
> And we will win out all right.
>
> Let's keep the darn mill standing
> No matter what they all say
> Then we will soon see a dawning
> For us, a brand new day.

NTWU organizers Beal and Pershing were again mentioned by name, for whom the strikers should "just be patient." But "old Baugh," the Loray mill manager, will ultimately let "out a squeal," begging the strikers to return to work and recognizing their union.

> We must look to our union then
> Stick with it thru thick and thin,
> Then you will hear the boss let out a cry—
> "If you don't give in I'm going to die."
> So just be patient with Pershing and Beal
> Until old Baugh let's [*sic*] out his squeal.
> "Please come back, we'll recognize you
> As a union thru and thru."

So to the union we send our call
For we need you most of all.[34]

As the strike proceeded, the Communist Party sent representatives from its various component agencies to Gastonia: the Workers International Relief (WIR), the International Labor Defense (ILD), the Young Communist League, the Young Pioneers, and the *Daily Worker*. What the average millhand thought of all this is difficult to guess, but it is important to remember that the initial call for a walkout was from the workers themselves and not the NTWU. Beal and the NTWU were simply forced to seize the situation as it presented itself, unable to do much to control events. Nonetheless, the NTWU and the Communist Party showed great resolve in their desire to see the strike succeed. With equal resolve, and more firepower, Loray management and community leaders wanted to see the strike fail.[35]

It became difficult for the workers to "stick to it," as Knight's song implored. With relief funds low and strikebreakers successful in crossing picket lines, the strike collapsed. As if to crush any potential for future disruption, an angry mob destroyed the union hall and commissary on the night of April 18. Although the National Guard encampment was within earshot of the fracas, the troops did nothing to stop the demolition. They arrived only after the mob had left, arresting a group of strikers who had been guarding the property. The charges against them were too preposterous for even the Gastonia authorities, however, and they were soon released. No effort was ever made to find the true perpetrators. Governor Gardner ordered the troops removed two days later—not because they failed to stop the mob but only because their "services" were no longer necessary. In their absence, the Loray mill owners organized a Committee of One Hundred, the majority deputized as sheriffs or special policemen. Additionally, the Gastonia city council issued antiparade ordinances to stop the union's picketing and demonstrations.[36]

On May 6, the company's management evicted sixty-two families from their homes. The union responded by housing the families in a tent colony on the edge of town. Life there was quite primitive, but the tent colony did provide shelter for those who had been put out of their homes. To keep up their spirits and to pass the idle hours, the strikers often sang. While some of the songs were strike songs, others were not. These were a people with a rich musical tradition. Sometimes they sang old favorites they had brought from their homes in the Appalachian hills, while other times they sang religious hymns. As union organizer Vera Buch observed: "In general, while there seemed to be little churchgoing among the people, there was much quiet religious feeling, which showed itself in hymn singing after the meetings or in the evenings when some of them would gather in the headquarters."[37] Certainly, the favorite singer among the strikers was Ella May. And her best-loved and most requested song was "Mill Mother's Lament." Beal described a typical evening in the tent colony:

> No evening passed without getting a new strike song from our Ella May, the minstrel of our strike. She would stand somewhere in a corner, chewing tobacco or snuff and fumbling over notes of a new poem scribbled on the back of a union leaflet. Suddenly some one would call for her to sing and other voices would take up the suggestion. Then in a deep, resonant voice she would give us a simple ballad. . . . The crowd would join in with an old refrain and Ella May would add verse after verse to her song. From these the singers would drift into spirituals or hymns and many a "praise-the-Lord" would resound through the quiet night.[38]

Some of those who had been evicted from their mill homes, in fact, had returned to their jobs. But because they were suspected of union activity, they were evicted anyway. "Let Me Sleep in Your Tent Tonight, Beal," another song by the eleven-year-old striker Odel Corley, describes workers who had scabbed but were evicted nonetheless. Modeled after "May I Sleep in Your Barn Tonight, Mister?," a song that expresses sentiments of desperation and uprootedness, Corley's composition similarly tells of being left "out on the ground." Contrite for having backslid, the singer asks for forgiveness, promising to "scab . . . no more."

> Let me sleep in your tent tonight, Beal,
> For it's cold lying out on the ground,
> And the cold wind is whistling around us,
> And we have no place to lie down.
>
> Manville Jenckes has done us dirty,
> And has set us out on the ground,
> We are sorry we did not join you,
> When the rest walked out and joined.
>
> Oh Beal please forgive us,
> And take us into your tent;
> We will always stick to the union,
> And not scab on you no more.

The last verse made reference to the April 18 attack on the union's headquarters and the destruction of its cache of food. Obviously, "you" in this verse was not referring to Beal or the union but to those forces combating the strike and the union.

> You have tore up our hall and wrecked it
> And you've went and threw out our grub,
> Only God in heaven,
> Knows what you scabs done to us.[39]

A striker one day might be a scab the next and vice versa. This, and the fact that many of the workers were related to each other, established an unusual attitude on the part of the strikers toward the scabs. A scab was viewed as a potential striker; all he or she needed was some friendly persuasion. Songs provided such persuasion. Another song by Corley, this one put to the tune of "Casey Jones," beckons scabs to return to the ranks of the strikers. In the first verse, the personification of Manville-Jenckes into a "cruel millionaire" accentuated the influence the mill had over legal and civil authorities in Gastonia.

> Come all you scabs if you want to hear
> The story of a cruel millionaire.
> Manville Jenckes was the millionaire's name,
> He bought the law with his money and frame [frame-up]
> But he can't buy the union with his money and frame.

The second verse mentioned specific tactics the bosses had used to break the strike and intimidate the union's leaders. But unlike the ill-fated engineer in the original song, Beal avoids disaster.

> Told Violet Jones if she'd go back to work
> He'd buy her a new Ford and pay her well for her work.
> They throwed rotten eggs at Vera and Beal on the stand,
> They caught the man with the pistol in his hand,
> Trying to shoot Beal on the speaking stand.

Violet Jones was a striker who had been sent to New York as a speaker to raise relief funds. Her husband, Troy Jones, was a scab and had charged Beal with abduction. When Violet Jones testified in court she had gone to New York voluntarily, charges were dropped. On another occasion, her husband tried to throw a stick of dynamite at George Pershing while he was addressing strikers from a speaker's stand. Although Troy Jones was caught in time, the authorities only gave him a warning. Whether Violet Jones was ever actually offered a new Ford for returning to work, as the song suggests, cannot be substantiated by any of the accounts of the strike.[40]

How easy or hard it was to convince a scab to return to the strike is difficult to measure. Undoubtedly, it would have varied from individual to individual and from one time in the course of the strike to another. But this short little verse by Corley certainly gave the impression that a scab could easily be won over (or bought). "I Bought a Scab for Fifty Cents" was sung to the popular World War I tune "Mademoiselle from Armentières."

> I bought a scab for fifty cents, parlie voo,
> I bought a scab for fifty cents, parlie voo,
> I bought a scab for fifty cents,
> The son of a gun jumped over the fence,
> Hinky Dinky, parlie voo.[41]

Even though most workers had returned to their jobs within a month of the outbreak of the strike, the NTWU persevered. On June 7, the NTWU conducted a demonstration during the change in shifts. After a scuffle, five policemen entered the strikers' tent colony without a warrant. An armed guard had been maintained at the tent colony to keep it from meeting the same fate as their union headquarters. Furthermore, the union had written Governor Gardner on May 16 informing him that they had constructed a new headquarters and intended to defend it against hostile forces. A confrontation took place; gunshots were fired; and four officers were wounded, Chief O. F. Aderholt mortally. One Communist organizer, Joseph Harrison, was shot.[42]

The shooting of Chief Aderholt sent the people of Gastonia into hysterics. A mob led by the Loray mill's attorney descended upon the tent colony and destroyed it. Though many escaped into the woods, more than a hundred of the residents were jailed. Beal, Harrison, and K. O. Byers, Beal's bodyguard, fled, seeking medical attention for Harrison. After getting him to the hospital, Beal and Byers escaped to Charlotte and then to Spartanburg, South Carolina. There they were apprehended by police and returned to Gastonia. Beal, Byers, Harrison, and thirteen others were charged with conspiracy leading to murder.[43]

Those accused of the murder of Chief Aderholt spent nearly two months in jail before the case went to trial. Initially, authorities rounded up anyone associated with the strike, and both NTWU organizers and strikers were hauled off to jail. In fact, many of those arrested did not even know Aderholt had been shot. Not knowing why they were being incarcerated increased their anxiety. Vera Buch remembered how the women were crowded into a small cell in the Gastonia jailhouse. To pass the time and quell their fears, the women sang. As Buch recounted in her autobiography, *A Radical Life*:

> How long we would have to stay here was our principal concern. Sophie [Melvin] and Edith [Miller, two NTWU organizers,] started some singing to cheer the strikers up; we staff kept our worries to ourselves. . . .
>
> We passed the interminable days with talk and with ballad singing. Gladys Wallace, [one of the strikers] whose voice was normally somewhat raucous, sang the entire ballad of Barbry Allen musically and with feeling. I remembered how my mother used to sing that ballad long ago. All of the women knew any number of ballads, most of them rather mournful . . . or was it the misery, the uncertainty, the worry of our circumstances that made them seem so?
>
> How lustily we sang, all joining in, all crowded together as we were in that little cell, how much feeling we threw into each verse! Anything to forget for a moment our bodily aches and discomforts, above all our anxiety.[44]

Another organizer, Amy Schechter, contributed to the music, which offered a temporary escape from their worries. From "a refined, cultured, rather prim environment" in England, her personal repertoire had come across the Atlantic with her.

> Amy was a graduate of Barnard College and had spent some time working for the labor bureau in London. From her English days she had a stock of songs with a Cockney accent:
> Oh girls, oh girls, take warning and never let it be.
> Never let a sailor go higher than your knee.[45]

The shooting of Chief Aderholt not only inspired singing among those imprisoned for his murder, but the event itself and the subsequent destruction of the tent colony were chronicled in two songs by Ella May. "Chief Aderholt" was modeled on the mountain ballad "Floyd Collins," about a young man trapped in a cave. Ella May's song tells the story of the police chief's shooting and the imprisonment of the strikers and their organizers. Just as the unfortunate victim in the original song explores a cave against his parents' wishes and perishes when rescue efforts fail, Chief Aderholt ventures into the tent colony against his better judgment and meets "his fatal doom."

> Come all of you good people, and listen while I tell;
> The story of Chief Aderholt, the man you all knew well.

> It was on one Friday evening, the seventh day of June,
> He went down to the union ground and met his fatal doom.

Understandably, more sympathy and concern are expressed for the strike leaders than for the fallen police chief. Although those arrested have been "shoved . . . into prison" and "refused . . . bail," the song implores the workers to support their imprisoned leaders.

> They locked up our leaders, they put them into jail,
> They shoved them into prison, refused to give them bail.
> The workers joined together, and this was their reply,
> "We'll never, no, we'll never, let our leaders die."

Another verse refers to the change of venue for the upcoming trial to Charlotte, while expressing hope for their leaders' freedom and a call for unionization.

> They moved the trial to Charlotte, got lawyers from every town;
> I'm sure we'll hear them speak again upon the union ground.
> While Vera, she's in prison, Manville Jenckes is in pain.
> Come join the Textile Union, and show them you are game.

Indeed, this promise of a union was not for just the Loray mill or Gastonia or even the larger Carolina Piedmont, but rather it was a promise for "all over the South." As with her most popular song, "Mill Mother's Lament," the connection between worker solidarity and the ability to do better for one's family was again affirmed. In this way, issues of class and gender are once more conjoined. If "we stand together" with the union's leaders and the union, "we can wear good clothes, and live in a better house."

> We're going to have a union all over the South,
> Where we can wear good clothes, and live in a better house;
> No we must stand together, and to the boss reply,
> "We'll never, no, we'll never, let our leaders die."

Ultimately, it would be one of the leaders who would die, Ella May herself, but that tragic episode in the strike was still to come.[46]

Regarding the ballad Ella May modeled for "Chief Aderholt," Henry M. Belden and Arthur Palmer Hudson, the editors of *Folk Ballads from North Carolina*, note: "Perhaps no American ballad owes, for its wide diffusion, to the phonograph than does 'Floyd Collins.'" The song was recorded by Vernon Dalhart (Columbia, 1925) and sold approximately 300,000 copies. On the other side was the topical ballad "Little Mary Phagan," the model of Ella May's "Mill Mother's Lament." In addition, Ella May modeled her "All Around the Jailhouse," discussed later in this chapter, on "Waiting for a Train" (variant title, "All Around the Watertank"), popularized by country music singer Jimmie Rodgers (Victor, 1928). It is apparent that the phonograph, or Victrola as it was called, had entered the world of the millhands. Radio and motion pictures, too, were undoubtedly instrumental in bringing such folk songs and ballads into the Piedmont region. Kermit Harden's "Union Boys" modeled "Sonny Boy," a million-selling hit record that Al Jolsen had performed in the "talkie" motion picture "Singing Fool (1928). It is important to remember, however, that many of the folk ballads that Tin Pan Alley marketed on record and over the airwaves were already familiar to the people, if but in a less polished and commercial form. This makes it difficult to assess the relative importance of the emerging mass consumer culture on song-making during the strike. But certainly it had some influence.[47]

Ella May's "Two Little Strikers," set to the tune of the folksong "Two Little Children," describes a brother and sister orphaned by the attack on the tent colony. In the original song, the orphaned siblings fall asleep outside a church door, freeze to death, and are carried off to heaven to be reunited with their mother. In Ella May's song, the children's mother has been jailed and their father injured and missing. Again, family disruption is at the heart of this song, for the children "have no mother, no home." In their time of need, they turn to the union for shelter. Considering Ella May's own fate, this song is also bitterly ironic. The lyrics foreshadow her own death and her children being orphaned.

> Two little strikers, a boy and a girl,
> Sit by the union hall door.
> The little girl's hand was brown as the curls
> That played on the dress that she wore.
>
> The little boy's head was hatless,
> And tears in each little eye.
> "Why don't you go home to your mama," I said
> And this was the children's reply.
>
> "Our mama's in jail they locked her up,
> Left Jim and I alone,
> So we come here to sleep in the tents, tonight,
> For we have no mother, no home.

"Our papa got hurt in the shooting Friday night,
We waited all night for him,
For he was a union guard you know,
But he never came home any more."[48]

The approaching trial of those accused of Chief Aderholt's murder strained the coffers of the ILD, which provided legal counsel. Songs were employed to assist in the soliciting of funds. Ella May's "ILD Song" called workers to "join the textile union" and "join the ILD." Membership in the union and the ILD "will help to win the victory."

Toiling on life's pilgrim pathway,
Wheresoever you may be.
It will help you, fellow workers,
If you will join the ILD.

REFRAIN:
Come and join the ILD
Come and join the ILD
It will help to win the victory,
If you join the ILD.

In the second verse, workers were reminded of their reduced pay, having experienced two 10 percent wage cuts under mill manager Johnstone.

When the bosses cut your wages,
And you toil and labor free,
Come and join the textile union,
Also join the ILD.

As in "Chief Aderholt," hope was expressed that the imprisoned union leaders would "soon be free."

Now our leaders are in prison,
But I hope they'll soon be free.
Come and join the textile union,
Also join the ILD.

Also similar to "Chief Aderholt," this was a struggle of the entire South, not just one mill or locale. For the Communist Party, the strike at the Loray mill was critical for future successes in the South. As one Communist spokesperson declared, "North Carolina is the key to the South, Gaston County is the key to North Carolina, and the Loray Mill is the key to Gaston County." Whether Ella May's reference to "the South" was made with this linkage in mind is impossible to know, but it may well have been that she had come to understand the struggle at the Loray mill in those larger terms.

> Now the South is hedged in darkness,
> Though they begin to see.
> Come and join the textile union,
> Also join the ILD.[49]

Another one of Ella May's songs from this period of the strike was "The Big Fat Boss and the Workers." Following the tune of "Polly Wolly Doodle," Ella May juxtaposed the comfortable conditions and wealth of the "boss man" with the poverty and misery of the workers. The "boss man" enjoys "a big fine car" and "a big fine bed," while the worker "has to walk" and "sleeps in a old straw bed." Once again, living conditions were the measure by which the workers' oppression was gauged.

> The boss man wants our labor, and money to pack away,
> The workers wants a union and the eight-hour day.

> The boss man hates the workers, the workers hates the boss,
> The boss man rides in a big fine car, and the workers has to walk.

> The boss man sleeps in a big fine bed, and dreams of his silver and gold.
> The workers sleeps in an old straw bed and shivers from the cold.

In the fourth verse, Ella May sang not of the misery of the workers but that of Fred Beal. With this shift, she connected the plight of Beal to that of the workers. Indeed, in the song Beal has it worse. He is "a-sleeping on the floor" while the workers at least have "an old straw bed." But any effort to create a martyr out of Beal is short-lived, for in the next line it is proclaimed, "he will soon be free again, and speak to us some more."

> Fred Beal he is in prison, a-sleeping on the floor,
> But he will soon be free again, and speak to us some more.

So there was hope. By joining the union and the ILD, workers will "show the bosses that we have starved too long." Once again, the appeal is for worker solidarity and unity.

The union is growing, the ILD is strong,
We're going to show the bosses that we have starved too long.[50]

Ella May's "All Around the Jailhouse" describes her own dedication to the strike. Modeled after "Waiting for a Train," the song expresses Ella May's lack of fear of the police and her resolve to support the union. Unlike the hobo in the original song who is a thousand miles from home, Ella May is but "one mile from the union hall." Despite the fact that her "tent now is empty," her "heart is full of joy," which contrasts sharply with the pain-ridden hobo in "Waiting for a Train." With the same hope for the union's success that is revealed in her other songs, Ella May is not just "waiting for a trial" but also "a-waiting for a strike."

All around the jailhouse
Waiting for a trial;
One mile from the union hall
Sleeping in the jail.
I walked up to the policeman
To show him I had no fear;
He said, "If you've got money
I'll see that you don't stay here."

"I haven't got a nickel,
Not a penny can I show."
"Lock her up in the cell," he said,
As he slammed the jailhouse door.
He let me out in July,
The month I dearly love;
The wide open spaces all around me,
The moon and stars above.

Everybody seems to want me,
Everybody but the scabs.
I'm on my way from the jailhouse,
I'm going back to the union hall.
Though my tent now is empty
My heart is full of joy;
I'm a mile away from the union hall,
Just a-waiting for a strike.[51]

By the time the trial date arrived, charges had been dropped against all of the women except Vera Buch, Sophie Melvin, and Amy Schechter. The trial attracted the attention of the entire nation and much of the rest of the world. The *Nation*, the *New Republic*, and other periodicals compared the trial to the not-yet-forgotten Sacco and Vanzetti affair. The Communist Party likewise claimed the trial to be a "frame-up." The ILD defended those charged, although as historian Irving Bernstein has written, they "behaved as though the defendants were more useful convicted than acquitted." The ILD lawyers were assisted by volunteers from the American Civil Liberties Union (ACLU). The ACLU lawyers were less inclined to accept the ILD's "frame-up" defense, thus causing some dissension among the lawyers themselves.[52]

John G. Carpenter led the prosecution. Among the other prosecuting attorneys were Clyde R. Hoey, Governor Gardner's brother-in-law, and A. L. Bulwinkle, the Manville-Jenckes attorney who had led the Committee of One Hundred. (In 1939 Hoey would become governor of North Carolina; as governor he would reject a plea for pardon for Beal, though he would reduce his sentence by seven years.) The presiding judge, M. V. Barnhill, agreed to a defense motion to have the trial moved. As mentioned, the new site was Charlotte, in neighboring Mecklenburg County.[53]

Carpenter went to great lengths in the trial. At one point he uncovered a wax model of the fallen chief of police dressed in his bloody uniform. This fantastic ploy was derived from the contemporary movie *The Trial of Mary Dugan*, which had recently run in both Charlotte and Gastonia, though in the movie the defense had employed this trick. When one of the jurors "went mad," the judge declared a mistrial. Several of the jurors told the press that based upon the evidence thus far presented, they would have acquitted the defendants.[54]

News of the mistrial brought further intimidation to the NTWU and ILD sympathizers and further destruction to their property. An angry mob invaded the tent colony, terrorizing the occupants. As the mob laid siege on the tent colony, they sang "Praise God from Whom All Blessings Flow," giving their actions the assumed legitimacy of a religious crusade. Ben Wells, a British Communist, and Cliff Saylor and C. M. Lell, two union organizers, were driven to a woods, beaten, and left. Following this incident, eight Communists were arrested in Charlotte, including Saylor and Lell, for conspiring to revolt against the state of North Carolina. Wells was able to identify five of his assailants.

Though tried, they were never convicted; Wells's testimony was impeached on the ground that he was an atheist.[55]

Such intimidation prompted the NTWU to call a meeting, but the opposition was committed to stop it. On September 14, vigilantes fired at a truckload of union supporters en route to the NTWU meeting. Pregnant with her tenth child, Ella May, the minstrel of the Gastonia strike, was killed. Although Ella May was killed in broad daylight with more than fifty witnesses present, the five Loray employees charged with her murder would be acquitted. Once again, justice would not be served.[56]

The killing of Ella May did not stop the singing, however. Another striker, Daisy McDonald, wrote two songs that related the events that took place during this period of the strike. "The Speakers Didn't Mind" and "On a Summer's Eve" were both set to the tune of the folksong "The Wreck of the Old Ninety-Seven." The original song details the 1903 wreck of a mail train, which ran between Washington, D.C., and Atlanta. In a number of the versions of that song, catastrophe occurs when the engineer acts recklessly because his wife had earlier spoken harshly to him. In "The Speakers Didn't Mind," it is the union leaders who are harassed and intimidated.

> On a summer night as the speaking went on,
> All the strikers were satisfied,
> The thugs threw rotten eggs at the speakers on the stand,
> It caused such a terrible fright.
>
> The speakers didn't mind that and spoke right on,
> As speakers want to do,
> It wasn't long till the police came,
> To shoot them through and through.

McDonald's song further describes the destruction of the tent colony, again causing family disruption. With the men arrested, leaving the women "to do the best they can," children "were left in the streets to roam." But despite this brutal treatment, the workers would continue to fight for better conditions because they have the assistance of the WIR.

> On that very same night the mob came down
> To the union ground you know,
> Searching high and low for the men,
> Saying "Damn you, come on, let's go."

"Mill Mother's Lament"

"We'll take you to jail and lock you up,
If you're guilty or not we don't care;
Come git out of these tents, you low down dogs,
Or will kill you all right here."

They arrested the men, left the women alone,
To do the best they can;
They tore down the tents, run them out in the woods,
"If you starve we don't give a damn."

Our poor little children they had no homes,
They were left in the streets to roam;
But the WIR put up more tents and said,
"Children, come on back home."

Encouraged that a number of their leaders were "already free," charges having been dropped against them in the murder case of Chief Aderholt, the song goes on to express hope that "all the rest will be soon" free. The song also reminded workers that "Fred Beal and Sophie [Melvin] and all the rest" were their "best friends," because "they c[a]me to the South to organize / When no one else would go."

Some of our leaders are already free
Hoping all the rest will be soon,
And if they do we'll yell with glee,
For the South will be on a boom.

Fred Beal and Sophie and all the rest,
Are our best friends, we know;
For they come to the South to organize
When no one else would go.

Heartened by such stalwart leaders, McDonald beseeched the strikers to "help them organize." Again, the connection between unionization and improved living conditions is made. With a union, mill workers will "have more money and better homes, / And live much better lives."

They've been our friends and let's be theirs,
And help them organize,

> We'll have more money and better homes,
> And live much better lives.[57]

In a similar fashion, "On a Summer Eve" recounts the setbacks the strikers and their leaders had endured. Despite the daunting prospect that "Fred Beal's in jail with many others, / Facing the electric chair," the song encourages workers to join the union and the ILD.

> On a summer eve as the sun was setting
> And the wind blew soft and dry,
> They locked up all our union leaders
> While tears stood in our eyes.
>
> Fred Beal's in jail with many others,
> Facing the electric chair,
> But we are working with the ILD
> To set our leaders clear.
>
> Come on fellow workers and join the union,
> Also the ILD
> Come help us fight this great battle
> And set our leaders free.

McDonald also made specific mention of the killing of Ella May. Herself a mill mother with a family of nine to support on $12.90 a week, McDonald could well identify with the struggle of Ella May's life. In the song, McDonald bemoans the domestic disruption created with Ella May's "five children in this world to roam." However, the ILD had once again come to the rescue, giving them "a brand new home." But the ILD needs the support of the workers to continue its fight, so McDonald implored the workers to "join the ILD."

> Come listen fellow workers about poor Ella May;
> She lost her life on the state highway.
> She'd been to a meeting as you all can see,
> Doing her bit to get our leaders free.
> She left five children in this world to roam,
> But the ILD gave them a brand new home.
> So workers come listen and you will see,
> It pays all workers to join the ILD.

With Beal and others "facing the electric chair" and Ella May dead, McDonald described the struggle for union as one for life itself. Only by joining the union can workers fight against bosses who would "rather see us hang on the gallows high."

> If we love our brothers as we all should do,
> We'll join the union help fight it through.
> We all know the boss don't care if we live or die,
> He'd rather see us hang on the gallows high.
>
> Our leaders in prison are our greatest friends,
> But the ILD will fight to the end.
> Come on fellow workers join the ILD
> And do your part to set our leaders free.
>
> We need them back on the firing line,
> To carry on the work that they left behind,
> When they were put in the dirty cell,
> In the Gastonia jail we all know well.[58]

The Communist Party would also invoke the spirit of Ella May. Hoping to capitalize on her death, the *Daily Worker* described her as the "Fearless Class War Fighter" who had been gunned down by the "mill owners' gangsters." The party called for a one-day strike and mass protests to mark her death, though neither would occur. Less than one week after her murder, the *Daily Worker* ran an article entitled "Ella May, Murdered, Lives in Her Songs of Class Strife." The *Labor Defender*, the monthly publication of the ILD, printed a likeness of the martyred minstrel on the cover of its October issue. Inside, among articles about the Gastonia strike and the trial of Chief Aderholt's alleged murderers, were two pictures of her five orphaned children. An article by Bill Dunne also included the lyrics of "Mill Mother's Lament." There the song appeared with two additional verses, which are also in Dorothy Myra Page's *Gathering Storm: A Story of the Black Belt*, a proletarian novel based upon the Gastonia strike, published in 1932. The following two verses precede the last two in Ella May's song.

> Now listen to me, workers,
> Both women and men,
> We are sure to win our Union
> If all will enter in.

> I hope this will be a warning,
> I hope you will understand,
> And help us win our victory,
> And lend to us a hand.

These two verses shift the emphasis from the plight of mothers and their children to concern for the union. It is the union here, not the children, that needs "help" and "a hand." It is quite probable that Ella May did not write these two verses. Dunne's Communist affiliation suggests the possibility that they were written by him or some other party member wishing to strengthen the call to union in Ella May's best-loved song.[59]

The next month the *Labor Defender* ran a letter Ella May had written entitled "What I Believe." The *Nation*, *New Masses*, and *North American Review* also ran stories about the killing of Ella May and the music she had composed. All three articles were written by Margaret Larkin, who had become fascinated by Ella May during the course of the strike and who was deeply troubled by her death. But neither the songs of Daisy McDonald nor the attention given to the slain musician in the liberal press could revive the strike in Gastonia. The workers' struggle in that mill town, like Ella May, was dead. All that was left to be determined was the fate of Chief Aderholt's accused murderers.[60]

By the time their second trial got under way, the prosecution had dropped charges against nine of the defendants and reduced the charges against the seven others from first- to second-degree murder. When one of the witnesses from the Young Communist League denounced religion from the witness stand, the prosecution successfully shifted the issue of the trial from murder to heresy. That was all the prosecution needed to ensure victory, and the jury delivered a guilty verdict against the accused. Beal and the other three northerners received the stiffest sentences, seventeen to twenty years. The southerners convicted were given sentences that ranged from five to fourteen years. Ironically, on the same day those convictions were handed down, a jury in Gastonia failed to indict any of the five accused of shooting Ella May.[61]

The ACLU put up $27,000 bail for the seven and the case was appealed to the North Carolina Supreme Court. In the meantime, the seven traveled to the Soviet Union. When the state's highest court refused their appeal, they forfeited their bail and remained in Russia. Eventually, the one person with the shortest sentence returned to serve his time.[62]

LABOR DEFENDER

Oct. 1929   10¢

ELLA MAY

Cover of the *Labor Defender* memorializing Ella May. Originally published in the *Labor Defender*.

Fred Beal finally returned to the United States in 1933 and went underground. Disillusioned, he denounced the ideology he once so fervently embraced. In 1938 he was arrested and imprisoned. After Beal made several

The Fighting Spirit of Ella May Lives On!

THE TEXTILE MILL BARONS, THEIR COURTS, THEIR THUGS, YEARS OF OPPRESSION, HAVE NOT KILLED IT.

Ella May fought shoulder to shoulder with her fellow-workers in the National Textile Workers' Union to obtain for herself and her five children, for her fellow-workers and for their children, freedom from mill slavery and better conditions.

She was a leading spirit in organizing the textile workers of the South. This struggle is the struggle of the unorganized workers in the steel, coal, automobile, oil and other industries.

She and the 23 Gastonia prisoners facing the electric chair and long terms in prison fought to assure better conditions for the new generation, children like the five of Ella May left orphaned by the mill bosses.

THE MILL BARONS, WITH ALL THEIR FASCIST TERRORISM COULD SUBDUE ELLA MAY ONLY WITH A BULLET IN HER BREAST.

The Textile Workers of the South Are Fighting On in the Spirit of Ella May

NEITHER BULLETS, ROPE, NOR THE WHOLE APPARATUS OF CAPITALIST OPPRESSION HAS TERRORIZED THEM. THEIR STAND SHOULD BE THE STAND OF WORKERS THROUGHOUT THE LAND.

Fight in the Spirit of Ella May for the Freedom of the Gastonia Prisoners!

The trial of the 23 strikers and union organizers facing the electric chair and long imprisonment has begun all over again. Again thousands of dollars are needed daily.

WORKERS, SWELL THE DEFENSE FUNDS

Collect in the factories, in the streets, in the homes, arrange mass meetings, form defense committees.

HELP ORGANIZE THE 300,00 SOUTHERN TEXTILE WORKERS!

HELP THE WORKERS DEFEND THEMSELVES AGAINST THE FASCIST MOBS!

RUSH FUNDS AND SEND FOR LITERATURE TO

THE GASTONIA JOINT DEFENSE AND RELIEF COMMITTEE
80 EAST 11TH STREET — NEW YORK, N. Y.

Originally published in the *Labor Defender*.

pleas for a pardon, his sentence finally was reduced, and he was released from prison in January 1942.[63]

Not only had the NTWU failed to achieve lasting gains for the Gastonia millhands, but the revolution the Communists had so earnestly hoped for was not to be realized. Although much had gone on in those few short months, little had changed. Tom Tippett described the Loray mill village after his visit in the winter of 1930: "In the winter of 1930 I visited the Loray Mill village. There was no open activity of the National Textile Workers. The union had been driven completely underground. The huge Manville-Jenckes mill was working its usual 12-hour shifts; the wages had been further reduced; the operatives were as undernourished and as miserable as before the strike. Ella May Wiggins was the only one at peace."[64]

Ella May may have been dead, but in the process of attempting to bring unionization to the textile mills of Gastonia, something had been born among the workers. They had become class conscious and aware of the need for collective action. No longer self-sufficient pioneer farmers imbued with an ethic of individualism, the realities of industrial labor had engendered within them a spirit of worker solidarity. Their desire to provide a better life for their families had pitted them against the mill owners and bosses, and during their struggle, they expressed their strength and resolve in song.

These powerful statements from the workers themselves reveal their class consciousness and gender identity. In their songs, workers voiced their discontent with their situation and their determination to fight for justice. They related the events of their strike, creating a sense of community and shared experience among the workers. Singing instilled in the workers a sense of their own strength, empowering them to "stand together," as Ella May implored. By adapting mountain ballads to express these thoughts and feelings, class consciousness and worker solidarity were given cultural legitimacy. Grafting new ideas to traditional cultural forms, as Larkin observed, gave these songs a "strange persuasiveness. . . . Their curious mingling of old and new is the true reflection of the lives of the workers."[65] These songs, indeed, were their own story.

Chapter 2

"Dreadful Memories"

Harlan County, Kentucky, 1931–32

In the course of such fights, songs expressed people's
feelings in a manner that allowed them to stand
together. . . . Rather than walking up to a gun thug and
saying, "You're a bastard," which might have resulted in a
shooting, we could express our anger much more easily
in unison with song lyrics.

—Jim Garland, *Welcome the Traveler Home*

Four years had passed since the National Miners Union (NMU) had withdrawn
defeated from the coalfields of Harlan County, Kentucky. Aunt Molly Jackson
was gone as well. The most famous troubadour of the Harlan County miners of
the early Depression years had moved to New York City's Lower East Side, leaving her home and family behind. But her memories were still with her. She had
witnessed too much pain and suffering to ever forget. They were terrible memories, to be sure, memories of grief and loss, torment and anguish, hate and
struggle. They were memories of dying infants. With such painful events etched
in her heart, Aunt Molly recalled:

> Thirty-seven babies died in my arms in the last three months of 1931. Their lit-
> tle stomachs busted open; they was mortified inside. Oh, what an awful way
> for a baby to die. Not a thing to give our babies to eat but the strong soup from
> soup beans, and that took the lining from their little stomachs, so that they
> bled inside and mortified, and died. And died so hard that before we got help
> from other states my nerves was so stirred up for four years afterward by the
> memory of them babies suffering and dying in my arms, and me sitting by their
> little dead bodies three or four hours before daylight in the dark to keep some
> hungry dog or cat from eating up their little dead bodies. Then four years later
> I still had such sad memories of these babies that I wrote this song.

From such horrific experiences that miners and their families endured, Aunt
Molly sang in mournful tones:

> Dreadful memories! How they linger,
> How they fill my heart with pain;

Oh, how hard I've tried to forget them,
But I find it all in vain.[1]

The songs of Aunt Molly Jackson and others are an integral part of the
story of Bloody Harlan. They tell a bitter tale. The music of these song-poets
describes the hard-bitten lives Kentucky miners led as the country entered the
Depression. Some of the songs are sad laments, a form of catharsis in tough
times. Others are filled with defiance and rebellion, calling for economic justice
in an unjust world. Some retell the events of the strike, praising the courage of
the miners' leaders. Still others, like the ballad above, provided solace and con-
solation years later for those who lived with the "dreadful memories" of Bloody
Harlan. Used in all these ways, songs helped give meaning to the lives of those
who composed them, sang them, and heard them.

What these songs offer, then, is a valuable historical source for understanding the lives of the miners and their families who lived through this struggle. As
products of their experience, the songs they wrote and sang give insight into
their working-class identity. Written primarily by women—Aunt Molly Jackson,
Sarah Garland Ogan Gunning, and Florence Reece—these songs provide the
unique perspective of those who watched their fathers, husbands, and brothers
slave in the mines for pennies a day. How these women perceived their situation
and how they responded to it can be found in the lyrics. The domestic disruption,
the poverty and hunger, the want of children are all told in these songs.

What is discovered in these songs' lyrics is a people defiant against the
seemingly indestructible power of the coal company and its bosses. Contrary to
the "ingrained individualism" attributed to southern workers, these miners and
their families remained steadfast in their efforts to unionize. Even though the
unions they joined and championed seemed to offer little hope of success, the
workers were relentless in their determination to organize their ranks. They
understood the importance of collective action in their struggle to provide a
decent living for their families from the coal operators who so controlled their
lives. It is noteworthy that in Sarah's version of "Dreadful Memories," a song
that told of the poverty, hunger, and death of miners and their families, her
last verse implored workers to organize. She understood well the need for collective action in the miners' struggle for higher wages and better working conditions.

We will have to join the union,
They will help you find a way

How to get a better living
And for your work get better pay.[2]

These songs reveal not only how the strikers and their families came to understand their situation, but the songs also served as the very means by which they expressed and communicated that understanding. The songs that came out of Bloody Harlan both articulated the claim to justice striking miners made against the coal operators and promoted that claim among the miners themselves. In so doing, songs helped create a shared identity of attitudes and values. As Jim Garland recalled, "songs expressed people's feelings in a manner that allowed them to stand together."[3] By employing traditional melodies and religious hymns so familiar to them, these songs expressed the workers' thoughts and feelings in an idiom deeply rooted in their own culture. "Dreadful Memories," for example, was modeled on the hymn "Precious Memories." As expressions of worker consciousness, the songs striking miners wrote and sang fused an ideology of collective action to traditional cultural forms. In this way, the ideals of unity and solidarity were advanced as compatible with the workers' own culture and values.

While the claim to justice striking miners expressed in their songs was given legitimacy by adopting traditional cultural forms, mine operators attempted to discredit the strikers and their union by red-baiting and charges of atheism. Similar to the mill owners in Gastonia, the mine operators challenged the strikers' patriotism and religious beliefs. Unionism was depicted as a foreign ideology promoted by godless Communists. As Garland remembered, "The opposition's battle cry—that the National Miners Union posed a Communist threat in Kentucky—made us realize that this strike was going to be different from previous ones, more of a political struggle than simply a battle for better wages."[4]

But like the striking millhands who were defeated in Gastonia a few years earlier, the striking miners in Harlan County were up against more than accusations of atheism and Communism. The coal operators' ability to blacklist miners suspected of union activity and evict them from their homes in company towns rendered the strikers virtually helpless in their efforts to unionize the mines. Moreover, the operators enjoyed considerable influence on local government and the press. Harlan County Sheriff John Henry Blair and his deputies acted as an arm of the coal operators in their efforts to crush union activity. But by opposing unionism in the name of God and country, the coal operators were able to justify their intimidation and violence against striking miners as the actions of the patriotic and God-fearing.

Singing also had practical benefits for striking miners. On the picket lines, songs lifted the spirits of the strikers, instilling in them the strength and resolve to persevere in their fight. Singing was "good for marching," Garland recalled, "it fits well with unionization."[5] Singing was also used to raise much needed relief funds for the unemployed strikers and their families. Both Garland and Aunt Molly traveled to New York City and other places to sing and solicit funds on behalf of the miners.

Undoubtedly, many of the songs that filled the air during those years have been lost forever. But fortunately, many have been preserved, captured by the tape recorders of folklorists who recognized the importance of these songs of protest. It is through this music, then, that the miners' struggle in Harlan County will be reexamined. As expressions of worker consciousness, the songs of Bloody Harlan offer insight into the thoughts and feelings of the striking miners and their families as they battled against the coal operators. Their songs tell their story.

Aunt Molly was by far the most important of the balladeers to emerge from the Harlan County labor struggles of the late 1920s and early 1930s. Mary Magdalene Garland, as she was named, was born to Oliver Perry Garland and Deborah Robinson Garland in 1880 in Clay County, Kentucky. When she was three years old the family moved to neighboring Laurel County, where her father opened a general store, selling groceries and dry goods to miners on credit. His business failed within two years, forcing him into the mines to support his family. He became involved in union activities, often bringing his young daughter with him to union meetings and picket lines. Aunt Molly's father had also been ordained a Baptist minister, so when he was not digging coal and preaching the gospel of unionism, he was preaching the gospel of Jesus. Aunt Molly summarized the influence her father had on her: "My dad was a strong union man and a good minister, so he taught me to be a strong union woman. . . . Just before he died my father asked me to carry on after he was gone, so if I live to be one hundred I will teach unity all of my days—one for all and all for one."[6] As Aunt Molly's comments suggest, her fundamentalist religion and her efforts for social and economic justice were intertwined. This relationship between her Baptist upbringing and her union organizing is implicit in the first stanza of one of her songs, "Little Talk with Jesus."

While fighting for my Savior here
The Devil tries me hard
He uses all his powers
My progress to retard
He's up to every move,
And yet through all I prove
A little talk with Jesus makes it right, all right.[7]

Aunt Molly's talent for putting her thoughts into verse was evident at a very early age. When she was only four she composed her first song, inspired by the Bible reading of her mother. Although one must be careful not to read too much into the lyrics crafted by a four-year-old, they do suggest a sense of solidarity with others engendered by her religious upbringing.

My friends and relations, listen if you will;
The Bible plainly tells us we shall not kill

If you love your neighbor, he will love you;
Do unto others what you want them to do to you.

If I love you, and you love me,
Oh, how happy we all would be!

But if I hit you and you will fall,
Then you won't answer me when I call,

Because you will be so mad at me
You will not want to play under my walnut tree.

So I want to be good to you so you will be good to me,
Then we can all be happy—don't you see?[8]

When Aunt Molly was six years old her mother died, survived by four children and a husband. Within a year Oliver Garland remarried; he would have eleven more children by his second wife, Sarah Elizabeth Lucas. Two of those children would also compose songs about the miners' fight to unionize, Jim and Sarah Garland. Because of the demands of such a large family, Aunt Molly received little formal education but nonetheless did learn to read and write.[9]

Aunt Molly's first brush with the law came when she was only ten. While visiting her grandfather Garland on Christmas at his farm in Clay County, she played a practical joke on some children. She blackened her face, put on a pair of her grandfather's breeches, and grabbed her grandfather's rifle. Feigning the persona of a black boy, she hoped to scare the children and have a laugh. Unfortunately for her, a writ was taken out against her by the victimized family. She was brought before a magistrate and sentenced to ten days in jail. As with so many other experiences in her life, she would capture this ordeal in song. "Mr. Cundiff, Won't You Turn Me Loose?" tells the story of her prank and punishment.[10]

At the age of fourteen, Aunt Molly married a young coal miner, Jim Stewart. By the time she was seventeen, she had given birth to two sons. During those years she had also completed a course of training as a registered nurse and midwife. After working at the Clay County hospital for ten years, she set up her own practice in Harlan County, which she maintained until a bus accident left her with a permanent disability in 1932. In her thirty-four years as a nurse and midwife, she delivered 884 babies. This work was what undoubtedly gained her the name "Aunt Molly." In the lyrics of one of her songs, she offered a sarcastic commentary on the prolific coal miners who fathered so many children.

> These Lost Creek miners
> Claim they love their wives so dear
> That they can't keep from giving them
> A baby or two every year.[11]

The dangers of mining were too familiar to the Garland family. After twenty-three years of marriage, Aunt Molly lost her husband when he was killed in a rock fall. Her father had his optic nerve destroyed from a piece of falling slate that hit his head. One of her brothers was crushed by a boulder. A rock and slate slide killed one of her sons. The grief of these losses simply compounded the bitterness that she harbored for the coal operators, whose greed forced workers to risk their lives in unsafe mines while keeping their families in poverty. Years later Aunt Molly recalled:

> I still hear hungry children cry. I held them in my arms and saw them die with the diseases of poverty—T.B., pellagra, and the bloody flux. I saw my own sister's little fourteen-month-old baby girl starve to death for milk while the coal operators was riding around in fine cars with their wives and children all dressed up in diamonds and silks, paid for by the blood and sweat of the coal miners. Oh, how can I forgive when I can never forget?[12]

Aunt Molly held the pain and anguish of these experiences in her heart. During the labor unrest in the Harlan County mines in the early Depression years, she expressed her anger toward the coal operators and her resolve to overcome their oppression. Indeed, her involvement in union activities during those years would force her out of Kentucky, along with other blacklisted organizers. Coming from a large family and having witnessed "the diseases of poverty" that afflicted the hundreds of babies she helped bring into the world, it is not surprising that so many of her songs about the miners' struggle to organize capture the hard lives of their families. For Aunt Molly, the harsh realities of miners' lives were inextricably connected to the exploitation by the bosses. Children without enough to eat, ill-clothed, living "in log cabins full of cracks so big you could throw big cats and dogs through" were all the bitter manifestations of coal operators who cared more for profits than people.[13] The songs of this troubadour of labor, and others like her, give voice to those Harlan County miners and their families.

Founded in 1819, Harlan County, Kentucky, remained an isolated area of the Southern Appalachian region throughout the nineteenth century. Situated between the Pine and Black Mountain ranges of the Cumberlands, the county borders Virginia, just northeast of the historic Cumberland Gap. In 1910 this secluded area was penetrated when the Louisville & Nashville Railroad extended a spur line into the county, and with the advent of the railroad came the development of the county's rich coal deposits.[14]

Growth was rapid. By 1928 the county boasted fifty-nine mines that produced nearly 15 million tons of bituminous coal valued at over 25 million dollars. The population grew as well. Between 1910 and 1930 the population increased over sixfold, jumping from ten thousand to sixty-four thousand. During that same period, the number of coal miners climbed from under two hundred to almost twelve thousand. Because the labor to work these mines was recruited from surrounding areas, the county's population remained distinctively homogeneous. In 1930, 90 percent of the county's residents were native-born, 9 percent were black, and only 1 percent were foreign-born whites. Noteworthy is the fact that many of the African Americans and almost all of the immigrants lived at United States Steel Corporation's camp in Lynch.[15]

Harlan's high-quality coal and a favorable freight rate structure had induced a number of large corporations to open subsidiary mines in the county during this period. Among the corporate giants were International Harvester,

Koppers Company, Detroit-Edison, United States Steel, Peabody Coal Corporation, Insull, and Ford Motor Company. These firms were particularly attracted by the lack of unionism in Harlan County. Except for a brief period during World War I when the United Mine Workers (UMW) organized the region, unionism was absent from Harlan County's mines. Most miners believed, and not without good reason, that union affiliation would result in their being fired, blacklisted, and evicted from their quarters in the company town. It was the high unemployment, low wages, and deteriorating working conditions brought on by the Great Depression that resuscitated unionism in Harlan County.[16]

Between 1929 and 1931 coal production plummeted and with it workers' income. Although work-sharing kept the number of miners employed from falling drastically, the average number of days worked by a Harlan County miner fell from 259 in 1929 to 175 in 1931. As a result, the average annual earnings of a miner dropped from $1,235 to $749. The human misery that accompanied these grim statistics made the times ripe for unionism. The final straw came in February 1931 when mine owners announced a 10 percent wage cut. The frustration that drew many miners toward unionism was expressed quite succinctly: "We starve while we work; we might as well strike while we starve."[17]

On the heels of the 10 percent reduction in wages, the UMW held a meeting on March 1 in Pineville, the Bell County seat. More than two thousand miners from Bell County and neighboring Harlan County attended the gathering, where UMW national vice president Philip Murray exhorted the miners to organize themselves under the UMW banner. Many of the miners took Murray's advice and signed up. Company spies at the meeting informed owners, who responded immediately by firing union members and evicting them from company towns. UMW District 19 president William Turnblazer urged the miners to hang tough and promised food and financial support for a strike. Heartened by Turnblazer's pledge of assistance, more than eleven thousand miners joined the union, and the mines closed.[18]

Many of the union miners who were discharged and evicted from the company towns moved to Evarts, one of only three noncompany towns in the county. When the relief promised by the UMW failed to materialize, desperate miners looted stores. In an effort to maintain order, scores of newly deputized mine guards converged on Evarts. Tensions mounted, and on May 5 a tragic confrontation between a group of armed miners and deputies took place. The Battle of Evarts, which lasted but thirty minutes, resulted in four dead, three deputies and one miner. In the wake of the bloody affair, Governor Flem D.

Evarts, Kentucky in the wake of the Battle of Evarts. Courtesy of Walter P. Reuther Library, Wayne State University.

Sampson met with Turnblazer. According to the terms of their agreement, National Guard troops would be dispatched to the area; food would be distributed to the miners and their families; union miners would be reemployed; deputized mine guards would be relieved; and the UMW would end its organizing efforts. In short, the union was raising the white flag. Nonetheless, the mine operators would not accept the terms of the agreement. Four hundred National Guard troops arrived on May 6, but they were used to break up union demonstrations and protect the mines. Even so, Sheriff Blair refused to disarm or dismiss his deputized mine guards.[19]

Less than two weeks after the Battle of Evarts, Blair and his deputies conducted a raid on the UMW offices in Evarts, allegedly discovering International Workers of the World materials. This allowed authorities to impose Kentucky's criminal syndicalism law, charging the accused with conspiracy to overthrow the government. Arrests were also made in connection with the deaths of the three deputies. In the end, forty-three union members, including Turnblazer, were indicted and jailed for the slayings. Charges of robbery and banding and confederating (associating for the purpose of illegal activity) were also brought against over a hundred unionists.[20]

Against these forces of intimidation, the UMW gave up its efforts to organize the Harlan County miners. Calling their strike a "wildcat," Turnblazer told the miners to return to work. No explanation was ever given for this sharp reversal, but once again the UMW retreated from Harlan County. Into this vacuum stepped the Communist Party's NMU.[21]

The struggle of the Harlan County miners against the coal operators appeared to have all the elements of the class war that Marx had predicted. Here in the isolated coal communities of eastern Kentucky, the oppressed proletariat was wresting itself from exploitative bourgeoisie capitalists. For workers feeling betrayed by the UMW, which had failed in its organizing efforts, the NMU brought renewed hope. However, the coal operators, who had just succeeded in defeating the UMW, were not about to allow the more radical NMU a foothold.[22]

The NMU organizers entered Harlan County weary from their defeats in western Pennsylvania, eastern Ohio, and northern West Virginia. In those coalfields the NMU had led forty thousand miners in the largest strike ever conducted by the Communist Party. Despite their valiant efforts, they ultimately failed, and they moved into Harlan County tired and cautious. Feeling betrayed by the UMW, the miners of Harlan County were not cautious but instead had grown increasingly impatient for change.[23]

The UMW strike was completely dead when the first of the NMU organizers, Dan Slinger, alias Dan Brooks, arrived in Harlan County on June 19. Brooks was followed by others who disseminated radical literature and established soup kitchens for the starving miners. In mid-July a delegation led by Brooks traveled to Pittsburgh for the NMU convention. At the convention, the NMU's national secretary, Frank Borich, extended a charter to the Harlan County miners and promised that a strike would be called at the next convention. Until then, relief efforts were to accompany union organizing in the county.[24]

Toward that end, the miners built soup kitchens to help feed their families. During the spring and summer months when their gardens were producing and neighboring farmers could contribute, they were able to get by. But by autumn, food was in short supply. Aunt Molly recalled the situation:

By the middle of October we was desperate; we did not see how we was going to live. For two or three days we did not have anything to make soup out of. On the 17th morning in October my sister's little girl waked me up early. She had 15 little ragged children and she was taking them around to the soup kitchen to try to get them a bowl of soup. She told me some of them children had not eat anything in two days. It was a cold rainy morning; the little children was all bare-footed, and the blood was running out of the tops of their little feet and dripping down between their little toes onto the ground. You could track them to the soup kitchen by the blood. After they passed by I just set down by the table and began to wonder what to try to do next.[25]

The song inspired by this experience, "Kentucky Miner's Wife" ("Ragged Hungry Blues"), not only poignantly expressed the horrible misery of the coal-mining families, but Aunt Molly's comments offer a glimpse into her creative process at work. As she put it: "Then I began to sing out my blues to express my feeling. This song comes from the heart and not just from the point of a pen."

> I'm sad and weary, I got those hungry ragged blues;
> I'm sad and weary, I got those hungry ragged blues;
> Not a penny in my pocket to buy one thing I need to use.
>
> I woke up this morning with the worst blues I ever had in my life;
> I woke up this morning with the worst blues I ever had in my life;
> Not a bite to cook for breakfast, poor coal miner's wife.[26]

It was not laziness or an unwillingness to work that had resulted in the miners living in such deprivation. As Aunt Molly intimated in the third stanza: "When my husband works in the coal mine he loads a car most every trip." He was "denied his scrip" because a substantial portion of his pay went "to pay his mine expense." It was common practice in the mining industry to subtract the cost of workers' expenses from their pay. These expenses were for such things as carbide for making a light and the sharpening of their picks and augers. Workers also had their pay docked for rent for their company-owned housing and a fee for the company doctor, regardless of whether a family needed a physician's care. As Aunt Molly remembered:

In 19 and 31 the Kentucky coal miners was asked to dig coal for 33 cents a ton and they had to pay the company for the carbide to make a light and coalite to shock the coal. And they had to pay for their picks and augers to be sharpened—the coal company took one dollar from each man's wages every month for a company doctor even if he did not have to call the doctor once. All we had to make a light in our shacks was kerosene lamps, and after the miners was blacklisted for joining the union March 5, 1931, the company doctor refused to come to any of the coal miner's families unless he was paid in advance. So I had to nurse all the little children till the last breath left them, and all the light I had was a string in a can lid with a little bacon grease on it.[7]

The mention of "scrip" in the song refers to the company-issued currency with which the miners were paid. Company scrip could only be used at the company-owned stores, where prices were often higher than independently run establishments. The inflated prices that miners were consequently forced to pay compounded their economic woes while simultaneously strengthening the control mine owners had over their workers. In fact, during particularly depressed periods in the coal industry, companies often realized greater profits from their monopoly on stores, commissaries, and housing than they did from their coal sales.[28]

When my husband works in the coal mine he loads a car most every trip;
When my husband works in the coal mine he loads a car most every trip;
Then he goes to the office that evening and gets denied his scrip.

Just because he took all he made that day to pay his mine expense;
Just because he took all he made that day to pay his mine expense;
A man that'll work for coalite and carbide ain't got a lick of sense.[29]

Written from the perspective of a "poor coal miner's wife," "Ragged Hungry Blues" directly links the exploitation of the miners by the company bosses to the desperation of mothers unable to care properly for their children. It is this human dimension of poverty and want "pictured on every face" that made Aunt Molly's song so compelling.

All the women in this coal camp are sitting with bowed-down heads;
All the women in this coal camp are sitting with bowed-down heads;
Ragged and barefooted, and their children are a-crying for bread.

This mining town I live in is a dead and lonely place;
This mining town I live in is a dead and lonely place;
Where pity and starvation are pictured on every face.

In another verse, Aunt Molly juxtaposed the dangers of coal mining, dangers she knew well from tragedies that struck her own family, with wages that paid for "just coalite and carbide."

> Oh, don't go under that mountain with the slate a-hanging
>   over your head;
> Oh, don't go under that mountain with the slate a-hanging
>   over your head;
> And work for just coalite and carbide and your children
>   a-crying for bread.

> Oh, listen, friends and workers, please take a friend's
>   advice;
> Oh, listen, friends and workers, please take a friend's
>   advice;
> Don't go load no more, don't pull no more, till you get
>   a living price.

Even in this song so filled with suffering and desperation—"Where pity and starvation are pictured on every face"—there is still present a spirit of defiance and rebellion: "Don't load no more, don't pull no more, till you get a living price." While this was hardly intended as a song that would motivate the workers to go out on strike, shut down the mines, and rally around the union, it does suggest something of Aunt Molly's will and determination. Even during these darkest times, she never succumbed to the intimidation of the owners. She never accepted defeat; her struggle would always continue, as implied by her comment, "I just set down by the table and began to wonder what to try to do next."[30]

Although "Ragged Hungry Blues" might not have roused the miners to organize and strike "till they get a living price," Aunt Molly's "I Am a Union Woman" was such a song. Like so many other labor songs to come out of the Appalachian hills, it was modeled after a familiar broadside ballad, "Jackie Frazier." In so doing, union membership was given cultural legitimacy, tying unionization to music familiar to the people. Florence Reece used the same melody for "Which Side Are You On?" the most famous of all the songs to emerge from the Harlan County coalfields. Aunt Molly sang "I Am a Union Woman" before speaking at union rallies.

> I am a union woman,
> As brave as I can be;
> I do not like the bosses,
> And the bosses don't like me.

CHORUS:
Join the NMU,
Come join the NMU.[31]

The coal operators often attempted to discredit union activity by insinuat-
ing that it was un-American, the product of northern radicals. Red-baiting was
a particularly potent tool against unions in Kentucky, since the state had criminal syndicalism statutes. To be called a "Rooshian Red," then, carried with it
potentially severe consequences. As the third verse mentions, Aunt Molly's
husband, Bill Jackson, was refused employment because of his wife's union activity and her being labeled a "Rooshian Red." In fact, he divorced Aunt Molly
in 1931 to escape reprisals against her.

I was raised in old Kentucky,
In Kentucky borned and bred;
And when I joined the union
They called me a Rooshian Red.

When my husband asked the boss for a job
These is the words he said:
"Bill Jackson, I can't work you sir,
Your wife's a Rooshian Red."

Accusations of being a Communist incensed Aunt Molly. As she later said: "I've
been framed up and accused of being a Red when I did not understand what
they meant. I never heard tell of a Communist until after I left Kentucky—then I
had passed fifty—but they called me a Red. I got all of my progressive ideas
from my hard tough struggles, and nowhere else." Nonetheless, Aunt Molly's
class consciousness is clearly evident in the last verse. It is "with blood" that
the miners' claim to justice is made, while the bosses' "banner is a dollar sign."

The bosses ride fine horses
While we walk in the mud;
Their banner is a dollar sign
While ours is striped with blood.[32]

Certainly the NMU was led by a number of Communist Party members. But
it was not a shared Communist ideology that attracted Harlan County miners to
the NMU's ranks, it was the promise of higher wages and better working condi-

tions that unionization might achieve. The striking miners had only the foggiest notions of what Communism represented, though they knew well what a union could mean. As Jim Garland later commented: "People were already calling us names they themselves didn't understand; even some of the working people were calling us the Communist party. If you had at this time said to a group of average mountain men, 'I'm a Communist,' they more than likely would have answered, 'I'm a Baptist,' or 'I'm a Mason.'"[33]

Many of the miners who joined the NMU had previously thrown their lot in with the UMW and would later join the Committee for Industrial Organization (CIO), and the miners' protest songs suggest something of the fluidity of their allegiance.[34] Later in the 1930s, when John L. Lewis and the CIO attempted to organize the mines, the refrain of "I Am a Union Woman" was changed accordingly. As Aunt Molly herself said: "When I was organizing the miners around Bell and Harlan Counties in 19 and 31, I sang this song. I used it in my organizational work; I always sung this before giving my speech. In those days it was 'Join the NMU.' But later on, John L. Lewis started a real democratic organization, so I changed it to 'Join the CIO.'"[35]

Regardless as to whether the miners themselves perceived their efforts as a Marxist revolution in the making, a number of northern intellectuals were intrigued by the prospects. Foremost among the groups that traveled to Harlan County on the heels of the NMU's arrival was the Dreiser Committee. Led by leftist writer Theodore Dreiser and accompanied by such literary giants as John Dos Passos and Sherwood Anderson, they came to investigate the conditions in Harlan County. During the course of their stay, they met Aunt Molly and listened to her sing. Aunt Molly testified before the visiting committee regarding malnutrition and diseases affecting miners' families. Following her testimony, she sang "Ragged Hungry Blues." Committee members were quite taken by what they heard. What attracted the Dreiser Committee to Aunt Molly's songs was the sense of class oppression they so poignantly captured. Here it was, the Dreiser Committee believed, the rugged articulation of workers rising up in rebellion against bourgeoisie capitalism. So touched were they by these bitter musical laments that they included Aunt Molly's "Kentucky Miners' Wives Ragged Hungry Blues" (a variant title of her "Ragged Hungry Blues") in the preface of the published product of their inquiry, *Harlan Miners Speak*. Indeed, Jim Garland commented years later: "The Dreiser people were so impressed by her that they thought she was just about the whole Kentucky strike."[36]

The Dreiser Committee also asked Aunt Molly and Jim Garland to travel to New York to help raise funds for the miners' relief. Willing to do anything to help the miners, they agreed. Their first appearance was in 1932 before an estimated twenty-one thousand people in New York's Bronx Coliseum. As a way of introducing herself to the crowd, Aunt Molly composed the following song:

> I was born and raised in old Kentucky;
> Molly Jackson is my name.
> I came up here to New York City,
> And I'm truly glad I came.
>
> I am soliciting for the poor Kentucky miners,
> For their children and their wives,
> Because the miners are all blacklisted
> I am compelled to save their lives.

Unionization, as Aunt Molly described it in this song, was a direct response to the wage cuts miners had experienced at the hands of the coal operators. Blacklisted for joining the union, unemployed miners were unable to provide for their families, resulting in hunger and death.

> The miners in Bell and Harlan counties organized a union;
> This is all the poor coal miners done,
> Because the coal operators cut down their wages
> To 33 cents and less a ton.
>
> All this summer we have had to listen
> To hungry children's cries;
> Through the hot part of the summer
> Our little babies died like flies.

By contrasting "coal operators and their wives" who "dressed in jewels and silk" with "poor coal miners' babies / Starved to death for bread and milk," Aunt Molly expressed her sense of class consciousness in a most fundamental manner and made her appeal to the crowd in the most human of terms.

> While the coal operators and their wives
> All went dressed in jewels and silk,
> The poor coal miners' babies
> Starved to death for bread and milk.

> Now I appeal to you for tender mercy
> To give us all you have to give,
> Because I love my people dearly
> And I want them all to live.[37]

Aunt Molly and Jim Garland's appeal that night was eminently successful. Over nine hundred dollars was collected for the miners and their families. Emphasizing the importance of song, Aunt Molly recalled the collection that evening:

> I collected hatfuls of bills that night, and my youngest brother, Jim Garland, pulled off his two socks and filled them full of silver, and next morning we sent over $900 to the starving miners and their families. The songs that I composed of the true conditions of the miners in Kentucky in 1931 and 1932 helped me to collect thousands of dollars that saved hundreds of lives and helped them to build the strong coal miners' union that they have today.[38]

In all, Aunt Molly toured thirty-eight states soliciting funds for Kentucky miners.[39] Although the travels of this Appalachian troubadour were quite profitable, separation from her home and family were often difficult. Two weeks after she began her tour, Aunt Molly was "feel[ing] blue and lonesome and homesick for home."[40] In typical fashion, she composed a song that came from her heart and expressed how she was feeling at the time. As with so many of her other songs, the theme of family predominated.

> I'm nine hundred miles away from home
> I'm nine hundred miles away from home
> I'm nine hundred miles away from my home,
> I love coal miners, I do.
>
> I love coal miners, I do
> I love coal miners, I do
> I've lived among them all their lives,
> With their children and their wives,
> I dearly love a coal mining man.

Subsequent verses make specific reference to Aunt Molly's own kin who worked, and died, in the mines.

> My father was a coal mining man
> My father was a coal mining man

Then it ought be plain for you to understand
Just why I love a coal mining man.

I love coal miners, I do
I love coal miners, I do
I've lived among them all their lives,
With their children and their wives,
And I'll love 'em 'til the day I die.

I have two brothers dead and gone,
I have two brothers dead and gone,
One was killed by the slate a-fallin' down,
I love coal miners, I do.

I love coal miners, I do,
I love coal miners, I do,
I've lived among them all their lives,
With their children and their wives,
And I'll love them till the sea runs dry.[41]

While making appeals in Ohio in late 1932, Aunt Molly was seriously
injured when a bus in which she was riding crashed. The damage suit she insti-
tuted against the Toledo Express Company proved fruitless, as the company
went bankrupt while the case moved slowly through the courts.[42]

The efforts of Aunt Molly and Jim Garland to raise funds for the NMU were
more successful than the NMU's endeavor to organize the miners. During the
summer and fall of 1931, even before a strike was called by the union, organizers who came into Harlan County and the blacklisted miners who joined the
NMU met with fierce opposition. Red-baiting, intimidation, and violence were
the tools of union busting in Harlan County. The local press, county officials,
and Harlan County coal operators sought to undermine the NMU's organizing
efforts by making the union's Communist connections the central issue.
Employing Kentucky's criminal syndicalism statute, NMU organizers and members had their homes raided in search of radical literature.[43]

Sam Reece was one of the miners who had joined the NMU. Knowing that
he was being targeted by the coal operators and their hired thugs, he had been
lying low. Feeling that she "just had to do something to help," Sam's wife, Flo-

rence, composed "Which Side Are You On?"[44] The song was written on the back of a calendar since "we didn't have any stationery cause we didn't get nothing, we was doing good to live."[45] Fusing a militant battle cry with a traditional melody, this song would become the anthem of the Harlan County miners. It would also be used years later during other chapters in their labor struggle, as well as being adopted and adapted by workers in other industries.[46]

Unlike so many of Aunt Molly's compositions, which described the class division between the coal operators and the miners, Reece's famous song addressed the split between the miners themselves. "I was asking the miners," she later recalled, "all of them, which side they were on. They had to be on one side or the other; they had to be for themselves or against themselves." The song's question, "Which Side Are You On?," summoned the miners to take a stand. As Reece saw it, one was either for the union or against it; neutrality was not an option. "You'll either be a union man / Or a thug for J. H. Blair."

> Come all you poor workers
> Good news to you I'll tell
> How the good old union
> Has come in here to dwell.
>
> CHORUS:
> Which side are you on?
> Which side are you on?
>
> We're starting our good battle
> We know we're sure to win
> Because we've got the gun-thugs
> A-lookin' very thin.
>
> If you go to Harlan County
> There is no neutral there
> You'll either be a union man
> Or a thug for J. H. Blair.[47]

But similar to many of Aunt Molly's songs, the miners' struggle to form a union was fundamentally an effort to better provide for their families. As Reece later recalled the effects of malnutrition that plagued the miners and their families, "The little children, they'd have little legs and a big stomach. Some men staggered when they walked, they were so hungry." Indeed, in the song class distinction is characterized in terms of the coal operators' children who "live in luxury," and the miners' children who are "almost wild." To "be a man," then, was to join the union and defend one's family against those who would "take away our bread."

> They say they have to guard us
> To educate their child
> Their children live in luxury
> Our children almost wild.
>
> With pistols and with rifles
> They take away our bread
> And if you miners hinted it
> They'll sock you on the head.
>
> Gentlemen, can you stand it?
> Oh, tell me how you can?
> Will you be a gun thug
> Or will you be a man?

Also like Aunt Molly, in the last verse Reece made reference to her own family.

> My daddy was a miner
> He's now in the air and sun
> He'll be with you fellow workers
> Till every battle's won.

The phrase "in the air and sun" meant being blacklisted. By the time the NMU began its organizing in Harlan County, any miner with known union affiliation had been denied work, which severely crippled the NMU's attempt to build a strong union. The miners who were willing to join the NMU were not working, and those who had returned to the mines were not willing to join.[48]

The coal operators' strategy of violence and intimidation was working, as scores of union members were rounded up and imprisoned. Before she left on her fund-raising tour, Aunt Molly had been one of them. As with so many of her other experiences, she expressed her feelings in song. Once again, song-making was a hybrid process, grafting new lyrics to an old mountain ballad. "I picked up the melody and then composed the words to fit the melody." The result was "Lonesome Jailhouse Blues." In the song, Aunt Molly not only bemoaned being "locked up in prison" with "the worst kind of blues" she "ever had," but she declared she was "framed up" for having "joined the union."

> Listen, friends and workers,
> I have some very sad news;
> Your Aunt Molly's locked up in prison
> With the lonesome jailhouse blues.
>
> You may find someone will tell you
> The jailhouse blues ain't bad;
> They're the worst kind of blues
> Your Aunt Molly ever had.
>
> I joined the miners' union,
> That made them mad at me.
> Now I'm locked up in prison
> Just as lonesome as I can be.
>
> I'm locked up in prison
> Walking on a concrete floor.
> When I leave here this time,
> I don't want to be here no more.
>
> Because I joined the union
> They framed up a lot of lies on me;
> They had me put in prison
> I am just as lonesome as I can be.

In "Lonesome Jailhouse Blues," Aunt Molly promoted the various arms of the Communist Party that were active in the strike, the NMU and the International Labor Defense (ILD). The ILD provided legal assistance to those accused of the Evarts murders and to those charged with violating Kentucky's criminal syndicalism laws.

> I am locked up in prison,
> Just as lonesome as I can be;
> I want you to write me a letter
> To the dear old ILD.

> Tell them I am in prison
> Then they will know what to do.
> The bosses had me put in jail
> For joining the NMU.

What is perhaps most striking about "Lonesome Jailhouse Blues" is the defiant attitude and fighting spirit expressed. Even in a song in which she lamented her imprisonment for union activity, Aunt Molly remained combative; she had not resigned herself to the power of the bosses. In the last verse, Aunt Molly entreated others to join the union.

> This NMU means union
> Many thousand strong;
> And if you will come and join us,
> We will teach you right from wrong.[49]

While "Lonesome Jailhouse Blues" is about the intimidation and imprisonment that Aunt Molly herself experienced, her "Kentucky Miners' Dreadful Fate" tells the story of the violence met by others associated with the NMU. In the first part of the song, Aunt Molly related the ordeal of organizer Tom Myerscough and Jim Grace, a preacher and local union contact. The two were picked up by authorities in Neon, Kentucky, in neighboring Letcher County and handed over to Harlan County "gun thugs," who drove them to a mountaintop near Larue, Virginia. "Jim Grace and I were 'invited' to fight by three heavily armed Harlan County gun thugs to whom we had been turned over by the thugs of Letcher County," Myerscough related. Fearing for his life, Myerscough managed to escape under the cover of darkness and a heavy rain, only to be picked up by the "law" hours later in Virginia. Grace was also able to get away but not before being badly beaten.

> Dear Comrades, listen to my song,
> A story I'll relate
> About the old Kentucky hills,
> And the miners' dreadful fate.
>
> The coal operators have robbed the miners,
> Of their food and daily bread,
> And then they send their gun thugs 'round
> To shoot and kill us dead.

The gangsters rove from town to town,
They went from place to place,
Until they came on comrade Tom
And also comrade Grace.

They drove them onto a mountain top,
"Get out of this car they said.
"We know you both are union men,
And we aim to kill you dead."

At first they beat up comrade Tom,
And bruised up his head and face,
And left him on the spot to die,
Then turned on comrade Grace.

And when they turned on comrade Grace,
"Your time is next," they said.
They also beat this comrade up,
And left him there for dead.

Despite their ordeal, both Myerscough and Grace ended up in jail. As in "Lonesome Jailhouse Blues," Aunt Molly credited the ILD for its work in getting imprisoned unionists released from jail.

Both comrade Tom and comrade Grace
Was placed in a lousy jail.
And the gangsters told them to their face
They could not have no bail.

So then the union miners said,
"Our comrades must go free."
So they sat down and wrote a letter
To the dear old ILD.

The ILD sets prisoners free
And takes them out of jail.
Now they are out of the gun thugs hands
For they don't need no bail.[50]

This long, episodic song also refers to the destruction of the union's soup kitchens. The Workers International Relief (WIR) had set up seven soup kitchens for the starving miners and their families, but these feeding stations became favorite targets of the gun thugs who roamed the countryside. On the evening of August 30, Deputy Lee Fleenor arrived at the Clovertown soup kitchen. He fixed his headlights on the building but was himself concealed by the darkness. With guns drawn, three frightened men—Joe Moore; Julius Baldwin, a NMU local secretary; and his brother, Jeff Baldwin—stepped into the glare of the headlights. Shots were exchanged. When it was over, Moore and Julius Baldwin were dead and Jeff Baldwin was seriously wounded; Fleenor escaped injury. After a county political shake-up a year later, Fleenor was finally tried for murder. He was acquitted by a jury, however, after they deliberated only five minutes.

> Last August at the WIR kitchen
> The gun thugs drove up to the door
> They shot and killed our comrade Baldwin,
> And also comrade Moore.
>
> So when the miners' children starved
> And deprived of feeds and bread
> The operators send their gun thugs 'round
> To fill them full of lead.

Again as in "Lonesome Jailhouse Blues," Aunt Molly concluded "Kentucky Miners' Dreadful Fate" with a call for collective action. Despite the repression she described in the song, she maintained her determination to support the union.

> So, comrades, you have heard my song,
> And every word is true.
> Why don't you miners come along
> And join the NMU.
>
> Join the dear old ILD
> As well as the NMU
> And we'll whoop and yell and fight like hell
> Just what we ought to do.[51]

As a result of this campaign of repression, in September the NMU transferred its base of operations to neighboring Bell County. In the Straight

Creek section of Bell County and the Brush Creek section of Knox County, the NMU enjoyed a positive response among the miners. Thereafter, those counties became the focus of the union's investigations, rallies, and strikes. It was after this move that the Dreiser Committee traveled into the region to investigate and publicize the conditions in the Harlan and Bell County coalfields. Although publication of *Harlan Miners Speak* came too late to aid the NMU strike effort, the national attention the Dreiser Committee's November visit brought to the region resulted in some immediate relief. It also encouraged the miners who joined the union to press for a strike. NMU leaders hesitated, knowing their membership was largely unemployed, blacklisted miners. But when 250 local NMU delegates met in Pineville on December 13, a strike was planned. "Thus," as John W. Hevener has noted in *Which Side Are You On?*, "the writers' visit gave an impetus to a futile strike that ultimately resulted in even greater unemployment and destitution among the miners."[52]

The NMU called a general strike for January 1, 1932. The union's strike demands included $4.80 per day wages for skilled workers, $3.60 to $4.80 for unskilled workers, and $.50 per ton for loaders. These rates represented a return to pre-Depression pay, approximately twice the existing levels. The NMU also demanded an eight-hour day; pay for dead work; freedom to trade at other than company stores; payment in cash rather than scrip; election of checkweighmen; reemployment of all blacklisted miners; dismissal of all privately paid mine guards; release of all miners and union leaders jailed for strike activity; freedom to picket, strike, and join the NMU; and recognition of the NMU as the miners' bargaining agent.[53]

With so few NMU members actually working in the mines, the strike was doomed to failure. On Monday, January 4, the strike's peak in Harlan County, only eighty-three miners were out on strike, little more than 1 percent of Harlan County's miners. Within a week, nearly all of the Harlan strikers either had returned to work or had been replaced. In both Bell and Knox Counties, the NMU enjoyed a slightly better response. Approximately nine hundred miners in that two-county area struck, representing 10 percent of the miners. Four mines in each of those two counties were forced to close temporarily, but within six weeks all eight mines had been reopened.[54]

The repression that coal operators used against NMU members and organizers broke the strike almost as soon as it began. On the first day of the strike, deputies dispersed a crowd of 150 miners and their allies who attempted to hold a rally in Harlan. Three days later, on January 4, a raid on strike headquarters led to the arrest of nine strike leaders. At the subsequent court hearings, one of the arrested, Doris Parks, was questioned regarding her religious views. She answered, "I believe in the religion of the workers. These workers have relied on your religion for bread and butter, and now they are starving. How can you ask them again to believe in religion?" The *Pineville Sun* and other local papers attacked the religious beliefs of the union's organizers, driving away more than half the membership. Jim Garland recalled, "The local papers continued to hammer on the religious theme to such an extent that, I believe, this issue bruised us more than any other." The eviction of a number of striking miners from company housing and a raid on the WIR warehouse served further to intimidate the miners and undermine the strike effort. In addition, the mine operators were granted a federal court injunction that prohibited mass picketing, circulating strike literature, advocating strikes, or entering company property.[55]

Even though the strike was stillborn, northern radicals continued to tour the depressed area. On February 10, a nineteen-year-old Young Communist League and NMU organizer named Harry Hirsh, alias Harry Simms, set out to meet writer Frank Waldo and a visiting committee in Pineville. Born into a Jewish working-class family in Springfield, Massachusetts, Simms had been involved in unemployment demonstrations in Waterbury, Connecticut, and Communist youth work in Chattanooga, Tennessee. Soon after coming to Harlan County in late 1931, Simms began staying with Garland, who was also active in organizing the miners. "Harry and I hit it off immediately," Garland later recalled; "soon he was staying in my house and we were organizing together." As Simms and a cohort, Green Lawson, were walking along a railroad right-of-way on their way to Pineville, they were met by deputy sheriffs riding a handcar. One of them shot Simms in the abdomen. After bleeding by the tracks for hours, he was finally taken to the Barbourville hospital, but it was too late; he died the next day. Only after Barbourville authorities deputized a large force and prohibited all demonstrations was Simms's body released. A three-person escort placed it aboard a train bound for New York City, where Simms lay in state at Communist headquarters.[56]

Garland believed that "Harry had taken the bullet that was meant for me there on Brush Creek." Shortly after attending the funeral, Garland wrote a song eulogizing Simms. "The Ballad of Harry Simms," Garland later related, "tells the story of his death and . . . describes the feelings belonging to a man [Garland] who loved and respected him." By capturing the event in song,

Garland helped memorialize the murder of Simms, certainly to the delight of the Communist Party, which depicted Simms as a martyr for the cause.

> Comrades, listen to my story,
> Comrades, listen to my song.
> I'll tell you of a hero
> That now—is dead and gone.
> I'll tell you of a young boy
> Whose age was just nineteen.
> He was the bravest union man
> That ever I have seen.
>
> Harry Simms was a pal of mine,
> We labored side by side,
> Expecting to be shot on sight
> Or taken for a ride
> By the dirty coal operator gun thugs
> That roam from town to town
> To shoot and kill our Comrades
> Wherever they may be found.
>
> Harry Simms and I were parted
> At five o'clock that day.
> "Be careful, my dear Comrade,"
> To Harry I did say.
> "I must do my duty,"
> Was his reply to me.
> "If I get killed by gun thugs
> Please don't grieve over me."
>
> Harry Simms was walking down the track
> One bright sunshiny day.
> He was a youth of courage.
> His step was light and gay.
> He did not know the gun thugs
> Were hiding on the way
> To kill our dear young Comrade
> This bright sunshiny day.

Harry Simms was killed on Brush Creek
In nineteen thirty-two.
He organized the miners
Into the NMU.
He gave his life in struggle,
That was all that he could do.
He died for the union,
Also for me and you.

Similar to Aunt Molly's "Lonesome Jailhouse Blues" and "Kentucky Miners' Dreadful Fate," "The Ballad of Harry Simms" does not express submission and resignation in the face of the terror and repression that befell the union. The last verse renews the call for miners to organize. Moreover, the bitterness and anger Garland felt in the wake of Simms's murder seem transformed into a militant radicalism in the last two lines.

Comrades, we must vow today,
This one thing we must do—
We must organize all the miners
In the good old NMU.
We'll get a million volunteers
From those who wish us well,
And sink this rotten system
In the deepest pits of hell.[57]

Shortly after the murder of Simms, the NMU determined Garland could be of greatest benefit to the union by traveling north to raise relief funds. Warrants for such charges as banding and confederation, criminal syndicalism, and conspiracy to overthrow the government had been taken out against many of the union organizers, including Garland, so his usefulness in the field was limited. Before he attended Simms's funeral service in New York, Garland and a number of others from Kentucky traveled first to Washington, D.C., with ILD attorney Allan Taub and journalist Mary Heaton Vorse to testify before a Senate subcommittee investigating conditions in the eastern minefields. Garland arrived in New York in time for Simms's funeral service, which was held in the Bronx Coliseum. As mentioned, both he and Aunt Molly performed at the service, soliciting funds from the crowd of over twenty thousand. After this appearance, both of them would continue making speaking/singing appearances on behalf of the WIR, promoting the miners' cause and raising relief funds. They

Cover of the *Labor Defender* memorializing Harry Simms. Originally published in the *Labor Defender*.

spoke to students at colleges throughout the northeast, Mount Holyoke, Yale, and Harvard among them; made appeals on subway trains; and even addressed an audience from the rostrum at the Old South Meeting House in Boston. Their efforts were quite successful, raising an average of five hundred dollars per day. However, a bus accident outside Rye, New York, in April 1932 cut short their efforts. Additionally, Garland's wife, Hazel, who had been traveling with them, miscarried while they were in Washington, D.C., for a second round of Senate hearings. The next month Jim and his wife returned to Kentucky, but Aunt Molly remained in New York.[58]

Apprehensive about their return home, Garland wrote "Welcome the Traveler Home." With warrants against him, the song makes specific reference to "gun thugs," "an old judge in Bell County," Bell County Attorney Walter B. Smith, and a "jailhouse cell . . . a'waiting." The charges were later dropped for lack of evidence.

> For to welcome the traveler home,
> For to welcome the traveler home,
> The gun thugs they are waiting
> To welcome the traveler home.
> (Repeat after each verse)
>
> There's an old judge in Bell County,
> His nose is big and long,
> And the son-of-a-gun is a'waiting
> For to welcome the traveler home.
>
> There's Walter B. Smith the attorney,
> Why he's got Gils and Combs,
> And the son-of-a-gun is a'waiting
> For to welcome this traveler home.
>
> The beans and potatoes are ready
> For to feed the traveler home,
> And the jailhouse cell is a'waiting
> For to welcome a red-neck home.

But again, it is not with an attitude of submission or resignation that Garland described his homecoming. The last verse expressed his determination to continue to fight. Indeed, in the song he characterized his struggle as akin to the patriots during the American Revolution.

When I get back to Kentucky,
And I get my .45's on,
They'll be another Boston Tea Party
If they try to welcome this red-neck home.[59]

Shortly after Jim and Hazel Garland's return, the last of the NMU organizers left Harlan County. The fight to organize the eastern Kentucky mines not only resulted in the death of Harry Simms and a number of other unionists, it also sounded the death knell of the NMU in the Kentucky coalfields. However, recognizing his skills as an organizer and his commitment to the miners' cause, the union's national leadership did convince Garland to return to New York for six weeks of training in the organizing of unemployed councils. Once he returned, he led a forty-six-person delegation to Frankfort, Kentucky, to meet with Governor Ruby Laffoon. Although they did get an opportunity to speak to the governor, he promised no relief for the starving Kentucky miners and their families.[60]

Garland was not only frustrated by the governor's indifference, he also had "become disgusted" with the NMU and the Trade Union Unity League (TUUL), the federation of Communist-affiliated unions. He and three others who had been involved with the unemployed councils traveled to New York to request increased funding for their work. A meeting with the TUUL's leadership brought a promise of additional financial support, but it never materialized. For all intents and purposes, the NMU and the TUUL had decided to cut their loses in Kentucky.[61]

For two years Garland made ends meet by operating a small wagon mine, digging his own coal and delivering it to local folks. By 1935 Jim and Hazel had one child with another on the way. When the wagon mine collapsed, the family decided to move to New York where Aunt Molly was living. Jim's sister, Sarah Garland Ogan, and her family would also migrate to New York in 1935. There Jim got a job with the Works Progress Administration (WPA), supplementing that income by selling fruit and chestnuts from a pushcart. He also spent more time singing and playing the guitar. Through his association with a professor at New York University (NYU), Mary Elizabeth Barnicle, he lectured on Kentucky folklife and culture at NYU and for four months had his own radio program on the university's station. The program featured "Jim Garland and his Kentucky Mountain Folk Singers," which included Jim and Hazel, Sarah Garland Ogan, Mamie Quackenbush, and Dorothy Burton. Aunt Molly, Jim, and Sarah also gained the interest of folklorists Barnicle and Alan Lomax, who recorded them for the Library of Congress.[62]

Sarah, for her part, had not been directly involved in union organizing or relief work during 1931-32. Born in 1910, thirty years after her half-sister Aunt Molly, Sarah was nonetheless influenced by her husband, Andrew, and brother, Jim, both of whom were active in the union. Although her songs of discontent generally are not specific to that time and place, like the songs of Aunt Molly, Jim Garland, and Florence Reece, her music was affected by that bitter struggle. "I Am a Girl of Constant Sorrow," "Down on the Picket Line," "I'm Going to Organize, Baby Mine," "I Hate the Capitalist System" (later "I Hate the Company Bosses"), "Come All You Coal Miners," "Old Southern Town," "Long, Long Ago," and "Dreadful Memories" are among her compositions that, though written years later, were inspired, at least in part, by Bloody Harlan. Removed as they were from the events of the strike, they are not strike songs per se, but they do communicate something of the same concerns of those written at the time. The poverty and the suffering of the miners and their families are directly linked to the greed of the coal operators. And like the songs of her siblings, Sarah's class-conscious songs fused revolutionary lyrics to traditional mountain ballads and religious hymns.[63]

For example, "I Hate the Capitalist System" tells Sarah's own story of misery and heartache. In this autobiographical song, she mentions the deaths of her husband, one of her children, and her mother, attributing all three to the "capitalist system." Andrew died of tuberculosis in 1938, one of her children died from malnutrition, and her mother from pellagra. In his prefatory comments to the song in *Hard Hitting Songs for Hard-Hit People*, a collection of protest songs from the Depression, Woody Guthrie aptly described Sarah and her music. Guthrie identified the intimate relationship between Sarah's radical ideology and her concern for her family.

> Sara loved her husband. He's dead from hard work in the mines. She loved her baby that died. She loves the 2 she's still got, and she hates the system that wrecked her family. Hates the set up that robbed her kids mouths. Hates the guns of war that aim at her sons and daughters. Hates all of these big Crooks and Greedy Rich Folks, reason is because she Loves what She Loves, and she'll fight to protect her Home.[64]

Ogan told folklorist Archie Green that she made the music up herself. He maintains, however, the song is related to a Carter Family melody, "The Sailor Boy." Either way, the song is in the mountain tradition, grafting its radical message to an indigenous folk form.

> I hate the capitalist system,
> I'll tell you the reason why,

Harlan County, Kentucky, 1931–32

They caused me so much suffering
And my dearest friends to die.

Oh yes, I guess you wonder
What they have done to me
I'm going to tell you—
My husband had T.B.

Brought on by hard work and low wages
And not enough to eat,
Going naked and hungry,
No shoes on his feet.

I guess you say he's lazy
And did not want to work;
But I must say you're crazy,
For work he did not shirk.

My husband was a coal-miner,
He worked and risked his life
To try and support three children,
Himself, his mother, his wife.

I had a blue-eyed baby,
The darling of my heart,
But for my little darling
Her mother had to part.

These rich and mighty capitalists,
They dress in jewels and silk;
But my darling, blue-eyed baby,
She starved to death for milk.

I had a darling mother,
For her I often cried,
But with these rotten conditions
My mother had to die.

> "Well, what killed your mother?"
> I hear some capitalist say,
> 'Twas the debt of hard work and starvation
> My mother had to pay.
>
> "Oh, what killed your mother?
> Oh, tell us if you please."
> "Excuse me it was pellagra
> That starvation did breed."

But even in this song of personal tragedy and pathos, a spirit of resistance is declared. The last two verses express her radical ideology and her determination to fight. Indeed, record producer Moe Asch commented that it was the most radical composition he had ever heard.

> They call this a land of plenty,
> To them I guess it's true;
> But that's to the rich old capitalists,
> Not workers like me and you.
>
> "Oh, what can you do about it,
> To these men of power and might?"
> I tell you Mr. Capitalist,
> I'm going to fight, fight, fight.[65]

Similarly, in "Long, Long Ago" Sarah describes the expropriation of the land by the coal companies. Again, family disruption and radical ideology underscore this song, which relates how "land that our grandfathers owned . . . was stole away by the capitalist band."

> Where is the land that our grandfathers owned,
> Long, long ago, long long ago?
> The capitalists they stole it; now we have no homes,
> Long, long ago, long long ago.
>
> Our Grandfathers was farmers, and owned all the land,
> Long, long ago, long, long ago.
> It was stole away by the capitalist band,
> Long, long ago, long, long ago.

Now we are ragged, hungry and cold,
The operators made millions on our grandfathers coal.[66]

These songs by Sarah not only suggest the enduring legacy of Bloody Harlan, they also proved influential in the urban folk movement of the late 1930s and 1940s. Until World War II, during the period of the Popular Front, the Left, especially the Communist Party, became increasingly interested in folk music as a tool of political subversion. The Garland clan would continue writing songs of complaint and protest in the company of Woody Guthrie, Earl Robinson, Will Geer, Pete Seeger, Huddie Ledbetter, Burl Ives, Cisco Houston, and others. Years had passed since the NMU pulled out of Harlan County defeated, but the experience of that struggle had left its mark on the Garland family and their music. The Garland clan's musical expression of the hard-bitten lives articulated a powerful sense of class consciousness, and the Left recognized and promoted this. However, the impact of the Garland clan on the "proletarian renascence," as sociologist R. Serge Denisoff has called it, occurred years after the NMU's organizing efforts in eastern Kentucky and goes beyond the scope of this study. Suffice it to say that their music not only told the story of Bloody Harlan, it also influenced the likes of Woody Guthrie and Pete Seeger years later.[67]

The NMU struggled against insurmountable odds when it entered Harlan County in the summer of 1931. The coal operators' determination to keep the mines free of unions had already forced the UMW from the area; the NMU would fare no better. Both the local press and civil authorities allied themselves with the mine owners, providing them with formidable means of repression. Red-baiting, charges of atheism, eviction from company housing, and the violence of gun thugs combined to defeat unionism in eastern Kentucky in the early 1930s. Although many blacklisted miners joined the NMU, the union was unable to attract those still working the mines. Without their support, any strike effort was doomed to failure. Nonetheless, the union struggled to promote the cause of the starving miners and their families. And while miners battled the coal operators, they composed songs narrating the story of their struggle.

These songs relate the events of the strike, praising the bravery of the union's leaders and chastising the mine owners for their greed. They express the suffering and misery of the miners and their families, while declaring their determination to fight for justice. As powerful statements of worker conscious-ness, the songs reveal a strong sense of class solidarity, articulating the need for collective action in the miners' fight for higher wages and better conditions. Moreover, by utilizing traditional mountain melodies and religious hymns, the songs verbalized the workers' thoughts and feelings in an idiom deeply rooted in their own culture, helping legitimize their claim to justice.

Theodore Dreiser and other left-wing writers were struck by these bitter expressions of the miners' discontent. These intellectuals interpreted the defi-ance and determination voiced in the lyrics as the impassioned outpourings of a disgruntled proletariat. Hoping to make potent propaganda of these trouba-dours, Aunt Molly Jackson and Jim Garland were brought north to speak and sing at rallies. Though quite successful raising relief funds, these minstrels were not able to foment the revolution leftists anticipated.

Primarily the creations of women, these songs also offer insight into how the wives, daughters, and sisters of miners perceived their situation. Hungry children, dying infants, and abject poverty—these women knew well the domestic disruption "brought on by hard work and low wages." For them, this was a fight for home and family, a battle for their loved ones, an intersection of class and gender, and that was the clear message in their songs.

Chapter 3

"Sit Down! Sit Down!"

Flint, Michigan, 1936–37

> They said, "We're going in!" We said, "over our dead bodies!" Then they started to charge. Within seconds all of us were there. Down the street—women, children, old people! Row after row. We were singing. That's when we found out we were a union!
>
> —Member, United Auto Workers Women's Auxiliary, Quoted in Seeger and Reiser, *Carry It On!*

> When the boss won't talk, don't take a walk.
> Sit Down! Sit Down!
> When the boss sees that, he'll want a little chat.
> Sit Down! Sit Down!
>
> —Maurice Sugar, "Sit Down"

Less than four months after the successful conclusion of the General Motors (GM) sit-down strike in Flint, Michigan, Merlin Bishop, educational director for the United Automobile Workers Union (UAW), addressed the National Conference of Social Workers. Commenting on the use of singing and music in the union, he noted:

> Our purpose of arousing interest in [singing and music] is entirely different from that of the employing class. For years the employers have promoted and financed various cultural activities. . . . But for what reason? The answer is obvious. It was to give the workers a means of escape from the depressing economic and social conditions created by unsatisfactory working conditions and insufficient income. It was also to develop a loyalty to the employer. We, on the other hand, are hoping to develop a working class loyalty and strive for the enrichment of a real working class culture.

Bishop's interest in fostering music and singing within the UAW was born out of his experience at Flint and other sit-down strikes of the period. Music and singing "were extremely worthwhile during the sit-down strikes," he told the assembly of social workers. As the UAW's first educational director, he viewed the singing of labor songs as both a valuable tool for rousing workers during a strike and vital "for the enrichment of a real working class culture." Indeed, in the wake of the UAW's successful campaign to win collective bargaining rights within the automobile industry, much had been done to promote singing within the union. Bands and orchestras were formed, glee clubs were assembled, and songbooks were printed, and many of the songs found in those songbooks were written by workers and union leaders who sat down in Flint.'

The strike that began in late December 1936 and continued until mid-February 1937 inspired a great deal of songwriting and singing. While most of the songs written by strikers were familiar tunes with the lyrics rewritten, some were original in both melody and verse. Still others were old standard labor songs from the Wobbly tradition, like "Solidarity Forever" and the particularly applicable "Hold the Fort." As a relatively new enterprise, the automobile industry did not have the long tradition of labor songs that mining and textiles enjoyed. Nonetheless, the Flint experience produced dozens of songs, securing an important position for singing among autoworkers, as Bishop's comments suggest.

Music and singing played a major role at Flint, largely because of the nature of a sit-down strike. The very fact that workers were together, occupying a number of plants for over six weeks, made boredom and idleness commonplace. Writing and singing songs were effective ways of maintaining morale and passing the time. Singing filled the sit-downers' many empty hours.

Singing could also be heard among those who supported the strikers from outside the plants. Scores of volunteers, many of them the wives, daughters, and sisters of those inside the factories, assisted the strike effort. And they, too, composed songs. Both on the picket lines and in the union hall, their voices were lifted in song, promoting their crusade and championing the workers "hold[ing] the fort."

Like the workers at Gastonia and Bloody Harlan, strikers at Flint advanced their cause in the lyrics they sang. Songs provided the terrain on which strikers could stake their claim to justice. In the wake of New Deal legislation that guaranteed collective bargaining rights, the Flint strikers literally voiced their demand for union representation in their songs. In a simple yet very powerful way, their songs proclaimed the very reason why they were on strike and occupying the plants: union recognition.

Through singing the strikers' demand for a union contract gained currency.

As a performative expression, singing communicated among the sit-downers and their allies their principal demand of the corporation, collective bargaining rights, reinforcing that demand and strengthening their resolve to achieve it with every verse sung. Strikers also retold the events of the strike in their songs, celebrating their victories and delighting in their bosses' defeats. Songs promoted the workers' side of the strike story, fostering a sense of shared experience among the participants. In so doing, songs helped spread and preserve the strikers' common history, keeping alive the lore of their struggle.

Moreover, singing brought the strikers and their allies together, both physically and emotionally, providing them an opportunity to flex their psychic muscle. Singing instilled in the strikers a sense of their own strength and power, even when that was tenuous. By sharing feelings, thoughts, and values, singing contributed to the construction of community and class consciousness among the workers and helped create "working class loyalty."

Written during the course of the strike, these songs capture the thoughts, feelings, and perceptions of the workers and their allies as events unfolded. Because of this, these songs are a valuable source in the study of the strike that inspired them and the workers who wrote and sang them. As powerful statements from the workers themselves, they reveal the workers' class consciousness. In these songs workers articulated their need for united action and solidarity in their battle for collective bargaining rights and union recognition. By mocking company bosses and plant supervisors in their songs, workers expressed their class identity and interests as distinct from those of corporate management.

Additionally, the songs offer insight into gender relations between male strikers and their female allies. The men inside the plants wrote songs that reveled in the strength and vigor of union brotherhood. The value of men sticking together in their battle against the bosses was paramount in their lyrics, and a spirit of male solidarity and camaraderie emanated from the songs they wrote and sang. By contrast, those written by women supporting the strike articulated their part in the struggle as an extension of their roles as wives and mothers. The strike expanded the sphere of women's domestic responsibilities, and the songs expressed this. As women saw it (and sang it), the fight for union recognition was a battle for their homes and families, a campaign for financial security and a brighter future for their children.

It is through the lens of these songs, then, that the GM sit-down strike of 1936–37 will be examined. In so doing, a deeper understanding of the striking workers at Flint can be revealed.

. . .

Described by historian Sidney Fine as "the most significant American labor conflict in the twentieth century," the Flint sit-down strike profoundly changed the history of organized labor in the United States. Success at Flint not only opened wide the door for union contracts for autoworkers, it helped promote unionization in many related industries, including steel, rubber, and glass. Though it was not the first time workers had employed the tactic of a sit-down to advance their cause, Flint's success ushered in a wave of sit-downs in a variety of workplaces. From garment workers to department store clerks, workers used this successful new strategy in their fight to secure collective bargaining rights, higher wages, and better working conditions.[2]

A fledgling enterprise at the turn of the century, the auto industry had grown tremendously during the 1920s. In the front seat among automobile manufacturers sat GM, with more than 41 percent of new car registrations in the United States in 1928. But the stock market crash and the depression that followed devastated the industry, as new car and truck sales skidded. By 1932 GM had cut employment by almost 50 percent and reduced its payroll by approximately 60 percent.[3]

By 1936, however, the year the strike began, economic recovery for the corporation was well under way. Between 1932 and 1936, net sales of the corporation for its consolidated operations more than tripled to almost $1.5 billion. This figure represented a more than thirty-fold increase in net profits before taxes. Nearly 60 percent of these profits were from the corporation's motor-vehicle business. As car and truck sales to dealers in the United States quadrupled, GM's employment doubled to more than 230,000 workers. During this same four-year period, its payroll grew 168 percent. By the measures of sales, profits, and number of employees, GM was the largest manufacturing corporation in the world.[4]

Presiding over this colossus was the corporation's president, Alfred P. Sloan Jr. Guided by a principle of "decentralized operations with co-ordinated control," Sloan modeled GM's organization on that of its largest stockholder, the du Pont company. This approach left such matters as the speed of the assembly line and hiring and firing to local control. By giving a large degree of autonomy to division heads and plant managers, efficiency, productivity, and profits were maximized.[5]

With regard to unions, General Motors was relentless in its efforts to maintain open shops. Ostensibly to abide by the statutory protection for collective bargaining provided in Section 7(a) of the National Industrial Act of 1933 and the Wagner Act of 1935, GM set up employee associations. According to a GM source, by offering this form of employee representation, these company unions were designed to "render the militant outside union superfluous." Workers generally recognized company unions as instruments of management control, unable as they were to negotiate such concerns as wages and hours. Additionally, GM rejected majority rule in favor of proportional representation when determining employee representatives for negotiation. Such an interpretation of the federal code's guideline for "representatives of their own choosing" so diluted collective bargaining rights to ensure that no outside union such as the UAW could organize and represent GM workers.[6]

A much more direct means of ensuring open shops was GM's use of espionage. No other corporation came even close to the outlays GM made to private detective services and security agencies, spending over $1 million on espionage in the three-year period prior to the strike. Indeed, GM was the Pinkerton Agency's largest industrial client. Described by the Senate committee investigating labor issues, the La Follette Civil Liberties Committee, as a "far-flung industrial Cheka," the company's use of espionage constituted the "epitome of the process of union . . . busting."[7]

The corporation also sought to mollify its workers by embracing welfare capitalism. Savings and investment programs, group-insurance plans, educational and recreational activities, and sporting events were all sponsored by the company as a way of gaining the loyalty of its workers. Since participation in many of these welfare plans was tied to membership in the employee associations, the attraction of these benefits effectively promoted the company union. Against such a formidable adversary, the UAW fought to organize.[8]

Unionization in the automotive industry had only scant success before the victory at Flint. Not only was GM determined to resist outside unions, but the politics within and among the various unions laying claim to jurisdiction within the industry also hampered organization. The UAW under the AFL was hamstrung by the Executive Council's practice of restrictive jurisdiction. By the council's unwillingness to grant a charter allowing the UAW to draw members throughout the industry, the goal of a union that would include all autoworkers was undermined. Rank-and-file members also resented the Executive Council's insistence that it control UAW locals.[9]

Other unions, such as Mechanics Educational Society of America (MESA),

Automotive Industrial Workers Association (AIWA), and Associated Automobile Workers of America (AAWA), also competed for autoworkers' allegiance. The rivalry between the UAW and other unions intensified late in 1935 during a strike called against Detroit Motor Products. When the AIWA went on strike in a wage dispute, MESA quickly joined them in sympathy. UAW members broke rank, crossing picket lines and gaining the suspicion and spite of the two other unions.[10]

Despite these forces of disunity, most laborites in the auto industry recognized the need for amalgamation into one industrial union. The autoworkers' grievances were industry-wide, requiring a united front. As a result of annual model changes, autoworkers suffered from severe seasonal unemployment. So despite high hourly wages relative to other industries, autoworkers had low annual earnings. The "speed-up" of the assembly line was another source of constant complaint for operatives. Not only did it make the work exhausting, it reinforced the sense of power workers felt the company had over them. As William "Red" Mundale, the leader of the sit-down strikers in the Fisher Body No. 2 plant, succinctly put it: "I ain't got no kick on wages, but I just don't like to be drove." Workers believed the speed of production forced those over the age forty out of work, unable as they were to maintain the pace of the assembly line. Piece rates used in some of the plants and the absence of an equitable seniority system also caused discontent among autoworkers. In large part, the strength and determination the sit-downers displayed in the strike were drawn from the deep well of animosity such depersonalizing treatment engendered.[11]

Because of these shared complaints and concerns, autoworkers understood the need for one industrial union to represent them. When the Committee for Industrial Organization (CIO) emerged from the AFL's Atlantic City convention in the autumn of 1935, the automotive industry was prime territory for the CIO's efforts to organize across the industry. It would be under the CIO banner that the UAW would win the Flint strike. In December 1935, CIO director John Brophy sent Adolph Germer to Detroit as the CIO representative. His task was to unite the independents—MESA, AIWA, and AAWA—with the UAW into one union. After considerable internal conflict, the UAW leadership was wrested from the conservative Executive Council by young "progressives." Many of the UAW's most able leaders during the sit-down strike were Communists and Socialists, which created a good deal of dissension and disharmony among UAW and CIO leaders both during the strike and in the years following.[12]

Despite these obstacles, there were reasons for hope on the part of unionists. In 1936, the UAW successfully negotiated its demands with Chrysler on rehiring procedures after the summer layoffs at its Dodge plant. More important, Franklin Roosevelt defeated Alfred Landon in the November election. As Germer commented before the election, autoworkers were "still gripped by a feeling of fear," but "the election of Roosevelt will inject *some* stiffening in their backbone." In fact, membership in the UAW jumped in the closing months of 1936. An organizational drive involving mass meetings, solicitation at factory gates, and even home visits increased paid-up membership to approximately 13.7 percent of the average employment in the industry (460,000) in 1936. Many more workers were sympathetic to the UAW and were awaiting just the kind of victory Flint would provide to sign union cards of their own.[13]

As the center of General Motors production, Flint was critical to a UAW victory. Flint was home to Chevrolet and Buick, as well as Fisher Body and AC Spark Plugs. With an estimated 80 percent of Flint's families dependent on GM's payroll, Flint was a classic company town. Elected officials, local law enforcement authorities, and the *Flint Journal* allied themselves with the corporation, upholding the GM public relations' dictum: "what happens to general motors happens to me."[14]

The situation of Flint's local of the UAW (Local 156) mirrored the national picture. Enrollment had jumped from 150 members in June 1936 to 4,500 by year's end, but this still constituted merely 10 percent of Flint's GM workforce. UAW leaders understood that only a successful strike would open the floodgates for membership. That strike was soon to come. The UAW had already successfully struck Bendix, Midland Steel, and Kelsey-Hayes, using the sit-down as its weapon in all three. But a victory against a major automobile manufacturer in its heart of production would be necessary to win exclusive collective bargaining rights for the union.[15]

UAW workers were already striking GM in Atlanta and Kansas City when workers sat down at Cleveland's Fisher Body plant on December 28. Two days later, Flint workers in Fisher Body No. 1 and No. 2 sat down. For logistical reasons, the Cleveland plant was evacuated on December 31, but the strike continued. Although the strike against GM spread to other plants across the country, national focus remained on the sit-down in Flint. The strike at Flint proved pivotal both for the success (or failure) of these other strikes and the future of the UAW in general.[16]

. . .

Why the workers sat down at Flint when they did is still an open question. That a strike was imminent is most certain. Anticipating the importance of the governor in the impending struggle, many UAW and CIO leaders believed the strike would not occur until after January 1, when Frank Murphy would be sworn in as the new governor of Michigan. Viewed by unionists as a liberal sympathetic to labor, he would play a decisive role in the strike. In addition, in January the holidays would also have passed, and the workers would have collected their bonuses. However, with the critical Cleveland plant now out, the pressure on Flint to strike to maintain the union's momentum increased. Like so many other important decisions in the course of the strike, the initial call was made by local union leaders. Bob Travis, a UAW organizer brought in from Toledo, Ohio, allegedly received news that GM was loading dies on freight cars outside Fisher Body No. 1 bound for plants in Grand Rapids and Pontiac, Michigan. Believing this shipment was being effected in an effort to circumvent a strike at the Fisher plant, he called an emergency meeting of the shop stewards during the evening lunch hour on December 30. At that meeting, Travis reminded them how GM had moved machinery following the Toledo strike in 1935, which resulted in several hundred workers losing their jobs. Without a vote of the membership, they decided to call a strike immediately.[17]

Bud Simons, the chair of the Fisher Body No. 1 shop committee, later contended that the story of the dies being shipped was fabricated. By his telling, the local leaders were concerned the plant might be closed down before a strike could be called. Low on glass because of another strike, Fisher Body No. 1 chanced a shutdown because of supply problems. If this happened, the union would lose the initiative, appearing to "be the passive victim of a plant shutdown." Which story is true "remains a moot point," as Sidney Fine has written. "It is a perfectly apparent that the dies story was at most the *occasion* for rather than the cause of the strike. Travis was determined because of the Cleveland strike to shut down No. 1 as soon as it was possible to do so; and as he concedes, he would have found one pretext or another to initiate the strike."[18]

Nonetheless, in the verses of "The Fisher Strike," the Travis version is celebrated. Sung to the tune of "The Martins and the Coys," the song retold the story of the strike's beginning.

> Gather round me and I'll tell you all a story,
> Of the Fisher Body Factory Number One.

When the dies they started moving,
The Union Men they had a meeting,
To decide right then and there what must be done.

CHORUS:
These 4000 Union Boys,
Oh, they sure made lots of noise,
They decided then and there to shut down tight.
In the office they got snooty,
So we started picket duty,
Now the Fisher Body shop is on a strike.

Now this strike it started one bright Wednesday evening,
When they loaded up a box car full of dies.
When the union boys they stopped them,
And the Railroad Workers backed them,
The officials in the office were surprised.[19]

Published within a week of the event in the local UAW newspaper, the *Flint Auto Worker*, "The Fisher Strike" popularized and perpetuated a version of the strike's origin as "Union Men" heroically responding to a company action openly and deliberately hostile to the workers—the threat of production relocation. In so doing, the song enhanced the image of the union in the eyes of GM workers, union and nonunion, while depicting the corporation as conniving and sinister. This was no small matter. For both GM and the union, public image during the strike was critical. GM tried to present itself as the good employer that had become the captive victim of a radical minority. By forcing a halt in production, this radical minority was depriving the mass of workers access to their jobs. On the other hand, for the strike to be successful, the union had to increase its ranks by winning the minds and hearts of the workers, and this "epic song of the great strike" proved to be effective propaganda for that purpose. Moreover, by modeling the lyrics to the tune of "The Martins and the Coys," the strike took on the elements of a great industrial feud between workers and management, comparable only to the legendary feud bespoke of in the original song.[20]

The reference to "These 4000 Union Boys" in the chorus of "The Fisher Strike" is also revealing. While the Flint local of the UAW had approximately four thousand members at the time the strike broke out, there were by no

means that many members employed at Fisher Body No. 1. The implicit sugges-
tion, then, that the company's actions at Fisher Body No. 1 prompted union
members in all of GM's Flint plants to strike, is a gross overstatement. In fact,
the decision "then and there to shut down tight" was made by Travis and the
committee of shop stewards he assembled the evening of December 30. No
strike vote was ever taken by Flint's UAW Local 156 or the union members of
Fisher Body No. 1, despite such a requirement by the UAW constitution.[21]

The union well understood that its ability to draw new members was
directly related to its victory in the strike. The fact that the union could
successfully seize a key plant, bringing production to a standstill, provided impressive testimony to the union's power. Consequently, songs like "The Fisher
Strike," which applauded the union's ability to exert its influence over GM,
served to promote the union among the workers as an able representative of
their interests. At other critical junctures in the six-week strike, the union was
able to outwit and out-fight GM. When these episodes were retold in song, they
boosted the morale of the strikers and became potent propaganda in the
union's campaign to organize.

Another such event occurred when Flint police attempted to retake Fisher
Body No. 2. What came to be called the "Battle of the Running Bulls" was a violent confrontation between police and strikers. ("Bull" is slang for a policeman
or detective.) The sit-downers in Fisher Body No. 2 occupied only the second
floor of the plant, while company police controlled the main gate. On the cold
winter afternoon of January 11, the company turned off the heat in the factory.
That night the gates were blocked when the sit-downers' evening meal arrived.
(At the request of state authorities, the strikers had been allowed food and
warmth since the outset of the strike.) A group of about thirty of the
approximately hundred sit-downers descended to the gates. Without resistance
from the company police, they snapped the lock and forced the gates open.
When the guards then locked themselves in the ladies' restroom, the chief of the
Fisher Body plant police, Edgar T. Adams, called police headquarters to report
the guards had been "captured" and were being held "prisoners."[22]

A few minutes later the Flint police arrived and attempted to disperse the
crowd by discharging tear gas, only to have the wind carry the fumes back
toward them. One of the UAW organizers, Victor Reuther, directed the strikers'
defense from the union's sound car. Alternating commands with martial music,
Reuther encouraged the strikers to hold fast. From the factory, the strikers
turned high-pressure hoses on the police while also heaving two-pound car-

door hinges at them. The drenched policemen beat a hasty retreat, literally freezing as the temperature hovered around 16 degrees.[23]

A second assault by police was met with a barrage of bottles, rocks, and hinges, forcing the police to retreat again. This time though, as the police left the plant, they fired into the crowd, wounding fourteen strikers and strike sympathizers. Several policemen also sustained injuries from the strikers' "popular ammunition." When Sheriff Thomas Wolcott arrived, strikers and their allies overturned his car with him still in it. As he emerged from the vehicle, he was hit by a door hinge. Although an exchange of rocks and tear gas continued between the crowd and the police for some time, the police were unable to mount another assault on the plant.[24]

The Battle of Running Bulls was an important victory for the strikers. They had proven themselves capable of repelling the police and holding the factory. In celebration of their success on that January night, two strikers, Cecil Hubel and Clarence Jobin, composed new lyrics for "There'll Be a Hot Time in the Old Town Tonight." The song both heralded the courage of "the boys . . . sticking fast" and reveled in the humiliation of the police who "never ran so fast."

> Cheer, boys, cheer,
> For we are full of fun;
> Cheer, boys, cheer,
> Old Parker's on the run;
> We had a fight last nite
> And I tell you, boys, we won,
> We had a hot time in the old town last nite.
>
> Tear gas bombs
> Were flying thick and fast;
> The lousy police,
> They knew they couldn't last.
> Because in all their lives they never ran so fast,
> As in that hot time in this old town last nite.
>
> The police are sick
> Their bodies they are sore
> I'll bet they'll never

The roof of Fisher Body No. 2 the morning after the Battle of Running Bulls. Courtesy of Walter P. Reuther Library, Wayne State University.

Fight us any more;
Because they learned last nite
That we had quite a corps.
We had a hot time in the old town last nite.

Now this scrap is o'er;
The boys are sticking fast
We'll hold our grounds
And fight here to the last
And when this strike is o'er
We'll have our contract fast,
We'll have a hot time in the old town that nite![25]

Another song inspired by the Battle of Running Bulls relished the physical violence strikers used against the police. Referring to the melee as a "jolly sight," "The Battle of Bull's [sic] Run" applauded the strikers for inflicting "bruises, bumps, and jolts / From the storm of nuts and bolts." The song's chorus accentuated the strikers' humiliation of the police by sarcastically describing how police "came marching / Bravely, with tear-gas and with gun" only to be "socked . . . on the nose."

Oh, it was a jolly sight
On that wintry, chilly, night
When the bulls came out
To throw us from the fort.
But with bruises, bumps, and jolts
From the storm of nuts and bolts
They just turned about
And made a line for port.

CHORUS:
On, on the bulls came marching
Bravely, with tear-gas and with gun.
But we coupled up the hose
And we socked 'em on the nose.

The second verse tells of the attack on Sheriff Wolcott during the most violent phase of the affray. Though he did sustain injuries from the missiles hurled by the strikers and their allies, he also came perilously close to being engulfed in flames. When his car was overturned, an overly excited striker or strike sympathizer had to be kept from igniting the gasoline that had spilled from his vehicle. Again in the song, the public humiliation of the police is underscored, calling the event "a sight for all the town."

Oh! The sherriff [*sic*] fat and fine
He came right on with his line
But his solar-plexus caved
And let him down,
As with bottles, stones, and trash
Up-side down his car did smash.
Oh! It surely was a sight for all the town.

CHORUS:
Cheer, boys, cheer
We've got them going

"Sit Down! Sit Down!"

Come one all and join the fun.
Tho it's hard we have to fight
We'll remember well the night
Of the royal, mighty battle of bull's run.[26]

Although willing to use such violence against the police, the strikers hardly considered themselves lawbreakers. They understood their possession of the factory as a necessary means toward securing their right to bargain collectively. Indeed, the legality of the sit-down as a tactic was a matter of bitter contention between GM's management and the strikers. GM maintained that the occupation of its factories was a clear violation of the corporation's property rights. By trespassing on company property, the sit-downers were denying GM use of its plants while also refusing other workers access to their jobs. The strikers countered GM's claim to its property rights by asserting their "property right in their job." Contending their right to bargain collectively had been abrogated by GM, the strikers justified taking control of the factory and stopping production on legal grounds. Arguing against the corporation's claim that the strikers were in illegal possession of the plants, union lawyers maintained the company's many violations of the Wagner Act gave GM "unclean hands." Viewed in this way, the sit-down strike was a necessary means of securing the fundamental right of collective bargaining guaranteed by federal statute but denied by the corporation.[27]

On a less legal plane, the workers' long-standing complaints against the company justified the sit-down. The speed-up of the assembly line, an inequitable seniority system, and domineering managers were among the strikers' chief complaints. As one sit-downer, Francis O'Rourke, wrote on the first day of the strike in a diary he kept: "This strike has been coming for years. Speed-up system, seniority, over-bearing foremen. You can just go so far you know, even with working men. So let's you and I stick it out with the rest of the boys, we are right and when you're right you can't lose." In another entry, he asked rhetorically:

> Did you know we were breaking a law? . . . We have done no harm. We're just honest working men that have been pushed so far and so hard that we can't keep it up any longer. They say we're lazy workers. Is a man lazy if he has not missed a day's work in two years, has not been late, and kept up with a line manufacturing forty-five bodies an hour all that time? Most of these men have done just that and our employment records prove it. . . . We don't want violence and yet . . .[28]

A number of the songs written during the Flint strike articulated this theme of rights, so central as it was to the issues at hand. The line of one song puts it quite simply: "We're here for our own rights." Another song, "The Sweat Shop," sung to the tune of "Working on the Railroad," described the struggle as a fight "to win our rights" and gain some "say."

> We're on strike, to win our rights,
> While working in the factory.
> We're going to fight, with all our might,
> To have things satisfactory.
>
> CHORUS:
> We're tired of working in the sweat shop,
> All the live long day.
> We're tired of working in the sweat shop,
> Where the boss has all the say.
> Can't you hear the whistle blowing?
> Get read [sic] to start another day.
> Can't you hear the bosses shouting?
> Dig in if you want to stay.

The second verse expressed the strikers' determination to stand up to GM by sticking behind the union.

> We're for the union hundred per cent,
> And we'll be darned if we'll relent.
> Until GM meets our demands,
> For that is where the union stands.[29]

In still another song, this one to the tune of "Where the Silver Colorado Winds Its Way," GM's denial of the workers' collective bargaining rights was underscored. The lyrics tell the story. By forcing the workers to "renounce [their] union" and "forswear [their] liberties," they are condemned "to live and die in slavery."

> The trouble in our homestead
> Was brought about this way
> When a dashing corporation
> Had the audacity to say

"You must all renounce your union
And forswear your liberties,
And we'll offer you a chance
To live and die in slavery."[30]

It was the belief that their rights had been denied that emboldened the Flint strikers to sit-down. Although most historians have argued that "the strikers were without revolutionary intent," as Sidney Fine has written, one song did describe the strike in manifestly class-charged, militant language. "The Veterans Song," sung to the tune of "Yankee Doodle," positioned the strike historically alongside the Civil War and World War I. As but another instance of class antagonism, General Motors was depicted as the moral equivalent of slave owners and war profiteers. A song of "veteran union boys" who "uphold the Constitution," the verses articulate a radical message from those least likely to be called un-American. Moreover, by putting the lyrics to the tune of "Yankee Doodle," its class-conscious message wore a patriotic mantle.

We are veteran union boys
We uphold the Constitution
We'll help the boys to win this strike
By these great resolutions.

CHORUS:
Down with Capitalism first
Break that Wall Street power
Give the working class a chance
And victory is ours

We fought in 1861
To free the world from slavery
From capitalism that was strong
And won our first great victory.

We fought in 1916 then
For Wall Street's many millions
But since the Armistice was signed
They've run it up to Billions.

> And now we have to Fight again
> But this time for our Freedom
> From being General Motors Slaves
> We have to Join the Union.[31]

Few of the dozens of songs from the Flint strike were so ideological. What was a distinguishing characteristic of the songs that emerged from the strike was the contempt and disregard vocalized by the strikers toward their corporate bosses. Whether it was GM's president, Alfred Sloan; the head of the Chevrolet Division, William Knudsen; or the plant manager for Fisher Body No. 1 and No. 2, Evan Parker—the strikers scorned and jeered and chastised management. Indeed, if there is one overarching sentiment expressed in these songs, it is this confrontational, contentious attitude toward the bosses. Considering the control the corporation held over its employees through welfare capitalism, intimidation, and espionage, the ridicule voiced in these songs is particularly poignant. Whether it be "To hell with G.M., Papa Sloan, and Mister Knudsen too" or "We, got old Parker on the run, Parlee-voo," the lyrics workers contrived to fit familiar melodies were decidedly pugnacious. By addressing corporate heads by name, the overwhelming power of the corporation seemed somehow divested, as in the following verse from "Spirit of the Union."

> Knudsen's just another man, Parlee-voo
> Knudsen's just another man, Parlee-voo
> Knudsen's just another man,
> Who ought to be kicked in the can—Hinky,
> Dinky, Parley-voo.[32]

The mocking tone of "Oh, Mister Sloan," a parody of "Mr. Gallagher and Mr. Sheen," composed by Gilliland and Beck, is another example of the strikers' castigation of their bosses. The pretentious airs of the song made it a particularly effective for lampooning management. "Mister Travis" refers to Bob Travis, a union organizer.

> Oh, Mister Sloan! Oh, Mister Sloan!
> We have known for a long time you would atone
> For the wrongs that you have done,
> We all know, yes, every one.
> Absolutely, Mister Travis!
> Positively, Mister Sloan![33]

"Sit Down! Sit Down!"

Even before the strike began, a Flint autoworker proclaimed a new relationship between the workers and their bosses in a song-poem ominously entitled "We Are Coming." Published in the *Flint Auto Worker* in December 1936, a determination to stand up to the bosses is expressed. The first verse proclaimed:

> We do not ask for unearned wealth
> Nor for a life of ease,
> To no man do we bow our head,
> To none we bend our knees.
> We're coming, we are coming,
> We're coming, yes, we're coming,
> We're coming, we are coming,
> United we can win.

Not only is the strike foreshadowed with the repeated verse, "We're coming, we are coming," but a note that accompanied the song-poem's publication portended the benefit such creative expressions could have in the coming struggle:

Dear Sir:
   In reading the *Fling Auto Worker*, the words of this parody came to my mind, and I send them to you for what they are worth. Hoping they may be of use to you.
   —A Flint Auto Worker[34]

During the strike, a takeoff on "It Ain't Gonna Rain No More" expressed a similar resolve to "bow no more." Written by striker Walter H. Frost, the song declared an end to deference toward management.

> Oh, we aint gonna bow no more, no more
> We aint gonna bow no more
> We're on the track
> Get off our back
> We aint gonna bow no more.[35]

Feigning vulgarity while mocking their bosses, strikers rewrote the lyrics to "Sweet Violets" in a scatological vein. But even in its humorous tone, the song articulated the central issue of the strike, "union contracts," as in this verse:

> So now all our men, they are inside
> They have resolved there to sit.

> They won't come out of that factory
> Till Knudsen is covered with----
> UNION CONTRACTS[36]

After the strike was settled, this hostility toward the bosses continued to be expressed in song, such as "Victory Jingle," composed by Jessie Lloyd and set to the tune of "Jingle Bells." Published in the *United Automobile Worker* two weeks after the strike ended, the song attributed the misery of "the boss" to the "power" of the union. No longer would low pay and the speed-up have to be tolerated. Having won "the right to have our say," "we will tell him where to go." Beneath the lyrics, the *United Automobile Worker* noted the adaptability of this song, suggesting "Du Pont's" be substituted with "Knudsen's, Sloan is Morgan's, ad lib."

> In the union there is power
> That's why the boss looks sour:
> He's weeping every hour
> Because he loves his workers so-o:
> He loves to pay us small
> While he improves his haul;
> More speedup is his call
> But we will tell him where to go. Oh!
>
> CHORUS:
> Du Pont's mad—we are glad—
> Union's on the way!
> Oh what fun since we have won
> The right to say our say-ay!
> Time to breathe we'll achieve—
> Decent yearly pay;
> Firm and strong we march along
> And more join up each day![37]

The strength of the union was further communicated by the very melodies strikers chose as the models for their lyrics. Upbeat and high-spirited tunes prevailed. "Mademoiselle from Armentières," "When Johnny Comes Marching Home," "Working on the Railroad," and "Hot Time in the Old Town Tonight" are but a few examples of the songs to which strikers set their verses. Other songs adapted lyrics to college yells and songs like "On Wisconsin" and the Notre Dame fight song. Most important, these songs also had the distinct advantage of being familiar to virtually everyone, greatly assisting the spontaneity of the process. And by selecting lively melodies, the songs exuded confidence and enthusiasm.

One of the most popular songs of the strike expressed the workers' contempt for their superiors in an upbeat melody. Put to the tune of "Goody, Goody," the distress of the bosses was depicted as their just deserts for years of worker exploitation. With the tables now turned during the strike, the song celebrated the powerlessness of the bosses.

> We Union Men are out to win to-day,
>   Goody, Goody,
> General Motors hasn't even got a chance,
>   Goody, Goody,
> Old Sloan is feeling blue, and so is Knudsen, too,
> They didn't like the little sit-downs,
> Now what could they do?
> So they lie awake just singing the blues all night,
>   Goody, Goody,
> For the picket lines have given them a fright.
> Now all the workers boo 'em,
> They had it comin' to 'em.
> Boogy, Boogy, Old Sloan,
> Boogy, Boogy, Knudsen,
> And I hope they hang you both,
> You rascals, you.[38]

•   •   •

While these songs instilled a sense of strength and resolve in the strikers, they also served another purpose—passing the time. Much of the singing during the Flint strike, and there was a great deal, helped fill the long, idle hours for those inside. As Henry Kraus, the managing editor of the union newspaper during the sit-down, later described it in his account of the strike, *The Many and the Few*: "For the men in the plants, the long days and nights of the six-week vigil grew very heavy at times, making pastime a major function of the strike." Cards, checkers, reading, Ping-Pong, and the radio were among the di-

A striker doing a jig during a "homespun game." Courtesy of Walter P. Reuther Library, Wayne State University.

Women supporters of the strike dance in front of Fisher Body No. 1. Courtesy of Walter P. Reuther Library, Wayne State University.

versions sit-downers used to pass the time. Other amusements involved games of the workers own making. Kraus described "one homespun game that was very popular. A mob of men would gather around in a ring and someone would call a fellow's name. He'd have to sing, whistle, do a jig or tell a story." Many of the songs the strikers wrote were undoubtedly the product of such frivolity.[39]

Although outside talent was sometimes brought in for the strikers' entertainment, "best of all the strikers liked their own hillbilly orchestra which broadcast its nightly programs over the loudspeaker for the benefit of the many outsiders who gathered each evening to listen." Strikers had a variety of instruments brought to them, including guitars, mandolins, banjos, accordions, and mouth organs. Indeed, Francis O'Rourke's diary reveals that these kinds of amusements were part of the strike from the very beginning. The initial entry in his diary describes the activities of the first few hours of the sit-down in Fisher Body No. 2: "I never knew we had so many entertainers in this little shop. Some are dancing, others have found a quartet, fair singers too. Now a snake dance, everyone is asked to sing a song, do a dance, or recite a poem. So the day is passed."[40]

Some songs seemed particularly appropriate to accompany "housekeeping" tasks the strikers performed inside the plant. Maurice Sugar, one of the union's attorneys during the strike, wrote a number of songs the strikers sang. One that he wrote in 1931 during the depths of the Depression, the "Soup Song," was picked up by the strikers and became quite popular during mealtime. In a letter Sugar wrote to Pete Seeger ten years after the strike, he described hearing it sung during a visit he made to Fisher Body No. 1 during the sit-down:

> You know my "Soup Song?" Imagine the kick I got out of what I saw in the plant during the sit-down at the big Fisher Body plant in Flint. I had a "pass" from the workers which entitled me to "tour" the plant accompanied by an officially-designated "guide," who took me from floor to floor and pointed out all the highly interesting spots in the plant. . . . It was meal time and I was taken to the plant kitchen, where I observed a long line of workers with soup bowls in their hands, standing in line for mess, and having their bowls filled from the gigantic cistern as they passed. All the time they were singing the "Soup Song" with gusto!

Sung to the tune of "My Bonnie Lies over the Ocean," the second verse would have seemed particularly appropriate for the Flint strikers, who complained of the aging and debilitating effects of the speed-up.

I spent twenty years in the factory,
I did everything I was told,
They said I was loyal and faithful,
Now, even before I get old.

CHORUS:
Soo-oup, soo-oup,
They give me a bowl of soo-oup.
Soo-oup, soo-oup,
They give me a bowl of soo-oup.[41]

Another song written by Sugar playfully described the strikers in their new domestic situation. By assuming the snobbish airs of an upper class capable of affording servants, "Bring Me My Robe and Slippers, James" poked fun at the strikers' own living conditions in the plants while simultaneously mocking the pretensions of corporate bosses. The song also captured the irony of "peace and quiet, . . . / Free from the noise and din," now a reality during the strike in these usually deafening plants.

Bring me my robe and slippers, James
Pull up my easy chair
Bring me my pipe and cushions, James
I'm not going anywhere
Let me have peace and quiet, James
Free from the noise and din
And send my regrets to Mr. Sloan
Just tell him I'm staying in.[42]

There was also singing by those who supported the sit-down on the outside. Maintaining picket lines in front of the plants was a vital part of the union's strategy, serving as they did as a first defense against police eviction of the strikers inside. After the Battle of Running Bulls on January 11, the strikers maintained constant guard against future attacks, and the chances of such violence increased significantly late in the strike when a court injunction ordered the strikers out of the factories. For long hours in frigid temperatures, pickets paraded in front of the plants, singing to keep up the morale of the men inside as well as their own. Strikers and strike sympathizers sang old labor standards like "Solidarity Forever" as well as new creations while they walked the picket lines. Journalist Mary Heaton Vorse described a typical evening late in the strike when tensions were especially high.

> We went through the lines late one night. Snow was falling. A guard scrutinized our cards suspiciously. We walked down toward Chevrolet No. 4. Again we were challenged. This happened four times in a five minute walk.
>
> There is a fringe of heads at the windows of Fisher No. 2. It is nearly midnight but they are still cheering and singing "Hold the Fort." The streets are dotted with fires in salamanders. It is bitter cold. There is a fire in front of Chevrolet No. 4, the scene of the latest sit-down.[43]

"Hold the Fort," mentioned by Vorse, and "We Shall Not Be Moved," another labor standard, seemed particularly appropriate for the sit-down strike.[44] In addition, pickets sang songs like "To Hell with Scabs," "Oh, Mr. Sloan," and "Collective Bargaining in Our Shops." Among typed copies of a number of songs from the Flint strike, Henry Kraus noted some of the songs that "were sung a lot and made a great hit wherever they were introduced." These three songs were among them. "Collective Bargaining in Our Shops," composed by Vic Bush and sung to the tune of "Old McDonald Had a Farm," communicated its message quite succinctly.

> Collective Bargaining in our shops
> C-I-C-I-O—
> And in our shops it makes us strong
> C-I-C-I-O—
>
> CHORUS:
> With a Union here and a Union there
> Here a Union there a Union everywhere a Union
> Collective bargaining in our shops—
> C-I-C-I-O.—[45]

Though quite simple, songs like these were easy for the pickets to compose and sing. In *The Many and the Few*, Kraus recounted the group process of song-making on the picket line: "They were intoning songs of their own making and were all taken up with their creative endeavor. They would take some popular song and one would propose a line and another a second—and the collective effort kept them occupied and happy." One song, "After the Battle," actually mentions the act of singing on the picket line. When the song's lyrics appeared in the *United Automobile Worker*, it was noted that the "Words [were] composed on the Scene of Action." Put to the tune of "That Old Gang of Mine," a verse goes:

> All the boys are singing strike songs,
> They forgot "Sweet Adeline."
> Those union men are holding fast
> That old picket line.[46]

Besides picketing, supporters on the outside provided other assistance to the strikers in the plants. Cooking meals, delivering mail, collecting contributions, communicating with workers' families, soliciting new members, and many other tasks were performed by strikers and strike sympathizers. Many of those who served in these ways were women. The wives, sisters, daughters, and other female allies of strikers made a major contribution to the union's victory. A Women's Auxiliary was formed shortly after the strike began, and after the Battle of Running Bulls, Genora Johnson, whose husband was a local strike leader, organized the Women's Emergency Brigade. Organized along quasi-military lines, members of the Brigade were to be available in a moment's notice for picket duty or other activities. Women in the Auxiliary and the Brigade also wrote songs about the strike and their involvement in it. Bessie Garrison and Dorothea Mejia, two women active in the strike, wrote the "Women's Theme Song." With its verses put to "Marching Through Georgia," this martial tune "became the rallying anthem for their wonderful 'Brigade.'" The first verse and chorus went as follows:

> The men are in the factories sitting in a strike we know
> Holding down production so that we can get more dough,
> The Union's organizing, and we'll see that it is so,
> Shouting the Union forever!
>
> CHORUS:
> Hurrah, Hurrah! The Union makes us free
> Hurrah, Hurrah! It's all for you and me
> Organize your brothers and we'll win the fight you'll see,
> Shouting the Union forever!

In the second verse, the song articulated the role of women in the strike as an extension of their roles as "wife and mom and sister" as they "fight beside the men to help the cause along."

> The women got together and they formed a might throng,
> Every worker's wife and mom and sister will belong,

They will fight beside the men to help the cause along,
Shouting the Union forever![47]

The connection between the family responsibilities women bore and their participation in the strike pervades another song. Put to the tune of "Let's All Sing Like the Birdies Sing," the "Women's Auxiliary Song" explained that "women are in the fight . . . for their homes and their kiddies" as well as "for their Union men."

> Auxiliary women are in the fight
> In the fight to stay
> They will battle with all their might
> Onward every day
> For their homes and their kiddies too
> For their union men
> You can bet your last dime
> They'll be there every time
> Fighting to the end.

The second verse applauded the contributions of women by asking rhetorically: Who performs picket duty, prepares the food, and keeps up morale? In the context of the strike, women fulfilled their traditional responsibilities in new ways. By sustaining, supporting, and encouraging the strikers, women's traditional roles of wife and mother were performed.

> When the workers sit-in the plant
> Who stands on the line?
> When the workers must get their food
> Who gets it there on time?
> When the spirit is runing [sic] low
> Who will make it rise?
> It's the woman you know
> Who makes everything go,
> They are Union-Wise.

It is not in the name of collective bargaining rights that the song stakes its claim to justice but for "food and shelter and clothing . . . for the family." The third and last verse explained why "she joins in the fight."

> Every woman should have a house
> She can call her own

Decent living for every child
In a decent home
Food and shelter and clothing too
For the family
So she joins in the fight
For a cause that is right
Sharing Victory![48]

A cheer women strike supporters yelled portrayed their contribution to the strike effort in similar terms. It was in their familial roles as "wives" and "mothers" that they would "fight for [their] kith and kin."

We're the wives
We're the mothers
Of our fighting union brothers
We'll fight for our kith and kin
And when we fight,
We fight to win.
Rah! Rah! Rah![49]

In another song, "Strike Marches On," composed by Loretta Blazek and Mildred Skalika, the union itself is characterized in terms of the family. In this version of the romantic tune "Love Marches On," it is "[t]he strike," not love, that "meets a union boy, a union girl / And takes them by the hand." And as the union grows with each new member, it becomes "the mighty clan."

The strike marches on
And meets a union boy, a union girl
And takes them by the hand
And marches on.

The strike marches on
And soon another man, has taken the stand
And joins the mighty clan
And marches on.

Soon he will be joined by others
Who would like to be members too
All workers are welcomed
So won't you please join too?

> The strike marches on
> And when the battles fought
> Have all been won
> We'll join the mighty throng
> As the union marches on.[50]

The lyrics of these songs reinforced the union's own plea to women. In an effort to solicit the support of the wives, daughters, and sisters of strikers, the *Flint Auto Worker* made "An Appeal to the Women of Flint." The article asked, "What can the union mean to the home?" The response included "decent schooling," "a good place to live," and "security for her loved ones." The article described these as the things any "good woman" would want. "And they're [good women] all for the union." Supporting the strikers was understood simply as an extension of their familiar roles and responsibilities. Or as Vorse described it in *Labor's New Millions*:

> One and all were normal, sensible women who were doing this because they had come to the mature conclusion that it must be done if they and their children were to have a decent life. Inevitably they were behind their husbands as long as there was need, and they showed the same matter of course capability with which they got the children off to school. Today their job was "protecting their men."[51]

In sharp contrast, the songs written by men did not portray their involvement in the strike as husbands and fathers. Curiously absent from the lyrics they wrote was an explanation of the strike as it would relate to their role as breadwinner. What the union would mean to them in their efforts to feed, clothe, and house their families seldom surfaced in their songs. While an individual striker might explain his "staying in" to his wife in terms of better security for the family, this message was not expressed in the lyrics the men wrote. Common among the songs written by men was the emphasis on male camaraderie. The theme of union men sticking together and fighting together often emerged in the lyrics they composed. Even the songs the strikers chose as models communicated a sense of male togetherness, as in "That Old Gang of Mine," the model for "After the Battle," mentioned earlier. Indeed, Kraus noted, "Another song that was universal whenever strikers either 'came out' or 'sat down' was 'Hail, hail, the gang's all here.'"[52]

In "A Union Man," sung to the martial tune of "When Johnny Comes Marching Home," this emphasis on male solidarity and loyalty is preeminent. As industrial musketeers, "It's all for one and one for all."

A Union man is a loyal man
He's tried and true.
No matter how tough the going gets
He sees it through
He's always ready to hear the call
It's all for one and one for all.
Anyone can see
A loyal man is he.

The same sentiment is expressed in the strikers' version of "Shipmates Stand Together."

Shipmates stand together
Don't give up the shop
Fair or stormy weather
We won't give up the shop
Friends and pals forever
We will have to stick
We will never take a licking
They will always find us kicking
Don't give up the shop[53]

As Kraus observed, it was "the potent force of emulation, the fact that one could not do less than one's buddies," that largely "sustained these men." Loyalty and brotherhood toward one's coworkers greatly defined "a union man," and it is this notion of male togetherness and mutual support that pervades the songs they wrote. The spirit of "Friends and pals forever / We will have to stick" was the very glue by which the strike held together. As one striker wrote his wife: "Hunny Wayen and Sim and Pat is all in here. I could of came out wen they went on strike But hunny I just thought I join the union and I look pretty yellow if I dident stick with them."[54]

Union attorney Maurice Sugar understood the importance of "the potent force of emulation." Masculinity and worker loyalty are intimately intertwined in a song he wrote a few years before the strike, "Be a Man!" To "[b]e a man" is to answer "the fighting call of brother" and "strike."

There's a cry that starts them shaking
As they sit upon their thrones;
There's a cry that leaves them quaking

As a chill runs thru their bones;
There's a cry that serves them notice
That they can't do as they like.
It's the workers' call to action
It's the workers' call to strike!

CHORUS:
It's the call of fellow-worker
Be a man!
Not a man shall be a shirker
Be a man!
It's the fighting call of brother
We are fighting for each other
Every man shall help another
Be a man!
Strike![55]

．　　．　　．

As Sugar's musical contributions suggest, union leaders appreciated the value of singing to the strike effort. Although much of the songwriting and singing during the Flint sit-down was the spontaneous outpouring of emotion from striking workers and their allies, union leaders did their part to encourage singing. Copies of strike songs were mimeographed and distributed at union meetings and on the picket line. They were also reprinted during the strike in the union newspapers, the *Flint Auto Worker* and the *United Automobile Worker*. In fact, the January 22 issue of the *United Automobile Worker* dedicated an entire page to strike songs under the headline, "Strike Songs: Battle, Victory, Joy." A note that accompanied the songs described song-making by the strikers and applauded their "creative activity."

> The foregoing songs (except for the one ["Sit Down"] by Maurice Sugar) were all composed in Flint during the present strike.
> The practice, however, is universal, though we have not had time to compile those composed by strikers in other centers.
> Though basing their verse on other tunes, the songs, nevertheless, express a collective creative activity that is rare enough in American life.
> The words are often exceptionally apt and descriptive. There is no reason to believe that original tunes will not be created also as our composers gain confidence. There has been a veritable up-surge of creative activity along the

lines of letter-writing, poetry, drawing, etc., among our people since the
strikes began. But what work has already been done is only a slight indication
of the vast creative resources possessed by the American working people.

As the note implies, union leaders clearly understood the benefit of song-making to their organizing efforts and sought to promote it. Indeed, the February 6,
1937, issue of the *Flint Auto Worker* included a call for performers. The
announcement read: "WANTED: Entertainers and Musicians."[56] Moreover, on January 13, just two days after the union's victory in the Battle of Running Bulls, it
was agreed that all mass meetings should be opened and closed with a verse of
"Solidarity Forever," as if to serve as an invocation and benediction to the pro-
ceedings. Regarding such gatherings, Kraus recounted: "The hour before strike
meeting every evening was devoted to entertainment, sometimes with outside
talent."[57]

The many Communists and Socialists active in the strike brought their fa-
miliarity with labor songs to the Flint sit-down. Through these associations,
they were undoubtedly familiar with the songs in the *Rebel Song Book.*
Published by the left-leaning Rand School in New York, it contained dozens of
radical songs proclaiming class solidarity and revolution. When compiling
songs from the strike, Kraus noted: "I have copied out on the preceding five
pages all the songs I found at Flint that were new to me. In addition there were
mimeographed song sheets which contained some of the above [songs and yells
original to the strike] plus many familiar songs, in versions familiar from the
Rebel Song Book published by the Rand School in New York." Kraus listed ten
songs from the *Rebel Song Book* he found among the song sheets at Flint; he
marked three with asterisks. "Soup Song," "Hold the Fort," and "Solidarity Forever" (double asterisks) were "those a group of women in the Union Hall agreed
were 'the ones we really sang.' "[58]

In addition, two union organizers, Roy Reuther and Merlin Bishop, had attended Brookwood Labor College. There they were taught the value of singing
in the labor movement and learned a host of songs. Bishop later recalled his
days at Brookwood:

> We did a lot with labor songs and singing and trying to interest the worker in
> some of the old songs that portrayed the history of the labor movement.
> Brookwood, of course, instilled that into us, the value of music.[59]

Sociologist R. Serge Denisoff has also observed the part labor colleges such as
Brookwood played in the promotion of singing within the labor movement. In

Great Day Coming: Folk Music and the American Left he writes: "The significance of these labor colleges is that they served as transfer points by which songs and personnel were directed from one movement to another. Many graduates of Brookwood . . . joined the CIO and more ideological movements and used songs that they had learned and observed in use at their institutions."[60]

Indeed, Bishop, the first educational director for the UAW, recognized the benefit of singing during the Kelsey-Hayes strike just prior to the Flint sit-down. As an organizer at Kelsey-Hayes, he knew the value of singing in maintaining the strikers' morale. In his sixteen-page report from that "sit-in" strike, Bishop wrote: "Every morning the sit-downers were called at six o'clock and everyone appeared at the front gate to cheer the pickets and to make sure that no one tried to enter the plant at the regular working hour. The sit-down strikers did a splendid job singing labor songs at this hour of the morning. It was said that they could be heard blocks away." This lesson would not be lost. Kelsey-Hayes and other early sit-down strikes provided the UAW the necessary experience in conducting a strike of the same type against one of the major auto producers. And part of this experience would be the use of labor songs.[61]

During these earlier strikes, the union had also experimented with the sound car as a strike weapon. Over its speakers orders could be given, support rallied, encouragement extended, speeches made, and singing led. So vital were the sound cars to the strike effort at Flint, Vorse commented that "it is hard to know how a strike was ever conducted without [them]."[62] Because of their value to the union, Kraus explained, the loudspeaker system and sound cars "were always preciously guarded, day and night."[63]

Precautions were taken with good reason. On January 7, the first "open hostilities" in the strike occurred when Roy Reuther attempted to address workers as they left their shift in Chevrolet No. 9. A group including many foremen and supervisors rushed the crowd and smashed the loudspeaker system. During the Battle of Running Bulls, just four days later, a sound car was used to direct the strikers' defense of the factory. The exhortations and martial music coming from the sound car, one observer remarked, "dominated everything!" It delivered "one steady unswerving note" that "like an inexhaustible, furious flood pour[ed] courage into the men."[64]

It is not surprising, then, that to the strike's opponents the sound car was "that feared and hated symbol," as Kraus has written. "The sound car particularly attained nightmarish proportions to the authorities and company agents everywhere whose repeated attacks upon it almost partook of a religious fervor—as though this instrument were a new god or idol that must be destroyed." In fact, it was for their use of the sound car that a number of union organizers faced criminal charges following the Battle of Running Bulls. GM also used its influence with local officials to secure "anti-noise" ordinances in a number of cities, Flint included, where GM had factories. Efforts to silence the union even included a prohibition against children singing union songs at school.[65]

For more than six weeks the strikers held fast, despite all of GM's efforts to wrest them from the plants. Claiming the strikers were in "illegal possession" of the two Fisher plants, GM twice sought court injunctions ordering the evacuation of the sit-downers and an end to picketing. Although an injunction was granted in Genesee County Circuit Court just four days into the strike, the order was discredited when it was disclosed that the presiding judge, Edward Black, owned nearly $220,000 in GM stock. GM transferred the suit to the court of Judge Paul Gadola but did not immediately press the issue. Neither legal maneuvering nor physical force could expel the strikers, as the Battle of Running Bulls proved nine days after the first injunction was issued.[66]

The violence of January 11 prompted Governor Murphy to dispatch the National Guard to Flint to maintain order, and he invited union and management leaders to Lansing to negotiate. As a condition to these negotiations, the strikers were to evacuate the plants. For its part, GM promised not to operate the struck plants nor remove dies, machinery, or equipment from them. But when it was learned that GM had agreed to also meet with the Flint Alliance, a recently formed company union sponsoring a back-to-work movement, the UAW refused to leave the plants. Even subsequent efforts by Secretary of Labor Frances Perkins to bring GM's president Alfred Sloan together with CIO chieftain John L. Lewis failed to break the deadlock.[67]

In an effort to gain the initiative, the UAW made a bold move on February 1. The union feigned a sit-down strike at Chevrolet No. 9, drawing company police to that plant. The diversion allowed the UAW to seize and occupy Chevrolet No. 4, which produced Chevrolet car engines and was "the most important single unit in the General Motors framework." The capture of Chevrolet No. 4 proved decisive in the UAW's victory at Flint, underscoring the strength of the union while emphasizing GM's vulnerability.[68]

Singing played a critical role in the distraction created at Chevrolet No. 9. With both loud voices and the sound cars, the union orchestrated the successful

When the police discharged tear gas into Chevrolet No. 9 on February 1, the Women's Emergency Brigade broke windows in the plant to allow air inside. Courtesy of Walter P. Reuther Library, Wayne State University.

ruse. As Henry Kraus recounted: "The boys had been told as they were passing police headquarters to sing out as though in triumph and they did so well, hanging two deep on every vehicle and with pickets upraised, that they might easily have impressed observers that they were returning from victorious battle."[69]

Mary Heaton Vorse also noted the contribution singing made to the union's ploy. Emboldened by such songs as "We Shall Not Be Moved" and "Hold the Fort," members of the Women's Emergency Brigade were part of the diversion at Chevrolet No. 9 so critical to the union's strategy. When police arrived and discharged tear gas, the Brigade broke windows in the plant to allow air inside. "To all the crowd there was something moving about seeing the women return to the picket line after having been gassed in front of plant No. 9. A cheer went up; the crowd took up the song. The line of bright-capped women spread itself out in front of the high gate. Clasping hands, they struck up the song, 'We Shall Not Be Moved.' "[70]

Not only was singing integral to the union's strategy of diversion, but like other key events in the strike, the clever deception UAW leaders staged at Chevrolet No. 9 was retold in song. Put to the tune of "Trail of the Lonesome Pine," the "Chevy Battle Song" was printed in the *Flint Auto Worker* just five days after the fight. Describing the melee at Chevrolet No. 9, the song "gave the women credit for holding the picket line."

> There was a great big fight on Monday,
>   in front of Chevy nine.
> Where the gas shells were exploding
>   in the good old picket line.
> Where the policemen's clubs were swinging,
>   but we paid them no mind.
> And we'll give the women credit for
>   holding the picket line.[71]

In the wake of the February 1 coup, Judge Gadola issued an injunction ordering the UAW to evacuate the two Fisher Body plants. Again, the union refused to obey the court's mandate. Governor Murphy, wanting to avoid violence at all costs, resisted using the National Guard to enforce the court order and evict the strikers. The capture of Chevrolet No. 4, combined with the restraint of the governor, brought GM to the negotiating table.[72]

After a series of marathon sessions, GM agreed not to bargain or enter into agreements with any other worker organization for six months after production resumed. The union delegation led by Lewis effectively secured collective bargaining rights for the UAW for a period of six months. With this achieved, the sit-downers walked out of the plants on February 11. The forty-four-day strike was over.[73]

In celebration of their triumph, a number of strikers wrote songs. One song written by Walter H. Frost of Chevrolet No. 4 suggests something of the variety of functions labor songs served during the Flint strike. Sung to the tune of "It Ain't Gonna Rain No More," the first verse attempted to capitalize on UAW's victory by calling others to "join the ranks of labor / With the UAWA."[74] Indeed, the lyrics virtually guided the workers to the union hall to enroll, hinting that the most recent victory should quell any misgivings they might have.

> Come all you auto workers
> Wherever you may be
> Come join the ranks of labor
> With the UAWA.
>
> Come down to Third and Harrison
> On the third floor is the hall
> And nothing now should hinder you
> From making us a call.

Sit-downers in Fisher Body No. 1 mark the last day of the strike, February 11, on their strike calendar. Courtesy of Walter P. Reuther Library, Wayne State University.

While the first two verses were an obvious effort to attract nonunion autoworkers to the UAW, later verses praised the union's leaders for their courage and resolve. As if having proven their mettle in the course of the strike, the union leaders were promoted as able representatives of autoworkers. For example, UAW president Homer Martin "is always on the spot." Even the influence of John L. Lewis on behalf of the autoworkers was advanced in the song as reason "they'll get us what we want."

> Our president Homer Martin
> Is always on the spot
> With the helping hand of Lewis
> They'll get us what we want.
>
> We all know they are fighters
> There isn't any doubt
> The thugs and scabs of GMC
> Can never scare us out.

In another verse, while "the Reuther boys" were heralded as "scrappers too /
Their task they've always done," the victory at the Battle of Bulls Run was
remembered. By recalling that fateful night when "they [would] not back down,"
the song both asserted the strength of the union as well as assisted in immor-
talizing the event. Such a memory served as compelling propaganda as the
UAW sought new members in the months following the strike.

> The Reuther boys are scrappers too
> Their task they've always done
> They helped to win a victory
> In the battle of Bulls Run.
>
> The cops would like to drive them out
> But they will not back down
> We're going to stick together till
> We organize this town.

The song also took shots at the various forces that combated unionization. During the course of the strike, the UAW leaders were criticized by GM and the local newspaper, the *Flint Journal*, as not being representative of the
autoworkers. Claiming that they were "outside agitators," GM hoped to
discredit the union. This assertion was addressed in one of the verses.

> These men are auto workers
> The same as you and I
> The Journal calls them agitators
> But that is a lie.

As mentioned, GM did promote a company union, the Flint Alliance, as an alter-
native to the UAW. The strikers were never fooled by this effort by management
to undermine their union. As the song proclaimed, with the strike now won, the
Flint Alliance and its head, George E. Boysen, are "nearly through."

> Now the strike is over
> And our song is nearly through
> So is George E. Boysen
> And the Flint Alliance too.[75]

•   •   •

By the time that song was written in celebration of the union's victory over
General Motors, the strike had already inspired dozens of songs. Though the au-

tomobile industry had little tradition of singing and songwriting before the Flint sit-down, the strike generated an "up-surge of creative activity." The songs strikers wrote recounted the strike's battles, serving as a form of oral tradition for the lore of this epic struggle. The strikers' determination and the leaders' courage were retold in the lyrics. In so doing, these songs lifted the spirits of the strikers within the plants and boosted the morale of their allies on the picket lines.

Union leaders were well aware of the value of singing during the strike. From their experiences at Kelsey-Hayes and other earlier strikes, as well as their own training at Brookwood Labor College, they clearly understood the potential benefits of song. In the plants and on the picket lines, from the sound cars and inside the union hall, in the union newspapers and on mimeographed song sheets, union leaders promoted singing among the strikers and their supporters. And when UAW leaders attempted to break the stalemate in the strike by capturing Chevrolet No. 4, gaining a critical advantage for the union, singing played an important part in their diversionary tactics.

Though UAW leaders encouraged singing for its ability to rouse the strikers and foster organizing, much of the songwriting and singing during the Flint strike simply filled idle hours. Faced with time on their hands, the strikers in the plants composed songs as a means of escaping boredom. But in those moments, singing provided the strikers both the means and the opportunity to voice their claim to justice and articulate their demands. Singing provided the psychological arena necessary for nurturing community and class consciousness. Although the lyrics of their songs did not generally express "revolutionary intent," they did espouse a strong sense of class consciousness and class identity. By advancing their collective bargaining rights, by scorning and chastising their bosses, by championing the strikers occupying the plants, and by retelling the events of the strike, the songs strikers wrote and sang promoted their interests as different and distinct from those of the corporation and its management.

On the outside, the strikers' allies, particularly the members of the Women's Auxiliary and the Women's Emergency Brigade, also contributed to the verses produced during the strike. In these creations, a great deal is revealed about gender relations between the male strikers and their female allies. While the lyrics written by male strikers celebrated their brotherhood, solidarity, and camaraderie, those composed by women depicted their efforts in support of the strike as an extension of their familial roles as wives and mothers. The demands of the strike required that their domestic responsibilities as nurturers and helpmates be carried out in a new arena, and their songs reflect this perception of an expanded sphere.

These songs, then, provide a window into the lives of the strikers who wrote and sang them. They express the thoughts and feelings of workers who might otherwise have been deemed inarticulate. And they capture the struggle and triumph that was the Flint sit-down strike.

"Better Than a Hundred Speeches"

> They made songs. . . . They developed unsuspected pow-
> ers. . . . They became human beings at last, instead of lit-
> tle cogs in a frightened, mechanized world, and they
> learned the great lessons that all workers must learn,
> solidarity.
>
> —Merlin Bishop Bishop Papers, "Foreword,"

In 1963, twenty-six years after the strikers at Flint had walked out of the plants singing of their victory over General Motors, Merlin Bishop lamented the decline of singing among the members of the United Auto Workers (UAW). The former educational director of the UAW reflected: "One thing I think is lacking today is the use of songs. . . . People really sang. There was a real life and spirit. We have lost that in the CIO. I think there is a great need for it. Maybe if we had more of it, we would be growing instead of slipping backwards as we are at the present time."[1]

Two years after Bishop's commentary, folksinger Pete Seeger made a simi-lar observation. In an article in *Sing Out!*, Seeger asked, "Whatever happened to singing in the unions?" Like Bishop, Seeger remembered a time in American labor history when workers lifted their voices in song as they walked picket lines and held union rallies. He pondered the powerful benefits that singing once had for strikers as they demanded higher wages, improved working condi-tions, and recognition for their union. Both Bishop and Seeger bemoaned the absence of such a formidable tool for union organizing. Both remembered the dramatic labor struggles of the Depression and the important role singing had played.[2] They understood what journalist Margaret Larkin had recognized in 1929 as she listened to Ella May's "song ballets." Songs were "better than a hun-dred speeches."[3]

What, then, do the songs striking workers wrote and sang during the Depression era say? What do the verses speak of the workers who struggled for economic justice during such difficult times? What are the meanings of their lyrics? And what did singing mean to the strikers?

Whether from the Carolina Piedmont, the hills of eastern Kentucky, or the streets of Flint, the songs striking workers wrote and sang during the Depression were decidedly class conscious. The strike songs from all three labor conflicts reveal that workers understood the necessity of solidarity and collective action. Whether against mill owners, mine bosses, or corporate executives, striking workers knew they had to unite if they were going to increase their wages, better their working conditions, and gain a union contract. And this is exactly what they stated in their songs. In Gastonia Ella May beckoned striking millhands to "stand together, workers / And have a union here," while in Harlan County Aunt Molly called on miners to "Join the NMU / Come join the NMU." And in Flint sit-downers demanded, "Collective bargaining in our shops, / C-I-C-I-O." Workers in all three strikes sang of the importance of joining together as a union for their common benefit.

As a shared experience, the singing of songs not only sent the message of collective action and worker solidarity, it also provided the very means by which that message was communicated. Singing was a communal experience, whether on picket lines, at union rallies, or on shop floors. Singing provided the strikers at Gastonia, Harlan, and Flint the opportunity to vent their frustrations, voice their opinions, and stake their claim to justice. By providing the psychological space for striking workers to speak their minds, quite literally, singing nurtured a sense of community and class consciousness. And when strikers retold the events of their strike, as they did in songs from all three strikes, they spread and preserved their common history, further strengthening the bonds among them.

What is most significant, perhaps, about the songs workers wrote and sang during these three strikes is the difference gender made. In Gastonia Ella May sang her "Mill Mother's Lament," in Harlan County Aunt Molly bellowed "Kentucky Miners' Wives Ragged Hungry Blues," and in Flint women sang as "wife and mom and sister." Whether as strikers themselves, as in Gastonia, or as the strikers' allies, as in Harlan and Flint, women expressed their support for unionization in terms of familial concerns. Their responsibilities as wives and mothers came through clearly in their songs. Food and clothing for their families, financial security for the home, and a brighter future for their children were what women fought for, and sang for, in all three of these strikes.

By contrast, the songs men wrote and sang in the course of these strikes championed male solidarity and camaraderie. It was not for their children, wives, and homes that male strikers fought, but in the name of worker loyalty and brotherhood. In Flint the sit-downers proclaimed, "It's all for one and one for all," while in Harlan County Jim Garland sang of his fallen "comrade" Harry Simms, who "was a pal of mine, / We labored side by side." Even in Gastonia, where the majority of the millhands were female, striker Kermit Harden wrote:

> Crowd around me here, union boys,
> And lend me your ears, union boys.
> You've a way of knowing
> I've a way of showing
> What the union means, union boys.

When in "Which Side Are You On?" Florence Reece asked, "Gentlemen, can you stand it? / Oh, tell me how you can? / Will you be a gun thug? / Or will you be a man?," she understood to "be a man" as defending against those who would "take away our bread." On the other hand, when Maurice Sugar exclaimed, "Be a Man," he meant for striking workers to answer "the fighting call of brother." Workers during the Depression era definitely sang in gendered voices.

Writing strike songs was an impromptu activity. On the picket lines and on the shop floor, at the "speakings" and in the union hall, striking bards fashioned their new lyrics to well-known melodies to assist with the singing. In Harlan and Gastonia this meant borrowing from a rich stock of mountain ballads and religious hymns familiar among the workers. In so doing, the strikers' demands were articulated in idioms deeply rooted in their culture, lending their demands legitimacy. In Flint strikers used a wide range of popular tunes, from "Old McDonald Had a Farm" to "Hot Time in the Old Town Tonight," again assisting the spread of their lyrics.

Although the majority of the songs from all three strikes were the spontaneous outpourings of the strikers' thoughts and emotions, union organizers knew well the practical uses of strike songs. Singing boosted the morale of those on the picket lines and beckoned others to the union's ranks. Singing was used to raise needed strike funds and served as a diversionary tactic against company police. Strike songs stated the union's demands and provided potent propaganda for the cause. Songs were even used to open and conclude union meetings. Singing truly served a multitude of functions in union organizing during these strikes. With mimeograph machines and the left-wing press, sound cars and loudspeaker systems, union organizers promoted singing among the strikers.

Local authorities, too, understood the formidable strike weapon song was. An antiparade ordinance in Gastonia and an antinoise ordinance in Flint were efforts by local authorities to keep strikers from singing. In Flint school children were even prohibited from singing union songs. But intimidation and violence were much more effective at silencing singing strikers. In Flint the sound car was threatened and the loudspeaker system attacked. In Harlan County the singing Garland clan was forced to migrate from the land of their birth. And in Gastonia Ella May was shot "because she made up songs," her coworkers believed.

But even Ella May's murder could not stop the singing. Gastonia striker Daisy MacDonald commemorated the fallen minstrel in "On a Summer Eve," and Sarah Garland Ogan reminded audiences of Bloody Harlan in her militant "I Hate the Capitalist System." John Steinbeck was correct. "You can burn books, buy newspapers, you can guard against handbills and pamphlets, but you can't prevent singing." It is "the one statement that cannot be destroyed."[4]

Notes

"Their Sharpest Statement": Introduction

1. Maurice Sugar to Philip P. Mason, July 17, 1967, Maurice Sugar Papers, Box 14, Folder 22, Archives of Labor History and Urban Affairs, Wayne State University, Detroit (hereafter cited as ALHUA). In that letter, Sugar responded to Mason's query as to when "Sit Down" was written. Sugar wrote, "My guess is that I wrote it, and passed it out, in January, 1937." In fact, the song appeared in the *United Automobile Worker.* January 22, 1937, 7. The strike began on December 30, 1936, and ended on February 11, 1937.

2. Maurice Sugar to Pete Seeger, January 25, 1947, Sugar Papers, Box 14, Folder 24.

3. On Maurice Sugar's career as a labor lawyer, see Christopher H. Johnson, *Maurice Sugar: Law, Labor, and the Left, 1912–1950* (Detroit: Wayne State University Press, 1988), esp. 191–218.

4. Alan Lomax, Woody Guthrie, and Peter Seeger, eds., *Hard Hitting Songs for Hard-Hit People* (New York: Oak Publications, 1967; reprint, Lincoln: University of Nebraska Press, 1999), 244–45. As noted, "Sit Down," as well as a number of other songs from the GM strike, can be found in *Hard Hitting Songs.* There the lyrics appear with musical scores. When applicable, in addition to other sources, *Hard Hitting* Songs is cited for the benefit of the music and easy reference. See also Pete Seeger and Bob Reiser, *Carry It On!: A History in Song and Picture of the Working Men and Women of America* (New York: Simon and Schuster, 1985), 151. A recording of "Sit Down" is on *Songs for a Better Tomorrow* (United Auto Workers, Education Department, 1963; reissued 1986). "Sit Down" has also been recorded live on Earl Robinson, *Strange, Unusual Evening: A Santa Barbara Story* (United Auto Workers ER-101, 1971). There is also a recording by the Manhattan Chorus on compact disc on Ronald D. Cohen and Dave Samuelson, comps. and eds., *Songs for Political Action: Folkmusic, Topical Songs, and the American Left, 1926–1953* (Hamburg, Germany: Bear Family Records, 1996), disc 1.

5. The phrase "lean years" is a reference to Irving Bernstein, *The Lean Years: A History of the American Worker, 1920–1933* (Boston: Houghton Mifflin, 1960; reprint, Baltimore: Penguin Books, 1966).

6. For general works on the labor movement during the Depression years, see Bernstein, *Lean Years*; Irving Bernstein, *Turbulent Years: A History of the American Worker, 1933–1941* (Boston: Houghton Mifflin, 1970); Irving Bernstein, *A Caring Society: The New Deal, the Worker, and the Great Depression* (Boston: Houghton Mifflin, 1985); Lizabeth Cohen, *Making a New Deal: Industrial Workers in Chicago, 1919–1939* (Cambridge: Cambridge University Press, 1990); Alan Dawley, *Struggles for Justice: Social Responsibility and the Liberal State* (Cambridge: Belknap Press of Harvard University Press, 1991), 295–417; Mary E. Frederickson and Timothy P. Lynch, "Labor: The Great Depression to the 1990s," in *Encyclopedia of American Social History*, vol. 2, ed. Mary Kupiec Clayton, Elliott J. Gorn, and Peter W. Williams (New York: Maxwell Macmillan International, 1993), 1475–94; Walter Galenson, *The CIO Challenge to the AFL: A History of the American Labor Movement, 1935–1941* (Cambridge: Harvard University Press, 1960); Harvey Klehr, *The Heyday of American Communism: The Depression Decade* (New York: Basic Books, 1984); Harvey Klehr and John Earl Haynes, *The American Communist Movement: Storming Heaven Itself* (New York: Twanye, 1992), 59–95; F. Ray Marshall, *Labor in the South* (Cambridge: Harvard University Press, 1967), 41–294; David Milton, *The Politics of U.S. Labor: From the Great Depression to the New Deal* (New York: Monthly Review Press, 1982); Art Preis, *Labor's Giant Step: Twenty Years of the CIO* (New York: Pioneer Publishers, 1964); Studs Terkel, *Hard Times: An Oral History of the Great Depression* (New York: Pantheon, 1970); Robert H. Zieger, *American Workers, American Unions, 1920–1985* (Baltimore: Johns Hopkins University Press, 1986), 3-61.

7. Regarding song and contemporary social movements, in addition to the other works cited in this introduction, see Frank Adams with Myles Horton, *Unearthing Seeds of Fire: The Idea of Highlander* (Winston-Salem, N.C.: John F. Blair, 1975); Joan Baez, *And a Voice to Sing With: A Memoir* (New York: Summit Books, 1987); Carl Benson, ed., *The Bob Dylan Companion: Four Decades of Commentary* (New York: Schirmer, 1998); Peter Blood-Patterson, ed., *Rise Up Singing* (Bethlehem, Pa.: Sing Out Corporation, 1988); Oscar Brand, *The Ballad Mongers: Rise of the Modern Folk Song* (New York: Funk and Wagnalls, 1962); Guy Carawan and Candie Carawan, comps. and eds., *Sing for Freedom: The Story of the Civil Rights Movement through Its Songs* (Bethlehem, Pa.: Sing Out Corporation, 1990); Tristram Coffin, "Folksong of Social Protest: A Musical Mirage," *New York Folklore Quarterly* 14 (spring 1958): 3–10; Barbara Dane and Irwin Silber, comps. and eds., *The Vietnam Songbook* (New York: The Guardian; distributed by Monthly Review Press, 1969); R. Serge Denisoff and Richard A. Peterson, eds., *The Sounds of Social Change: Studies in Popular Culture* (Chicago: Rand McNally, 1972); David King Dunaway, "Music and Politics in the United States," *Folk Music Journal* 5 (1987): 268–94; David King Dunaway, *How Can I Keep from Singing: Pete Seeger* (New York: McGraw-Hill, 1981; reprint, New York: Da Capo, 1990); Josh Dunson, *Freedom in the Air: Song Movements of the Sixties* (New York: International Publishers, 1965; reprint, Westport, Conn.: Greenwood Press, 1980); Edith Fowke and Joe Glazer, *Songs of Work and Protest* (New York: Dover, 1973); Reebee Garofalo, ed., *Rockin' the Boat: Mass Music and Mass Movements* (Boston: South End Press, 1992); Tom Glazer, *Songs of Peace, Freedom and Protest* (New York: David McKay, 1970); Wayne Hampton, *Guerrilla Minstrels* (Knoxville: University of Tennessee Press, 1986); Elizabeth J. Kizer, "Protest Song Lyrics as Rhetoric," *Popular Music and Society* 9 (1983): 3–11; Ralph E. Knupp, "A Time for Every Purpose Under Heaven: Rhetorical Dimensions of Protest Music," *Southern Speech Communication Journal* 46 (summer 1981): 377–89; George H. Lewis, "Social Class and Cultural Communication: An Analysis of Song Lyrics," *Popular Music and Society* 5 (1977): 23–30; John McDonnell, ed., *Songs of Struggle and Protest* (Cork, Ireland: Mercier Press, 1979); Lloyd Miller, "The Sound of Protest," *Case Western Reserve Journal of Sociology* 1 (June 1967): 41–52; Jeffery J. Mondak, "Protest Music As Political Persuasion," *Popular Music and Society* 12 (fall 1988): 25–38; Marianne Philbin, ed., *Give Peace a Chance: Music and the Struggle for Peace* (Chicago: Chicago Review Press, 1983); David Pichaske, *A Generation in Motion: Popular Music and the Culture of the Sixties* (Granite Falls, Minn.: Ellis Press, 1989); Jerome L. Rodnitzky, "The Evolution of the American Protest Song," *Journal of Popular Culture* 3 (summer 1969): 35–45; Jerome L. Rodnitzky, "The Decline of Contemporary Protest Music," *Popular Music and Society* 1 (fall 1971): 44–50; Jerome L. Rodnitzky, "The New Revivalism: American Protest Songs, 1945–1968," *South Atlantic Quarterly* 70 (winter 1971): 13–21; Michael Schumacher, *There But for Fortune: The Life of Phil Ochs* (New York: Hyperion, 1996); Robert Shelton, *No Direction Home: The Life and Music of Bob Dylan* (New York: Beech Tree Books, 1986); Jerry Silverman, *The Liberated Woman's Songbook* (New York: Macmillan, 1971); Jerry Silverman, comp., *Songs of Protest and Civil Rights* (New York: Chelsea House, 1992); Hilda E. Wenner and Elizabeth Freilicher, *Here's to the Women: 100 Songs for and about Women* (New York: Feminist Press, 1991); Wanda Willson Whitman, *Songs That Changed the World* (New York: Crown, 1970).

8. Quoted in the preface to John Greenway, *American Folksongs of Protest* (Philadelphia: University of Pennsylvania Press, 1953; reprint, New York: Octagon Press, 1972), vii. This passage is also in John Steinbeck's foreword to Lomax, Guthrie, and Seeger, *Hard Hitting Songs*, 8.

9. Archie Green, "Labor Song: An Ambiguous Legacy," *Journal of Folklore Research* 28 (May-December 1991): 93-94.

10. For a discussion of George Korson's life and work see Angus K. Gillespie, *Folklorist of the Coal Fields: George Korson's Life and Work* (University Park: Pennsylvania State University Press, 1980); Angus K. Gillespie, "Folklore and Labor: An Intellectual Context for the Work of George Korson," *Keystone Folklore Quarterly* 23 (fall 1979): 11-27; Jay Anderson, ed., "George Korson

Memorial Issue," *Keystone Folklore Quarterly* 16 (summer 1971). Korson's collections of mining songs include George Korson, *Songs and Ballads of the Anthracite Miner* (New York: Grafton Press, 1927); George Korson, *Minstrels of the Mine Patch: Songs and Stories of the Anthracite Industry* (Philadelphia: University of Pennsylvania Press, 1938; reprint, Hatboro, Pa.: Folklore Associates, 1964); George Korson, *Coal Dust on the Fiddle: Songs and Stories of the Bituminous Industry* (Philadelphia: University of Pennsylvania Press, 1943; reprint, Hatboro, Pa.: Folklore Associates, 1965). A number of the field recordings made by Korson have been released on record by the Library of Congress. See *Songs and Ballads of the Anthracite Miners* (Library of Congress AFS L16, 1964); *Songs and Ballads of the Bituminous Miners* (Library of Congress AFS L60, 1965).

11. R. Serge Denisoff, *Songs of Protest, War, and Peace: A Bibliography and Discography* (Santa Barbara, Calif.: American Bibliographical Center, Clio Press, 1973). For other discographies of labor songs, see Richard A. Reuss, ed., *Songs of American Labor, Industrialization and the Urban Work Experience: A Discography* (Ann Arbor: Labor Studies Center, Institute of Labor and Industrialization, University of Michigan, 1983); David King Dunaway, "A Selected Bibliography: Protest Songs in the United States," *Folklore Forum* 10 (fall 1977): 8–25; Archie Green, "A Discography of American Labor Union Songs," *New York Folklore Quarterly* 17 (fall 1961): 186-93; Archie Green, "Folksong on Records," *Western Folklore* 27 (January 1968): 68–76; Archie Green, "Industrial Lore: A Bibliographic-Semantic Query," *Western Folklore* 37 (July 1978): 213–44. For discographies of labor songs of specific industries, see Archie Green, "A Discography of American Coal Miners' Songs," *Labor History* 2 (winter 1961): 101-15; Archie Green, "Born on Picketlines, Textile Workers' Songs Are Woven into History," *Textile Labor* 22 (April 1961): 3-5; Doug DeNatale and Glenn Hinson, "The Southern Textile Song Tradition Reconsidered," *Journal of Folklore Research* 28 (May-December 1991): 103-33.

12. This observation of Korson's work was made in Archie Green, "George Korson and Industrial Folklore," *Keystone Folklore Quarterly* 16 (summer 1971): 58-59. There Green noted that while some union organizers might well have been " 'from the outside,' " as Korson described them, many were not. Green explained that determining who is "folk" and who is not is a difficult task for the folklorist, "sketching the little-known relationship of polemical to industrial material." In *Ballad Makin' in the Mountains of Kentucky* (New York: Henry Holt, 1939), Jean Thomas, like Korson, eschewed the radical, class-conscious songs of Aunt Molly Jackson and other minstrels of Bloody Harlan. Both Korson and Thomas did, however, include in their works union organizing songs from the CIO drives of the late 1930s.

13. Greenway, *American Folksongs of Protest,* 21.

14. Stewart Bird, Dan Georgakas, and Deborah Shaffer, *Solidarity Forever: An Oral History of the IWW* (Chicago: Lake View Press, 1985), 21–24; *I.W.W. Songs: Songs of the Workers: To Fan the Flames of Discontent,* 1st–35th eds. (Chicago: I.W.W., 1909-76).

15. Joyce L. Kornbluh, ed., *Rebel Voices: An I.W.W. Anthology* (Ann Arbor: University of Michigan Press, 1964). See also Bird, Georgakas, and Shaffer, *Solidarity Forever;* Richard Brazier, "The Story of the I.W.W.'s 'Little Red Songbook,' " *Labor History* 9 (winter 1968): 91–105; Ralph Chaplin, *Wobbly: The Rough and Tumble Story of an American Radical* (Chicago: University of Chicago Press, 1948); Melvyn Dubofsky, *We Shall Be All: A History of the Industrial Workers of the World* (New York: Quadrangle, 1969); Philip S. Foner, *The Industrial Workers of the World, 1905–1917* (New York: International Publishers, 1965); Barrie Stavis and Frank Harmon, eds., *The Songs of Joe Hill* (New York: Oak Publications, 1960).

16. Philip S. Foner, *American Labor Songs of the Nineteenth Century* (Urbana: University of Illinois Press, 1975).

17. Archie Green, *Only a Miner: Studies in Recorded Coal-Mining Songs* (Urbana: University of Illinois Press, 1972); Archie Green, *Wobblies, Pile Butts, and Other Heroes: Laborlore Explorations* (Urbana: University of Illinois Press, 1993). See also Archie Green, "The Death of Mother Jones," *Labor History* 1 (winter 1960): 68-80; Archie Green, ed., *Songs about Work: Es-*

says in Occupational Culture for Richard A. Reuss (Bloomington: Indiana University Press, 1993).

18. R. Serge Denisoff, *Great Day Coming: Folk Music and the American Left* (Urbana: University of Illinois Press, 1995). See also R. Serge Denisoff, *Sing a Song of Social Significance*, 2nd ed. (Bowling Green, Ohio: Bowling Green State University Popular Press, 1983); R. Serge Denisoff, "The Proletarian Renascence: The Folkness of the Ideological Folk," *Journal of American Folklore* 82 (January-March 1969): 51–65.

19. Robbie Lieberman, *"My Song Is My Weapon": People's Songs, American Communism, and the Politics of Culture, 1930–1950* (Urbana: University of Illinois Press, 1989). See also Robbie Lieberman, "People's Songs: American Communism and the Politics of Culture," *Radical History Review* 36 (September 1986): 63–78; Irwin Silber, ed., *Reprints of the People's Songs Bulletin, 1946–1949* (New York: Oak Publications, 1961).

20. Richard A. Reuss, "The Roots of American Left-Wing Interest in Folksong," *Labor History* 12 (spring 1971): 259–79; Richard A. Reuss, with JoAnne C. Reuss, *American Folk Music and Left-wing Politics, 1927–1957* (Lanham, Md.: Rowman and Littlefield, 2000). See also Richard A. Reuss, "Folk Music and Social Conscience: The Musical Odyssey of Charles Seeger," *Western Folklore* 38 (October 1979): 221–38.

21. Cohen and Samuelson, *Songs for Political Action*. In addition to the works of Denisoff, Lieberman, and Reuss cited earlier, which examine the urban folk revival, see Benjamin Botkin, "The Folksong Revival: Cult or Culture?," in *The American Folk Scene*, ed. David A. De Turk and A. Poulin Jr. (New York: Dell, 1967), 95–100; Robert Cantwell, *When We Were Good: The Folk Revival* (Cambridge: Harvard University Press, 1996); Ronald D. Cohen, ed., *"Wasn't That a Time!": Firsthand Accounts of the Folk Music Revival* (Metuchen, N.J.: Scarecrow Press, 1995); Dunaway, *How Can I Keep from Singing*; David King Dunaway, "Unsung Songs of Protest: The Composers Collective of New York," *New York Folklore* 5 (summer 1979): 1–19; David King Dunaway, "Charles Seeger and Carl Sands: The Composers' Collective Years," *Ethnomusicology* 24 (1980): 159–68; Benjamin Filene, " 'Our Singing Country': John and Alan Lomax, Leadbelly, and the Construction of an American Past," *American Quarterly* 43 (December 1991): 602–24; Archie Green, "Charles Louis Seeger (1886–1979)," *Journal of American Folklore* 92 (October-December 1982): 391–99; Woody Guthrie, *Bound for Glory* (New York: E. P. Dutton, 1943; reprint, New York: Penguin, 1983); Louis Harap, *Social Roots of the Arts* (New York: International Publishers, 1949); Joe Klein, *Woody Guthrie: A Life* (New York: Alfred A. Knopf, 1980); Richard H. Pells, *Radical Visions and American Dreams: Culture and Social Thought in the Depression Years* (Middletown, Conn.: Wesleyan University Press, 1973); Ann M. Pescatello, *Charles Seeger: A Life in American Music* (Pittsburgh: University of Pittsburgh Press, 1992); Earl Robinson, with Eric A. Gordon, *Ballad of an American: The Autobiography of Earl Robinson* (Lanham, Md.: Scarecrow Press, 1998); Neil V. Rosenberg, ed., *Transforming Tradition: Folk Music Revivals Examined* (Urbana: University of Illinois Press, 1993); Doris Willens, *Lonesome Traveler: The Life of Lee Hays* (Lincoln: University of Nebraska Press, 1993); Charles Wolfe and Kip Lornell, *The Life and Legend of Leadbelly* (New York: Da Capo Press, 1999).

22. Jim Garland, *Welcome the Traveler Home: Jim Garland's Story of the Kentucky Mountains*, ed. Julia S. Ardery (Lexington: University Press of Kentucky, 1983); Shelly Romalis, *Pistol Packin' Mama: Aunt Molly Jackson and the Politics of Folksong* (Urbana: University of Illinois Press, 1999).

23. Just as folklorists were the first to collect and examine labor songs and songs of protest, they were also the first to recognize their value as historical sources. See B. A. Botkin, "Folklore as a Neglected Source of Social History," in *The Cultural Approach to History*, ed. Caroline F. Ware (Port Washington, N.Y.: Kennikat Press, 1940), 308–15; Archie Green, "American Labor Lore: Its Meanings and Uses," *Industrial Relations* 4 (February 1965): 51–69; Archie Green, "Working with Laborlore," *Labor's Heritage* 1 (July 1989): 66–75; Green, "Labor Song," 93-102;

Notes

John Greenway, "Folk Songs as Socio-Historical Documents," *Western Folklore* 9 (January 1960): 1–9; Bruce Jackson, ed. *Folklore and Society: Essays in Honor of Benjamin A. Botkin* (Hatboro) Pa.: Folklore Associates, 1966; reprint, Folcroft, Pa.: Folcroft Library Editions, 1978); Paul Rosenfeld, "Folk Music and Culture Politics," *Modern Music* 17 (October-November 1939): 18–24; Charles Seeger, "On Proletarian Music," *Modern Music* 11 (March-April 1934): 120–27; Charles Seeger, "Folk Music as a Source of Social History" in *Cultural Approach to History*, ed. Ware, 316-23.

24. The notion of the working class being deemed "inarticulate" is discussed in Jesse Lemisch and John K. Alexander, "The White Oaks, Jack Tar, and the Concept of the 'Inarticulate,'" *William and Mary Quarterly* 29 (January 1972): 109–42.

25. Roger D. Abrahams, *Singing the Master: The Emergence of African American Culture in the Plantation South* (New York: Pantheon Books, 1992; reprint, New York: Penguin Books, 1993); John W. Blassingame, *The Slave Community: Plantation Life in the Antebellum South*, rev. ed. (New York: Oxford University Press, 1979); Eugene D. Genovese, *Roll, Jordan, Roll: The World the Slaves Made* (New York: Pantheon, 1974; reprint, New York: Athens: University of Georgia Press, 1989); Lawrence W. Levine, *Black Culture and Black Consciousness: Afro-American Folk Thought from Slavery to Freedom* (New York: Oxford University Press, 1977). See also B. A. Botkin, ed., *Lay My Burden Down: A Folk History of Slavery* (Chicago: University of Chicago Press, 1945); John Lovell, "The Significance of the Negro Spiritual," *Journal of Negro Education* 8 (October 1939): 634-43; Eileen Southern, *The Music of Black Americans: A History*, 3rd ed. (New York: W. W. Norton, 1997); Sterling Stuckey, "Through the Prism of Folklore: The Black Ethos in Slavery," *Massachusetts Review* 9 (summer 1968): 417–37.

26. Stanley Elkins, *Slavery: A Problem in American Institutional and Intellectual Life*, 2nd ed. (Chicago: University of Chicago Press, 1968).

27. Frederick Douglass, *Narrative of the Life of Frederick Douglass, an American Slave* (1845; reprint, New York: Penguin Books, 1986), 57–58. Nearly sixty years after Douglass's *Narrative* was published, W. E. B. Du Bois made a similar observation regarding slave songs in *The Souls of Black Folk* (1903; reprint, New York: Bantam Books, 1989), 179–80. There he wrote: "What are these songs, and what do they mean? I know little of music and can say nothing in technical phrase, but I know something of men, and knowing them, I know that these songs are the articulate message of the slave to the world. . . . They are the music of an unhappy people, of the children of disappointment; they tell of death and suffering and unvoiced longing toward a truer world, of misty wanderings and hidden ways."

28. John R. Commons et al., *History of Labor in the United States*, 4 vols. (New York: Macmillan, 1918-35; reprint, New York: A. M. Kelley, 1966). See also Selig Perlman, *A Theory of the Labor Movement* (New York: Macmillan, 1928; reprint, Philadelphia: Porcupine Press, 1979.

29. Edward P. Thompson, *The Making of the English Working Class* (New York: Vintage, 1966).

30. Herbert G. Gutman, *Work, Culture, and Society in Industrializing America* (New York: Vintage, 1977).

31. On trends in American labor history, see Ava Baron, ed., *Work Engendered: Toward a New History of American Labor* (Ithaca, N.Y.: Cornell University Press, 1991); David Brody, "The Old Labor History and the New: In Search of an American Working Class," *Labor History* 20 (winter 1979): 111-26; Mari Jo Buhle and Paul Buhle, "The New Labor History at the Cultural Crossroads," *Journal of American History* 75 (June 1988): 151–57; Alan Dawley, "A Preface to Synthesis," *Labor History* 29 (summer 1988): 363–77; Melvin Melvyn Dubofsky, "Lost in a Fog: Labor Historians' Unrequited Search for a Synthesis," *Labor History* 32 (spring 1991): 295–300; Paul G. Faler, "Working Class Historiography," *Radical America* 3 (March 1969): 56–68; Leon Fink, *In Search of the Working Class: Essays in American Labor History and Political Culture* (Urbana: University of Illinois Press, 1994); Michael Kazin et al., "The Limits of Union-Centered History: Responses to Howard Kimeldorf," *Labor History* 32 (winter 1991): 104–27; Howard Kimeldorf, "Bringing Unions Back In (Or Why We Need a New Old Labor History)," *Labor History* 32 (win-

ter 1991): 91–103; Thomas A. Krueger, "American Labor Historiography, Old and New: A Review Essay," *Journal of Social History* 4 (spring 1971): 277–85; David Montgomery, "To Study the People: The American Working Class," *Labor History* 21 (fall 1980): 485–512; J. Carroll Moody and Alice Kessler-Harris, eds., *Perspectives on American Labor History: The Problem of Synthesis* (DeKalb: Northern Illinois University Press, 1989); Robert Ozanne, "Trends in American Labor History," *Labor History* 21 (fall 1980): 513–21; Joan Wallach Scott, "On Language, Gender, and Working-Class History," *International Labor and Working Class History* 31 (spring 1987): 1–13; Robert H. Zieger, "Workers and Scholars: Recent Trends in American Labor Historiography," *Labor History* 13 (spring 1972): 245–66.

32. Bernstein, *Lean Years*, 9, 49, 58, 61, 90, 294, 324, 358–59, 423–24, 476; Bernstein, *Turbulent Years*, 37, 79, 145–47, 305, 444, 501, 526–27, 594–95, 682–83, 768–69.

33. Clark D. Halker, *For Democracy, Workers, and God: Labor Song-Poems and Labor Protest, 1865-95* (Urbana: University of Illinois Press, 1991), 210.

34. The phrase "turbulent years" is a reference to Bernstein, *Turbulent Years*.

35. Bernstein, *Lean Years*, 335; Bernstein, *Turbulent Years*, 769.

Chapter 1. "Mill Mother's Lament": Gastonia, North Carolina, 1929

1. There is some confusion as to who sang "Mill Mother's Lament" at Ella May's funeral. According to Fred E. Beal, *Proletarian Journey: New England, Gastonia, Moscow* (New York: Hillman-Curl, 1937), 194, and Margaret Larkin, "The Story of Ella May," *New Masses* 5 (November 1929): 4; Katie Barrett sang it. In Vera Buch Weisbord, *A Radical Life* (Bloomington: Indiana University Press, 1977), 259, Gladys Wallace is credited with singing it. Ella May's funeral is also described in John A. Salmond, *Gastonia 1929: The Story of the Loray Mill Strike* (Chapel Hill: University of North Carolina Press, 1995), 131–33.

2. Larkin, "Story of Ella May," 3–4.

3. Weisbord, *Radical Life*, 218, 219.

4. Bernstein, *Lean Years*, 40.

5. On individualism and self-reliance as character traits of the Appalachian people, see Thomas R. Ford, "The Passing of Provincialism," in *The Southern Appalachian Region: A Survey*, ed. Thomas R. Ford (Lexington: University of Kentucky Press, 1962), 12–15. On individualism in the South in the nineteenth century, see Bertram Wyatt-Brown, *Southern Honor: Ethics and Behavior in the Old South* (New York: Oxford University Press, 1982); Edward L. Ayers, *Vengeance and Justice: Crime and Punishment in the 19th-Century American South* (New York: Oxford University Press, 1984).

6. Greenway, *American Folksongs of Protest*, 251–52. It is worth noting that although Ella May used the first-person plural "we" throughout her song, the title of the song is most often given as "Mill Mother's Lament," with "Mother's" in the singular possessive. In Weisbord, *Radical Life*, 259, the title of the song is given in the plural possessive, "The Mill Mothers' Song."

7. Beal, *Proletarian Journey*.

8. Ibid., 190–91; Weisbord, *Radical Life*, 255–56.

9. Weisbord, *Radical Life*, 225.

10. Mary Heaton Vorse, *Strike!* (New York: Horace Liveright, 1930; reprint, Urbana: University of Illinois Press, 1991), 90. Vorse wrote the novel *Strike!* while at Gastonia during the strike. Regarding Vorse's experience at Gastonia, see Dee Garrison, *Mary Heaton Vorse: The Life of an American Insurgent* (Philadelphia: Temple University Press, 1989), 213–32. Other novels based upon mill life and the strike in Gastonia include: Sherwood Anderson, *Beyond Desire* (New York: Horace Liveright, 1932); Fielding Burke Olive Tilford Dargan, *Call Home the Heart* (London: Longmans, 1932; reprint, New York: Feminist Press, 1983); Grace Lumpkin, *To Make My Bread* (New York: Macauley, 1932); Dorothy Myra Page, *Gathering Storm: A Story of the Black*

Notes

Belt (New York: International Publishers, 1932); William Rollins, *The Shadow Before* (New York: Robert M. McBride, 1934). For an examination of the Gastonia novel, see John M. Reilly, "Images of Gastonia: A Revolutionary Chapter in American Social Fiction," *Georgia Review* 28 (fall 1974): 498–517; Joseph R. Urgo, "Proletarian Literature and Feminism: The Gastonia Novels and Feminist Protest," *Minnesota Review*, n.s. 24 (spring 1985): 64–83.

11. For information on the growth of the textile industry in the Carolina Piedmont, and the Gastonia strike in particular, see Salmond, *Gastonia*; Christina Baker and William J. Baker, "Shaking All the Corners of the Sky: The Global Response to the Gastonia Strike of 1929," *Canadian Review of American Studies* 21 (winter 1990): 321–31; Bernstein, *Lean Years*, 1-43; Theodore Draper, "Gastonia Revisited," *Social Research* 39 (spring 1971): 3–29; John R. Earle, Dean D. Knudsen, and Donald W. Shriver Jr., *Spindles and Spires: A Re-Study of Religion and Social Change in Gastonia* (Atlanta: John Knox Press, 1976); Ronald D. Eller, *Miners, Millhands, and Mountaineers: Industrialization of the Appalachian South, 1880–1930* (Knoxville: University of Tennessee Press, 1982); Ellen Grigsby, "The Politics of Protest: Theoretical, Historical, and Literary Perspectives on Labor Conflict in Gaston County, North Carolina" (Ph.D. diss., University of North Carolina at Chapel Hill, 1987); Jacquelyn Dowd Hall, "Disorderly Women: Gender and Labor Militancy in the Appalachian South," *Journal of American History* 73 (September 1986): 354-82; Jacquelyn Dowd Hall et al., *Like a Family: The Making of a Southern Cotton Mill World* (Chapel Hill: University of North Carolina Press, 1987; reprint, New York: W. W. Norton, 1989); Jacquelyn Dowd Hall, Robert Korstad, and James Leloudis, "Cotton Mill People: Work, Community, and Protest in the Textile South, 1880–1940," *American Historical Review* 91 (April 1986): 245–86; Harriet L. Herring, *Welfare Work in Mill Villages* (Chapel Hill: University of North Carolina Press, 1929; reprint, New York: Arno Press, 1971); Robin Hood, "The Loray Mill Strike" (master's thesis, University of North Carolina, 1932); Charles W. Joyner, "Up in Old Loray: Folkways of Violence in the Gastonia Strike," *North Carolina Folklore* 12 (December 1964): 20-24; Jack Temple Kirby, *Rural Worlds Lost: The American South, 1920–1960* (Baton Rouge: Louisiana State University Press, 1987), 275–308; Lois McDonald, *Southern Mill Hills: A Study of Social and Economic Forces in Certain Textile Mill Villages* (New York: Alex L. Hillman, 1928); Melton Alonza McLaurin, *Paternalism and Protest: Southern Cotton Mill Workers and Organized Labor, 1875–1905* (Westport, Conn.: Greenwood Publishing, 1971); I. A. Newby, *Plain Folk in the New South: Social Change and Cultural Persistence, 1880–1915* (Baton Rouge: Louisiana State University Press, 1989); Dale Newnan, "Work and Community Life in a Southern Textile Town," *Labor History* 19 (spring 1978): 202-25; Dennis R. Nolan and Donald E. Jonas, "Textile Unionism in the Piedmont, 1901-1932," in *Essays in Southern Labor History: Selected Papers, Southern Labor History Conference, 1976*, ed. Gary M. Fink and Merl E. Reed (Westport, Conn.: Greenwood Press, 1977), 48-79; Liston Pope, *Millhands and Preachers: A Study of Gastonia* (New Haven, Conn.: Yale University Press, 1965); Robert A. Ragan, *The Pioneer Cotton Mills of Gaston County, N.C.: The First Thirty* (Charlotte, N.C.: Robert A. Ragan, 1973); Bruce Raynor, "Unionism in the Southern Textile Industry: An Overview," in *Essays in Southern Labor History*, ed. Fink and Reed, 80–99; Carl Reeve, "The Great Gastonia Textile Strike," *Political Affairs* 63 (March 1984): 37–40; George Brown Tindall, *The Emergence of the New South, 1913–1945* (Baton Rouge: Louisiana State University Press, 1967); Allen Tullos, *Habits of Industry: White Culture and the Transformation of the Carolina Piedmont* (Chapel Hill: University of North Carolina Press, 1989); David E. Whisnant, *All That Is Native and Fine: The Politics of Culture in an American Region* (Chapel Hill: University of North Carolina Press, 1983); David E. Whisnant, *Modernizing the Mountaineer: People Power and Planning in Appalachia*, rev. ed. (Knoxville: University of Tennessee Press, 1994); Gavin Wright, *Old South, New South: Revolutions in the Southern Economy since the Civil War* (New York: Basic Books, 1986; reprint, Baton Rouge: Louisiana State University Press, 1996), esp. 124–55; Samuel Yellen, *American Labor Struggles*, (New York: Harcourt, Brace, 1936), 303–16; Robert H. Zieger, "Textile Work-

ers and Historians," in *Organized Labor in the Twentieth-Century South*, ed. Robert H. Zieger (Knoxville: University of Tennessee Press, 1991), 35–59.

For accounts of the strike by NTWU organizers and others close to the union, see Beal, *Proletarian Journey*, 109–221; William F. Dunne, *Gastonia, Citadel of Class Struggle in the New South* (New York: Workers Library Publishers, 1929); Bertha Hendrix, "I Was in the Gastonia Strike," in *Working Lives: The Southern Exposure History of Labor in the South*, ed. Marc S. Miller (New York: Pantheon, 1980), 169-72; Dorothy Myra Page, *Southern Cotton Mills and Labor* (New York: Workers Library Publishers, 1929); Tom Tippett, *When Southern Labor Stirs* (New York: Jonathan Cape and Harrison Smith, 1931; reprint, Huntington, W.Va.: Appalachian Movement Press, 1972); Mary Heaton Vorse, "Gastonia," in *Rebel Pen: The Writings of Mary Heaton Vorse*, ed. Dee Garrison (New York: Monthly Review Press, 1985), 112–27; Vera Buch Weisbord, "Gastonia 1929: Strike at the Loray Mill," *Southern Exposure* 1 (fall-winter 1974): 185-203; Weisbord, *Radical Life*, 173–289.

12. Salmond, *Gastonia*, 7–10; Bernstein, *Lean Years*, 3–6. For a detailed account of early efforts to unionize southern textile mills, see McLaurin, *Paternalism and Protest*; Tippett, *When Southern Labor Stirs*, 35–53. For a discussion of the condition of southern agriculture and its impact on industrialization in the Piedmont, see Pope, *Millhands and Preachers*, 51–57. The migration of farmers to the textile mills is examined in Hall et al., *Like a Family*, 31–43.

13. See Hall et al., *Like a Family*; Tullos, *Habits of Industry*. See also Herring, *Welfare Work*, and Ann McDonald, *Southern Mill Hills* for descriptions of life in a typical mill village. These studies were conducted during the period just prior to the Gastonia strike. Pope, *Millhands and Preachers* details the place of churches and religion within the mill communities. Earle, Knudsen, and Shriver, *Spindles and Spires*, is a more recent reappraisal of religion and social change in Gastonia.

14. Bernstein, *Lean Years*, 8–10.

15. Ibid., 11–12; Salmond, *Gastonia*, 13; Tippett, *When Southern Labor Stirs*, 77.

16. For a discussion of the strike in Elizabethton, see Bernstein, *Lean Years*, 13–20; James A. Hodges, "Challenge to the New South: The Great Textile Strike in Elizabethton, Tennessee, 1929," *Tennessee Historical Quarterly* 23 (December 1964): 343-57.

17. Hall et al., *Like a Family*, 214–15; Salmond, *Gastonia*, 13–16; Bernstein, *Lean Years*, 20–21.

18. Bernstein, *Lean Years*, 20.

19. Ibid., 21–22.

20. Lynn Haessly, " 'Mill Mother's Lament': Ella May, Working Women's Militancy, and the 1929 Gaston County Strikes" (master's thesis, University of North Carolina at Chapel Hill, 1987), 1–4; Larkin, "Story of Ella May," 3.

21. Haessly, " 'Mill Mother's Lament,' " 4–19; Larkin, "Story of Ella May," 3. There is some confusion regarding Ella May Wiggins's name. Her name prior to marriage was "May." Insofar as she dropped her married name when John Wiggins deserted her, I have avoided using it and have referred to her as simply "Ella May." On Ella May and the music of the Gastonia strike, see also Mary E. Frederickson, "Heroines and Girl Strikers: Gender Issues and Organized Labor in the Twentieth-Century American South," in *Organized Labor in the Twentieth-Century South*, ed. Zieger, 84-112; Greenway, *American Folksongs of Protest*, 244–52; Patrick Huber, " 'Battle Songs of the Southern Class Struggle': Songs of the Gastonia Textile Strike of 1929," *Southern Cultures* 4 (summer 1998): 109–22; Margaret Larkin, "Ella May's Songs," *Nation* 129 (October 9, 1929): 382-83; *Let's Stand Together: The Story of Ella Mae [sic] Wiggins* (Charlotte, N.C.: Metrolina Chapter, National Organization for Women, 1979); Stephen R. Wiley, "Songs of the Gastonia Textile Strike of 1929: Models of and for Southern Working-Class Women's Militancy," *North Carolina Folklore Journal* 30 (fall-winter 1982): 87–98.

For more general treatment of the music and song of textile workers, see Evelyn Alloy, *Working Women's Music: The Songs and Struggles of Women in the Cotton Mills, Textile Plants and Needle Trades* (Somerville, Mass.: New England Free Press, 1976); DeNatale and

Hinson, "Southern Textile Song Tradition Reconsidered," 103-33; Green, "Born on Picketlines," 3-5; Green, *Wobblies, Pile Butts, and Other Heroes*, 275–319; Greenway, *American Folksongs of Protest*, 121–45.

22. Larkin, "Story of Ella May," 3; Larkin, "Ella May's Songs," 383; Greenway, *American Folksongs of Protest*, 251–52; Wiley, "Songs of the Gastonia Textile Strike," 93–95. Ella May was never recorded singing any of her songs, including "Mill Mother's Lament." The song has been recorded by Pete Seeger on *American Industrial Ballads* (Folkway Records FH 5251, 1956; reissued, Smithsonian Folkway SF-40058, 1992). Variations of "Little Mary Phagan" can be found in Henry M. Belden and Arthur Palmer Hudson, eds., *Folk Ballads from North Carolina*, vol. 2 of *The Frank C. Brown Collection of North Carolina Folklore*, ed. Newman Ivey White (Durham, N.C.: Duke University Press, 1952-64), 598–603; Mellinger Edward Henry, comp. and ed., *Folk-Songs from the Southern Highlands* (New York: J. J. Augustin Publisher, 1938), 336–37. Regarding the guilt of Leo Frank, the accused murderer of Mary Phagan, there is some question. See Leonard Dinnerstein, *The Leo Frank Case* (New York: Columbia University Press, 1968); Nancy MacLean, "The Leo Frank Case Reconsidered: Gender and Sexual Politics in the Making of Reactionary Populism," *Journal of American History* 78 (December 1991): 917–48.

23. Salmond, *Gastonia*, 58–60.

24. Ibid., 36, 65–68; Weisbord, *Radical Life*, 205, 208, 217–19, 260.

25. Greenway, *American Folksongs of Protest*, 135–36; Wiley, "Songs of the Gastonia Textile Strike," 90–91. Variations of "On Top of Old Smoky" can be found in Harry M. Belden and Arthur Palmer Hudson, eds., *Folk Songs from North Carolina*, vol. 3 of *The Frank C. Brown Collection of North Carolina Folklore*, ed. Newman Ivey White, 287–90; Henry, *Folk-Songs from the Southern Highlands*, 273–75; Mellinger Edward Henry, comp., *Songs Sung in the Southern Appalachians, Many of Them Illustrating Ballads in the Making* (London: Mitre Press, n.d.), 2–3; Dorothy Scarborough, *A Song Catcher in the Southern Mountains: American Folk Songs of British Ancestry* (New York: Columbia University Press, 1937; reprint, New York: AMS Press, 1966), 276–77. Two different spellings of Corley's first name, "Odel" and "Odell," appear in both the primary and secondary literature. I have consistently used the former to avoid confusion.

26. Christene Patton, "Loray Workers," *Daily Worker*, April 15, 1929, 6.

27. Will Truett, "Spring Time in Gastonia," *Daily Worker*, May 17, 1929, 4. Recreation among the mill owners and other "uptown people" is discussed in Pope, *Millhands and Preachers*, 66–67.

28. Beal, *Proletarian Journey*, 131–32.

29. Ibid., 132.

30. For the full text of "Solidarity Forever," see Greenway, *American Folksongs of Protest*, 181; Kornbluh, *Rebel Voices*, 26–27. The musical score, but not all of Ralph Chaplin's verses, are in Fowke and Glazer, *Songs of Work and Protest*, 12–13; Seeger and Reiser, *Carry It On!*, 112-13.

31. Beal, *Proletarian Journey*, 134–35. See also Weisbord, *Radical Life*, 187–88.

32. Bernstein, *Lean Years*, 22; Beal, *Proletarian Journey*, 142-43. See also Pope, *Millhands and Preachers*, 252–84, for a detailed discussion of the reaction to the strike by various elements within the community—employers, workers, uptown community, and ministers and churches.

33. Kermit Harden, "Union Boys," *Daily Worker*, April 15, 1929, 6. In the last verse, the line "So climb up on the ties, union boys" is a reference to the rail line near the mill where striking workers congregated.

34. Russell D. Knight, "We Need You Most of All," *Daily Worker*, April 15, 1929, 4; Weisbord, *Radical Life*, 186.

35. Bernstein, *Lean Years*, 22–23. With regard to the reaction of the millhands toward the Communists, Pope, *Millhands and Preachers*, 257, 262, observes: "In general, it may be said that the workers reacted favorably and in large numbers to the Communist leadership at the beginning and gradually reacted negatively as the real character of Communist proposals became more evident and the opposing pressure of community opinion and action more severe." Pope

goes on to suggest that "the factor which more than any other alienated the majority of the workers from the Communist leadership was the indifference, and occasional open contempt, of the organizers for religion."

36. Salmond, *Gastonia*, 41–45; Bernstein, *Lean Years*, 23–24; Tippett, *When Southern Labor Stirs*, 87–89.

37. Salmond, *Gastonia*, 56–57; Bernstein, *Lean Years*, 24; Weisbord, *Radical Life*, 184.

38. Beal, *Proletarian Journey*, 159.

39. "Strike Songs Show Spirit of Mill Hands," *Daily Worker*, July 27, 1929, 4; Greenway, *American Folksongs of Protest*, 137–38; Wiley, "Songs of the Gastonia Textile Strike," 91. Variations of "May I Sleep in Your Barn Tonight, Mister?" can be found in Belden and Hudson, *Folk Songs*, 420–23.

40. Salmond, *Gastonia*, 36–37; Beal, *Proletarian Journey*, 151. Corley's song is found in Larkin, "Ella May's Songs," 383. A variation of this song appeared in *Labor Defender*, August 1929, 152. Both of these variants included another verse, which made reference to Fred Beal being moved to a different jail once the trial of the alleged killers of Chief Aderholt was moved to Charlotte. This took place approximately two months after the incident with Violet Jones. A discussion of the shooting of Chief Aderholt is found later in this chapter. Greenway included a slight variation of the first two verses in *American Folksongs of Protest*, 138. Variations of "Casey Jones" can be found in John A. Lomax and Alan Lomax, eds., *American Ballads and Folk Songs* (New York: Macmillan, 1934; reprint, New York: Dover, 1994), 36–39; John A. Lomax and Alan Lomax, eds., *Folk Song U.S.A.: The 111 Best American Ballads* (New York: Duell, Sloan and Pearce, 1947; reprint, New York: New American Library, 1975), 315–19, 336–41.

41. "Strike Songs Show Spirit of Mill Hands," *Daily Worker*, July 27, 1929, 4; Salmond, *Gastonia*, 48–49, 68; Tippett, *When Southern Labor Stirs*, 91.

42. Salmond, *Gastonia*, 70–74; Bernstein, *Lean Years*, 24; Tippett, *When Southern Labor Stirs*, 95–96.

43. Salmond, *Gastonia*, 74–75; Bernstein, *Lean Years*, 24–25; Tippett, *When Southern Labor Stirs*, 96–97.

44. Salmond, *Gastonia*, 46–47; Weisbord, *Radical Life*, 224–25.

45. Salmond, *Gastonia*, 63, 90; Weisbord, *Radical Life*, 231.

46. Greenway, *American Folksongs of Protest*, 248; Larkin, "Ella May's Songs," 382; Wiley, "Songs of the Gastonia Textile Strike," 92; Bernstein, *Lean Years*, 25; Salmond, *Gastonia*, 101. See also Green, "Born on Picketlines," 4. "Chief Aderholt" has been recorded by John Greenway on *American Industrial Folksongs* (Riverside Records RLP 12–607, 1956). On the death of Floyd Collins, see Frederick Lewis Allen, *Only Yesterday: An Informal History of the 1920's* (New York: Harper & Brothers, 1931; reprint, New York: Perennial Library, 1964), 161–62. Variations of "Floyd Collins" can be found in Belden and Hudson, *Folk Songs*, 498–501; Henry, *Songs Sung*, 82–83.

47. Belden and Hudson, *Folk Ballads*, 498; Huber, "Battle Songs of the Southern Class Struggle," 121; Bill C. Malone, *Southern Music/American Music* (Lexington: University Press of Kentucky, 1979), 66. "Waiting for a Train" can be found in Belden and Hudson, *Folk Songs*, 428–29. Regarding the impact of a mass consumer culture on mill communities during this period, see Hall et al., *Like a Family*, 237–88.

48. A copy of Ella May's "Two Little Strikers" is in the Mary Heaton Vorse Papers, Box 122, ALHUA. A slightly different version appears in Weisbord, "Gastonia 1929," 189. See also Wiley, "Songs of the Gastonia Textile Strike," 92. "Two Little Children" can be found in Belden and Hudson, *Folk Ballads*, 394–95; a variation, "Two Little Orphans," can be found in Henry, *Songs Sung*, 126–27.

49. Bernstein, *Lean Years*, 20–21; Greenway, *American Folksongs of Protest*, 249–50. The Communist spokesperson is quoted in Hood, "Loray Mill Strike," 33–34. For background on the ILD, see Charles H. Martin, "The International Labor Defense," in *Encyclopedia of the American Left*, ed. Mary Jo Buhle, Paul Buhle, and Dan Georgakas, 2nd ed. (New York: Oxford University Press, 1998), 368–70.

50. Larkin, "Ella May's Songs," 383; Greenway, *American Folksongs of Protest*, 250.

51. Greenway, *American Folksongs of Protest*, 251; Wiley, "Songs of the Gastonia Textile Strike," 92–93; Belden and Hudson, *Folk Songs*, 428–29.

52. *Nation* 129 (July 30, 1929): 106; *New Republic* 59 (July 24, 1929): 244; Salmond, *Gastonia*, 84–85, 95; Bernstein, *Lean Years*, 25. See also "The Gastonia Strikers' Case," *Harvard Law Review* 44 (May 1931): 1118–24.

53. Salmond, *Gastonia*, 101; Bernstein, *Lean Years*, 25.

54. Salmond, *Gastonia*, 68, 117; Bernstein, *Lean Years*, 25–26; Beal, *Proletarian Journey*, 188–89; Tippett, *When Southern Labor Stirs*, 103–4.

55. Salmond, *Gastonia*, 122–27, 135–36, 151, 154-55; Bernstein, *Lean Years*, 26; Beal, *Proletarian Journey*, 191; Weisbord, *Radical Life*, 255–56.

56. Salmond, *Gastonia*, 127–30, 136, 155-66, 200; Bernstein, *Lean Years*, 26–27.

57. Greenway, *American Folksongs of Protest*, 136–37; Wiley, "Songs of the Gastonia Textile Strike," 91. Variations of "The Wreck of the Old Ninety-Seven" can be found in Belden and Hudson, *Folk Ballads*, 512–21; Henry, *Songs Sung*, 79–80. Two different spellings of Daisy's last name, "McDonald" and "MacDonald," appear in both the primary and secondary literature. I have consistently used the former to avoid confusion. For background on Daisy McDonald see Vorse, "Gastonia," 120; Margaret Larkin, "Tragedy in North Carolina," *North American Review* 208 (1929): 690.

58. Greenway, *American Folksongs of Protest*, 138-39; Wiley, "Songs of the Gastonia Textile Strike," 91–92; *Labor Defender*, November 1929, 226; Vorse, "Gastonia," 120; Larkin, "Tragedy in North Carolina," 690; Salmond, *Gastonia*, 56, 60, 63, 96, 104, 141. The Communist Party in fact announced that Ella May's children would be sent to the Young Pioneers School in Philadelphia. That did not happen; they were sent to the Presbyterian orphanage at Barium Springs, North Carolina. See Salmond, *Gastonia*, 131–33.

59. *Daily Worker*, September 16, 17, 18, 1929; Jessie Lloyd, "Ella May, Murdered, Lives in Her Songs of Class Strife," *Daily Worker*, September 20, 1929, 1, 3; Bill Dunne, "On the Gastonia Battle Front," *Labor Defender*, October 1929, 191–92; Page, *Gathering Storm*, 335–36. "Mill-Mothers Song" was one of five folksongs included in Granville Hicks et al., eds., *Proletarian Literature in the United States: An Anthology* (New York: International Publishers, 1935), 203–4. In this anthology, published by the Communist Party just five years after the strike, the song appeared without the two aforementioned verses. Regarding the Communist Party's interest in folksongs, see Cohen and Samuelson, *Songs for Political Action*; Denisoff, *Great Day Coming*; Denisoff, *Sing a Song*, 1–18, 40-47, 58–79, 97–117; Denisoff, "Proletarian Renascence," 51–65; Lieberman, *"My Song Is My Weapon"*; Lieberman, "People's Songs," 63–78; Reuss, *American Folk Music and Left-Wing Politics*; Reuss, "Roots of American Left-Wing Interest," 259–79; Reuss, "Folk Music and Social Conscience," 221–38.

60. Ella May, "What I Believe," *Labor Defender*, November 1929, 227; Larkin, "Ella May's Songs," 382–83; Larkin, "Story of Ella May," 3–4; Larkin, "Tragedy in North Carolina," 690.

61. Salmond, *Gastonia*, 138–53; Bernstein, *Lean Years*, 27.

62. Salmond, *Gastonia*, 167–68; Bernstein, *Lean Years*, 27–28.

63. Salmond, *Gastonia*, 168–72; Bernstein, *Lean Years*, 28.

64. Tippett, *When Southern Labor Stirs*, 108.

65. Larkin, "Ella May's Songs," 383.

Chapter 2. "Dreadful Memories": Harlan County, 1931–32

1. Greenway, *American Folksongs of Protest*, 274–75. Many of Aunt Molly's songs and stories were recorded for the Library of Congress, as well as for private collectors and folklorists. Some of these have since been released by commercial recording companies. "Dreadful Memories" is on John Greenway, *The Songs and Stories of Aunt Molly Jackson* (Folkways Records

FH 5457, 1961). However, on that record album, Aunt Molly's songs are sung by John Greenway, though her stories are told by herself. A complete discography of the songs of Aunt Molly Jackson, Sarah Ogan Gunning, and Jim Garland can be found in Garland, *Welcome the Traveler Home*, 209–23. In addition to their own recordings, their songs performed by other artists are included. Recordings of a number of songs of the Garland siblings can also be found on Cohen and Samuelson, *Songs for Political Action*, which was released after Garland's *Welcome the Traveler Home*, with its comprehensive discography.

2. Sarah Ogan Gunning's version of "Dreadful Memories" is on her *Girl of Constant Sorrow* (Folk-Legacy Records FSA-26, 1965) and George Tucker et al., *Come All You Coal Miners* (Rounder Records 4005, 1973). There is some question regarding the authorship of "Dreadful Memories." Both Aunt Molly and Sarah have claimed to have written "Dreadful Memories." Archie Green believes that Sarah probably had composed the song. In the liner notes to Gunning, *Girl of Constant Sorrow*, 17, Green comments: "In 1952, when John Greenway visited Aunt Molly Jackson at Sacramento, California, she sang for him a poignant song modeled on the familiar hymn 'Precious Memories.' Molly placed the date of the composition as 1935 and the 'experience' as 1931. It was an exciting find for the folklorist, since Molly had not given this piece to previous collectors Alan Lomax or Mary Elizabeth Barnicle in the 1930's. Greenway used 'Dreadful Memories' in *American Folksongs of Protest* and recorded it twice. Consequently, I was pleased and surprised to collect it from Sarah in 1963, for she generally eschewed her half-sister's material. Sarah told me that she composed the song in New York about 1938 and that Molly 'learned it from her' when the Gunnings visited California during World War II. There is no question in my mind as to the veracity of Sarah's statement (although to document my belief would require an analysis of Aunt Molly Jackson longer than this brochure). Here it can be said that folksong students are in debt to the two sisters for this excellent example of variation within a single family tradition." Whether it was Sarah or Aunt Molly who wrote the song seems less the point than the fact that such powerful memories could inspire such strong feelings years later and that it would be in and through song that these feelings would be recalled and expressed. See also Romalis, *Pistol Packin' Mama*, 142.

3. Garland, *Welcome the Traveler Home*, 161.

4. Ibid., 154.

5. Ibid., 161.

6. Greenway, *American Folksongs of Protest*, 254; Romalis, *Pistol Packin' Mama*, 60–61. On Aunt Molly Jackson, see also Archie Green, spec. ed., "Aunt Molly Jackson Memorial Issue," *Kentucky Folklore Record* 7 (October 1961); Archie Green, "A Great Rebel Passes On," *Sing Out!* 10 (December-January 1960–61): 31–32; Green, *Only a Miner*, 77–88, 419–23; John Greenway, "Aunt Molly Jackson and Robin Hood: A Study of Folk Re-creation," *Journal of American Folklore* 69 (January–March 1956): 23–38.

7. "Little Talk with Jesus" is on Aunt Molly Jackson, *Aunt Molly Jackson*, Library of Congress Recordings (Rounder Records 1002, 1972).

8. Greenway, *American Folksongs of Protest*, 254-55; Romalis, *Pistol Packin' Mama*, 61–62.

9. Greenway, *American Folksongs of Protest*, 255; Romalis, *Pistol Packin' Mama*, 62–68.

10. Greenway, *American Folksongs of Protest*, 255–57; Romalis, *Pistol Packin' Mama*, 68–71; Garland, *Welcome the Traveler Home*, 61–62. "Mister Cundiff, Won't You Turn Me Loose?" is on Greenway, *Songs and Stories of Aunt Molly Jackson*.

11. Greenway, *American Folksongs of Protest*, 255, 257, 260; Romalis, *Pistol Packin' Mama*, 72–76, 92. Romalis speculates that the accident might have been in 1933, not 1932.

12. Greenway, *American Folksongs of Protest*, 257–58.

13. Ibid., 257.

14. John W. Hevener, *Which Side Are You On?: The Harlan County Coal Miners, 1931–1939* (Urbana: University of Illinois Press, 1978), 1. The industrial development of Appalachia and eastern Kentucky is examined in Edward L. Ayers, *The Promise of the New South: Life after*

Notes

Reconstruction (New York: Oxford University Press, 1992), 104–31; Allen W. Batteau, *The Invention of Appalachia* (Tucson: University of Arizona Press, 1990), esp. 86–126; Guy Carawan and Candie Carawan, *Voices from the Mountains* (New York: Alfred A. Knopf, 1975; reprint, Athens: University of Georgia Press, 1996); Harry M. Caudill, *Night Comes to the Cumberlands: A Biography of a Depressed Area* (Boston: Little, Brown, 1963); Harry M. Caudill, *Theirs Be the Power: The Moguls of Eastern Kentucky* (Urbana: University of Illinois Press, 1983); Mabel Green Condon, *A History of Harlan County* (Nashville: Parthenon Press, 1962); Eller, *Miners, Millhands, and Mountaineers*; John Gaventa, *Power and Powerlessness: Quiescence and Rebellion in an Appalachian Valley* (Urbana: University of Illinois Press, 1980), esp. 47–121; James P. Johnson, *The Politics of Soft Coal: The Bituminous Industry from World War I through the New Deal* (Urbana: University of Illinois Press, 1979); G. C. Jones, *Growing Up Hard in Harlan County* (Lexington: University Press of Kentucky, 1985); Kirby, *Rural Worlds Lost*, 275–308; Priscilla Long, *Where the Sun Never Shines: A History of America's Bloody Coal Industry* (New York: Paragon House, 1989); Newby, *Plain Folk in the South*; Alessandro Portelli, *The Death of Luigi Trastulli and Other Stories: Form and Meaning in Oral History* (Albany: State University of New York Press, 1991), 195–238; Malcolm H. Ross, *Machine Age in the Hills* (New York: Macmillan, 1933); Crandall A. Shifflett, *Coal Towns: Life, Work, and Culture in Company Towns of Southern Appalachia, 1880–1969* (Knoxville: University of Tennessee Press, 1991); Tindall, *Emergence of the New South*; Whisnant, *Modernizing the Mountaineer*; Whisnant, *All That Is Native and Fine.*

15. Hevener, *Which Side Are You On?*, 3–4.
16. Ibid., 4–10. See also George J. Titler, *Hell in Harlan* (Beckley, W.Va.: BJW Printers, n.d.). Though Titler's book is essentially a memoir of his work as a UMW organizer in Harlan County between 1937 and 1941, he does describe the UMW's early years in Harlan County in the first three chapters.
17. Hevener, *Which Side Are You On?*, 10–11; Bernstein, *Lean Years*, 378.
18. Hevener, *Which Side Are You On?*, 33–34; Bernstein, *Lean Years*, 378; Tony Bubka, "The Harlan County Coal Strike of 1931," *Labor History* 11 (winter 1970): 45.
19. Hevener, *Which Side Are You On?*, 34–49; Bernstein, *Lean Years*, 378; Bubka, "Harlan County," 46–48. See also Bill Bishop, "1931: The Battle of Evarts," *Southern Exposure* 4 (spring-summer 1976): 92–101.
20. Hevener, *Which Side Are You On?*, 49–50; Bernstein, *Lean Years*, 378–79. For a discussion of the trials that followed the "Battle of Evarts," see Bubka, "Harlan County," 50–53; Titler, *Hell in Harlan*, 22–35; Paul F. Taylor, *Bloody Harlan: The United Mine Workers of America in Harlan County, Kentucky, 1931–1941* (Lanham, Md.: University Press of America, 1990), 18–25.
21. Hevener, *Which Side Are You On?*, 55–56; Bernstein, *Lean Years*, 379; Bubka, "Harlan County," 48–49; Theodore Draper, "Communists and Miners 1928–1933," *Dissent* 19 (spring 1972): 381. See also *The National Miners Union, Harlan and Bell Kentucky, 1931–32*, compilation from the *Labor Defender* and *Labor Age* (Huntington, W.Va.: Appalachian Movement Press, 1972).
22. Taylor, *Bloody Harlan*, 26; Bernstein, *Lean Years*, 379–80.
23. Hevener, *Which Side Are You On?*, 56–57; Draper, "Communists and Miners," 382–83.
24. Hevener, *Which Side Are You On?*, 57–58; Bernstein, *Lean Years*, 380.
25. Greenway, *American Folksongs of Protest*, 266–67. In this passage quoted in Greenway's *American Folksongs of Protest*, Aunt Molly incorrectly gave the year as "19 and 30," not 1931, the correct year.
26. Ibid., 267. Greenway entitles the song "Hungry Ragged Blues" in *American Folksongs of Protest* and in his recording of it on *Songs and Stories of Aunt Molly Jackson*. Shortly after arriving in New York City in December 1931, Aunt Molly herself recorded "Kentucky Miner's Wife" ("Ragged Hungry Blues"), which was released by Columbia as a two-sided record on 10 inch 78 RPM. It was rereleased on compact disc on Cohen and Samuelson, *Songs for Political Action*, disc 1. See also Romalis, *Pistol Packin' Mama*, 91–92.

27. Greenway, *American Folksongs of Protest*, 267, 273–74.

28. Hevener, *Which Side Are You On?*, 22, 77.

29. Greenway, *American Folksongs of Protest*, 267.

30. Ibid., 267-68.

31. Ibid., 269–70; Romalis, *Pistol Packin' Mama*, 10-11. "I Am a Union Woman" is on Greenway, *Songs and Stories of Aunt Molly Jackson*. Regarding "Jackie Frazier" as the model for "I Am a Union Woman," see note 46 of this chapter.

32. Greenway, *American Folksongs of Protest*, 261–62, 270; Romalis, *Pistol Packin' Mama*, 83.

33. Garland, *Welcome the Traveler Home*, 152.

34. In 1935 John L. Lewis, president of the UMW, and AFL affiliate, led the effort to form the Committee for Industrial Organization (CIO). Three years later, the AFL expelled CIO unions, the UMW among them, and the CIO reorganized as the Congress of Industrial Organizations. The AFL and CIO were joined in 1955 to form the AFL-CIO.

35. Guthrie, and Seeger, *Hard Hitting Songs*, 142. "Join the CIO," a variant of "I Am A Union Woman," is on Jackson, *Aunt Molly Jackson*.

36. Hevener, *Which Side Are You On?*, 63–68; Garland, *Welcome the Traveler Home*, 149; Romalis, *Pistol Packin' Mama*, 1, 39–42; National Committee for the Defense of Political Prisoners, *Harlan Miners Speak: Report on Terrorism in the Kentucky Coal Fields* (New York: Harcourt, Brace, 1932; reprint, New York: Da Capo Press, 1970), v-vii, 279–82. See also Lawrence Grauman Jr., " 'That Little Ugly Running Sore': Some Observations on the Participation of American Writers in the Investigations of Conditions in the Harlan and Bell County, Kentucky, Coal Fields, 1931–32," *Filson Club History Quarterly* 36 (October 1962): 340–54. The Dreiser Committee changed the title of the song to make it plural: "Kentucky Miners' Wives Ragged Hungry Blues." Whether this was a deliberate effort on the part of Dreiser and other members of the committee to present the song as the sentiments of a group, as opposed to simply those of one miner's wife, is impossible to know.

37. Greenway, *American Folksongs of Protest*, 259-60; Romalis, *Pistol Packin' Mama*, 89–92. The appearance at New York's Bronx Coliseum was part of the funeral services for NMU organizer Harry Simms who was murdered during the course of the strike. That episode in the strike is discussed later in this chapter.

38. Greenway, *American Folksongs of Protest*, 260.

39. Ibid., 259.

40. Lomax, Seeger, and Guthrie, *Hard Hitting Songs*, 146.

41. Ibid., 146–47. "I Love Coal Miners, I Do" is on Jackson, *Aunt Molly Jackson*.

42. Greenway, *American Folksongs of Protest*, 260; Romalis, *Pistol Packin' Mama*, 92.

43. Hevener, *Which Side Are You On?*, 59-60.

44. Ron Stanford, " 'Which Side Are You On?': An Interview with Florence Reece," *Sing Out!* 20 (July-August 1971): 15; in this interview, Reece incorrectly gave the year as 1930, not 1931, the correct year.

45. Kathy Kahn, *Hillbilly Women* (Garden City, N.Y.: Doubleday, 1973), 35.

46. Romalis, *Pistol Packin' Mama*, 10–11. Regarding the hymn used as the model for "Which Side Are You On?," there is some confusion. In her interview in Stanford, " 'Which Side Are You On?,' " 15, Reece related, "I've heard different people's ideas on where I got the tune for 'Which Side Are You On?,' but I think I got it from a hymn called 'I'm Going To Land On That Shore.' The first verse starts out, 'I'm going to land on that shore / And be saved forever more,' but I don't remember more, and I've looked everywhere." In Kahn, *Hillbilly Women*, 37, Reece said, "The music to the song is an old hymn. I can't remember what was the hymn, but I've got to look in the songbooks and find out what that was a tune to." In the liner notes to *They'll Never Keep Us Down: Women's Coal Mining Songs* (Rounder Records 4012, 1984), 4, she gave the tune as "Lay the Lily Low." In Greenway, *American Folksongs of Protest*, 169–70, the tune is also given as "Lay the Lily Low." However, folklorist Archie Green maintains the tune is most likely related

to the broadside ballad "Jackie Frazier." Regardless as to the particular song used as the model, it was a song in the mountain tradition familiar to the people.

47. Stanford, " 'Which Side Are You On?,' " 14–15. Another version of "Which Side Are You On?," with a slightly different order of the verses, appears in Greenway, *American Folksongs of Protest*, 170–71. "Which Side Are You On?" is on *They'll Never Keep Us Down: Women's Coal Mining Songs*. On that record, Reece herself sings her famous protest song. There it does not include the fifth verse which begins, "With pistols and with rifles."

48. Stanford, " 'Which Side Are You On?,' " 14–15; Hevener, *Which Side Are You On?*, 55–56.

49. Greenway, *American Folksongs of Protest*, 265–66. "Lonesome Jailhouse Blues" is on Jackson, *Aunt Molly Jackson*. The recorded version of "Lonesome Jailhouse Blues" is slightly different from the one that appears in Greenway's *American Folksongs of Protest*. It is worth noting that on the recorded version the first line goes, "Listen friends and comrades." Aunt Molly was quite adept at incorporating the radical vocabulary of the Communist Party into her songs. In so doing, she infused traditional mountain ballads with language charged with class consciousness. The role of the ILD during the Harlan County strike is discussed in Hevener, *Which Side Are You On?*, 57, 61–63, 68, 78–79. For background on the ILD see also Martin, "International Labor Defense," 368–70.

50. Draper, "Communists and Miners," 382; *Daily Worker*, September 1, 1931, 1; National Committee for the Defense of Political Prisoners, *Harlan Miners Speak*, 92–96; Lomax, Guthrie, and Seeger, *Hard Hitting Songs*, 150.

51. Hevener, *Which Side Are You On?*, 60; *Harlan Miners Speak*, 109-21; Lomax, Guthrie, and Seeger, *Hard Hitting Songs*, 151. Regarding the WIR, see Harry Gannes, *Kentucky Miners Fight* (n.p.: Workers International Relief, 1932).

52. Hevener, *Which Side Are You On?*, 62–63, 70–72, 75–76.

53. Ibid., 21-22, 76–77. "Dead work" refers to various tasks such as cleaning up the work site and setting timbers in the mines at the end of the day. These jobs required coal loaders, paid by the ton, to do extra work without additional compensation. "Checkweighmen" determined the tonnage a coal loader loaded. Loaders complained that they were often short-weighed by unscrupulous checkweighmen and thereby underpaid.

54. Ibid., 77–78.

55. Ibid., 78–79; Garland, *Welcome the Traveler Home*, 156, 158. For a Communist critique of the collapse of the NMU strike see Jack Stachel, "Lessons of Two Recent Strikes," *Communist* 11 (June 1932): 527–36.

56. Hevener, *Which Side Are You On?*, 79–80; Garland, *Welcome the Traveler Home*, xxvii-xxviii, 150, 165–69; Mary Elizabeth Barnicle, "Harry Simms: The Story behind This American Ballad," in liner notes to Pete Seeger, *Songs of Struggle and Protest: 1930–1950* (Folkways Records FH 5233, 1964), 3–4; Green, *Only a Miner*, 420–22.

57. Garland, *Welcome the Traveler Home*, 169–71; Preval Glusman, "Harry Simms—A Young Revolutionist," *Daily Worker*, May 8, 1934, 5. Jim Garland recorded "The Ballad of Harry Simms" on *Newport Broadside: Topical Songs of the Newport Folk Festival, 1963* (Vanguard Records VRS 9144 1963). In Greenway, *American Folksongs of Protest*, 271–73, a slightly different version appears, entitled "The Death of Harry Simms" and included among the songs of Aunt Molly Jackson. That variant is recorded on Greenway, *Songs and Stories of Aunt Molly Jackson*.

It should be noted that while the version quoted here from Garland's autobiography, *Welcome the Traveler Home*, begins, "Comrades, listen to my story, / Comrades, listen to my song," the other version cited above begins, "Come and listen to my story, / Come and listen to my song." Similarly, the line, "To shoot and kill our Comrades," in the other version appears, "To shoot and kill our union men." When the more class-conscious word "comrade" was first used by Garland is difficult to know, but it undoubtedly would have been encouraged by outside organizers with whom Garland had considerable association both during and after the strike. In fact, in *Welcome the Traveler Home*, Garland suggests this version is the original. Consequently, the word "comrade" may very well have been used from the very beginning. Garland also provides a variant of the last verse, which he says was composed later. That verse goes as follows:

Comrades, we must vow today,
There's one thing we must do—
We'll organize all the miners
Into the good old NMU.
We'll get a million volunteers
From those who wish us well,
And travel over the country
And Harry's story tell.

Both of these concluding verses are also different from the last verse that appears in Greenway's *American Folksongs of Protest* and is sung by Greenway on *Songs and Stories of Aunt Molly Jackson*. That version concludes:

The thugs can kill our leaders
And cause us to shed tears,
But they cannot kill our spirit
If they try a million years.
We have learned our lesson
Now we all realize
A union struggle must go on
Till we are organized.

For other recordings of "The Ballad of Harry Simms," as well as other songs recorded by the Garland clan of Aunt Molly Jackson, Jim Garland, and Sarah Garland Ogan Gunning, see the discography in Garland, *Welcome the Traveler Home*, 209-23. In addition to their own recordings, other artists' performances of their songs are included.

58. Garland, *Welcome the Traveler Home*, 64, 168–74; "Workers! Over the Murdered Body of Harry Simms, Rally and Fight for Victory," *Daily Worker*, February 13, 1932, 1; "Jim Garland, Kentucky Striker, Tells Story of Simms' Murder," *Daily Worker*, February 16, 1932, 4. Estimates of the attendance at the service range from 21,000 in Greenway, *American Folksongs of Protest*, 259, to "at least 25,000" in Garland, *Welcome the Traveler Home*, 169. Regarding the Congressional investigations, see U.S. Congress, Senate, Committee on Manufacturers, *Conditions in Coal Fields in Harlan and Bell Counties, Kentucky, Hearings*, Senate Report 178, 72nd Congress, 1st session, 1932.

59. Garland, *Welcome the Traveler Home*, 174.

60. Ibid., 175–81.

61. Ibid., 181.

62. Ibid., 181–84. For an account of Aunt Molly's years in New York City and subsequent move to Sacramento, California, see Romalis, *Pistol Packin' Mama*, 89–126. Regarding Aunt Molly's and Sarah's relationships with Barnicle and Lomax, see Romalis, *Pistol Packin' Mama*, 100–121, 146-47.

63. Regarding Sarah and her music, see Sarah Ogan Gunning, "My Name Is Sarah Ogan Gunning. . . ," *Sing Out!* 25 (July-August 1976): 15–17; Romalis, *Pistol Packin' Mama*, 127–48; Lomax, Guthrie, and Seeger, *Hard Hitting Songs*, 154–69; Green, in liner notes to Gunning, *Girl of Constant Sorrow*. See also Henrietta Yurchenco, "Trouble in the Mines: A History in Song and Story by Women of Appalachia," *American Music* 9 (summer 1991): 209-24. For a discography of the songs of Sarah Ogan Gunning, see Garland, *Welcome the Traveler Home*, 213–15. Two documentary films have been produced about Sarah Ogan Gunning: Guy Carawan and Candie

Carawan, eds., *Always Sing My Songs: Sarah Ogan Gunning at Highlander, 1972–1982* (New Market, Tenn.: Highlander Center for Social Research, 1983); Mimi Pickering, prod., dir., and ed., *Dreadful Memories: The Life of Sarah Ogan Gunning* (Whitesburg, Ky.: Appalshop Films, 1988).

64. Lomax, Guthrie, and Seeger, *Hard Hitting Songs*, 164; Green, in liner notes to Gunning, *Girl of Constant Sorrow*, 3, 12. Sarah married Joseph Gunning in 1941, becoming Sarah Garland Ogan Gunning.

65. Lomax, Guthrie, and Seeger, *Hard Hitting Songs*, 164–65; Green, in liner notes to Gunning, *Girl of Constant Sorrow*, 12–14. "I Hate the Capitalist System" is on Sarah Ogan Gunning, *The Silver Dagger* (Rounder Records 0051). Sarah also sings "I Hate the Capitalist System" in Carawan and Carawan's film documentary, *Always Sing My Songs*. "I Hate the Company Bosses," a later version of "I Hate the Capitalist System," is on Gunning, *Girl of Constant Sorrow*. Regarding this change in the song's title, Sarah is quoted in Romalis, *Pistol Packin' Mama*, 144, as stating that the original title made it sound "like I was a radical and I'm no radical. This thing that I did hate was the company bosses so it was better to change it to the real one I mean. At the time of the capitalist system I didn't even know what that meant. I had heard the word in New York City but thought all the rich coal operators was the system."

66. Lomax, Guthrie, and Seeger, *Hard Hitting Songs*, 160.

67. Romalis, *Pistol Packin' Mama*, 100–21, 151–73. See also Cohen and Samuelson, *Songs for Political Action*; Denisoff, *Great Day Coming*; Denisoff, "Proletarian Renascence," 51–65; Denisoff, *Sing a Song*, 1–18, 40–47, 58–79, 97–117; Lieberman, "My Song Is My Weapon"; Lieberman, "People's Songs," 63–78; Reuss, *American Folk Music and Left-Wing Politics*; Reuss, "Folk Music and Social Conscience," 231–38; Reuss, "Roots of American Left-Wing Interest," 259–79.

Chapter 3. "Sit Down! Sit Down!": Flint, Michigan, 1936–37

1. Page 5 of typed copy of address given by Merlin Bishop before a conference on workers' education at the National Conference of Social Workers, Indianapolis, Indiana, May 27, 1937, Merlin Bishop Papers, Box 1, ALHUA.

2. Sidney Fine, *Sit-Down: The General Motors Strike of 1936–1937* (Ann Arbor: University of Michigan Press, 1969), 341. The most comprehensive account of the Flint sit-down strike is Fine's *Sit-Down*. See also Sidney Fine, "The General Motors Sit-Down Strike: A Re-examination," *American Historical Review* 70 (April 1965): 691–713; Sidney Fine, *The Automobile Under the Blue Eagle: Labor, Management, and the Automobile Manufacturing Code* (Ann Arbor: University of Michigan Press, 1963); John Barnard, *Walter Reuther and the Rise of the Auto Workers* (Boston: Little, Brown, 1983), 18–53; Bernstein, *Turbulent Years*, 499–571; Ely Chinoy, *Automobile Workers and the American Dream* (Garden City, N.Y.: Doubleday, 1955); Bert Cochran, *Labor and Communism: The Conflict that Shaped American Unions* (Princeton, N.J.: Princeton University Press, 1977), 103–26; Ronald Edsforth, *Class Conflict and Cultural Consensus: The Making of a Mass Consumer Society in Flint, Michigan* (New Brunswick, N.J.: Rutgers University Press, 1987), 157–89; Nora Faires, "The Great Flint Sit-Down Strike as Theatre," *Radical History Review* 43 (January 1989): 121–35; Galenson, *CIO Challenge to the AFL*, 134–43; David Gartman, *Auto Slavery: The Labor Process in the American Automobile Industry* (New Brunswick, N.J.: Rutgers University Press, 1986); Irving Howe and B. J. Widick, *The UAW and Walter Reuther* (New York: Random House, 1949; reprint, New York: Da Capo Press, 1973), 47–65; Thomas A. Karman, "The Flint Sit-Down Strike," *Michigan History* 46 (June, September 1962): 97–125, 223–50; Roger Keeran, *The Communist Party and the Auto Workers' Unions* (Bloomington: Indiana University Press, 1980), 148–85; Sidney Lens, *The Labor Wars: From the Molly Maguires to the Sitdowns* (Garden City, N.Y.: Doubleday, 1973), 291–317; Nelson Lichtenstein, "Auto Worker Militancy and the Structure of Factory Life, 1937–1955," *Journal of American History* 67 (September 1980):

335–53; Nelson Lichtenstein and Stephen Meyer, eds., *On the Line: Essays in the History of Auto Work* (Urbana: University of Illinois Press, 1989); Daniel Nelson, "How the UAW Grew," *Labor History* 35 (winter 1994): 5–24; Joyce Shaw Peterson, *American Automobile Workers, 1900–1933*, (Albany: State University of New York Press, 1987); Arthur Pound, *Turning the Wheel: The Story of General Motors through Twenty-Five Years* (Garden City, N.Y.: Doubleday, Doran, 1934); Robert Lyle Sandler, " 'You Can Sell Your Body but Not Your Mind': A Sociolinguistic Examination of the Folklore on the Automobile Factory Assembly Line" (Ph.D. diss., University of Pennsylvania, 1982); Stephen W. Sears, " 'Shut the Goddam Plant!': The Great Sit-Down Strike that Transformed American Industry," *American Heritage* 33 (April-May 1982): 49–64; Jack Stieber, *Governing the UAW* (New York: John Wiley and Sons, 1962); Kenneth B. West, " 'On the Line': Rank and File Reminiscences of Working Conditions and the General Motors Sit-Down Strike of 1936-37," *Michigan Historical Review* 12 (spring 1986): 57–82; Kenneth B. West, "Standard Cotton Products and the General Motors Sit-Down Strike: Some ` Forgotten Men' Remembered," *Michigan Historical Review* 14 (spring 1988): 57–73.

For women, blacks, and ethnic immigrants in the UAW during the time of the strike, see Nancy F. Gabin, *Feminism in the Labor Movement: Women and the United Auto Workers, 1935–1975* (Ithaca, N.Y.: Cornell University Press, 1990), 8-46; August Meier and Elliott Rudwick, *Black Detroit and the Rise of the UAW* (New York: Oxford University Press, 1979), 3–33; Steve Babson, *Building the Union: Skilled Workers and the Anglo-Gaelic Immigrants in the Rise of the UAW* (New Brunswick, N.J.: Rutgers University Press, 1991); Steve Babson, "Pointing the Way: The Role of British and Irish Skilled Tradesmen in the Rise of the UAW," *Detroit in Perspective* 7 (spring 1983): 75–95; Steve Babson, "Class, Craft, and Culture: Tool and Die Makers and the Organization of the UAW," *Michigan Historical Review* 14 (spring 1988): 33–55; B. J. Widick, ed., *Auto Work and Its Discontents* (Baltimore: Johns Hopkins University Press, 1976).

For examinations of union organizing at plant locations other than Flint, see Ray Boryczka, "Seasons of Discontent: Auto Union Factionalism and the Motor Products Strike of 1935–1936," *Michigan History* 61 (1977): 3–32; Peter Friedlander, *The Emergence of a UAW Local, 1936-1939: A Study in Class and Culture* (Pittsburgh: University of Pittsburgh Press, 1975); Neill Herring and Sue Thrasher, "UAW Sit-down Strike: Atlanta, 1936," *Southern Exposure* 1 (fall-winter 1974): 63–83; Claude E. Hoffman, *Sit-Down in Anderson: UAW Local 663, Anderson, Indiana* (Detroit: Wayne State University Press, 1968); J. G. Kruchko, *The Birth of a Union Local: The History of UAW Local 674, Norwood, Ohio, 1933–1940* (Ithaca, N.Y.: New York School of Industrial and Labor Relations, Cornell University, 1972).

For accounts of the strike by UAW leaders and others close to the union, see Henry Kraus, *The Many and the Few: A Chronicle of the Dynamic Auto Workers*, 2nd ed. (Urbana: University of Illinois Press, 1985); Edward Levinson, *Labor on the March* (New York: University Books, 1956), 141–68; Wyndham Mortimer, *Organize!: My Life as a Union Man*, ed. Leo Fenster (Boston: Beacon Press, 1971), 103–41; Victor G. Reuther, *The Brothers Reuther and the Story of the UAW* (Boston: Houghton Mifflin, 1976), 143–71; Mary Heaton Vorse, *Labor's New Millions* (New York: Modern Age Books, 1938), 59–90.

A number of documentary films have been made about the Flint sit-down strike. Among the best is *Sit Down and Fight: Walter Reuther and the Rise of the Auto Workers Union*, in *The American Experience* series, PBS, 1993. The role of women during the strike is told in the film by Lyn Goldfarb and Lorraine Gray, *With Babies and Banners: The Story of the Women's Emergency Brigade*, 1978.

3. Fine, *Sit-Down*, 20-21.

4. Ibid., 21–22; Bernstein, *Turbulent Years*, 510–11.

5. Fine, *Sit-Down*, 19; Bernstein, *Turbulent Years*, 511–12. See also Alfred P. Sloan Jr., *My Years with General Motors* (Garden City, N.Y.: Doubleday, 1964).

6. Fine, *Sit-Down*, 28–36, 42–47. See also Fine, *Automobile Under the Blue Eagle*.

7. Fine, *Sit-Down*, 37–42; Bernstein, *Turbulent Years*, 516–18.

Notes

8. Fine, *Sit-Down*, 23–27.

9. Ibid., 63–72.

10. Ibid., 71–72, 83–84; Bernstein, *Turbulent Years*, 503–6. For an examination of the Motor Products strike see Boryczka, "Seasons of Discontent," 3–32.

11. Fine, *Sit-Down*, 55–63; Kraus, *Many and the Few*, 43–45.

12. Fine, *Sit-Down*, 81–91; Bernstein, *Turbulent Years*, 502–9. For an examination of Communism and the UAW during the strike, see Keeran, *Communist Party and the Auto Workers' Union*, 148–85; Cochran, *Labor and Communism*, 103–26.

13. Fine, *Sit-Down*, 95–96, 98.

14. Ibid., 100–108; Bernstein, *Turbulent Years*, 519–20.

15. Fine, *Sit-Down*, 109, 118, 128–33; Bernstein, *Turbulent Years*, 523.

16. Fine, *Sit-Down*, 134–36, 138-39, 141-44; Bernstein, *Turbulent Years*, 522–25. For an examination of the UAW strike in Atlanta drawn from interviews, see Herring and Thrasher, "UAW Sit-down Strike," 63–83.

17. Fine, *Sit-Down*, 144–48; Bernstein, *Turbulent Years*, 524–26; Kraus, *Many and the Few*, 86–90. On Governor Frank Murphy's role during the strike, see Sidney Fine, *Frank Murphy: The New Deal Years* (Chicago: University of Chicago Press, 1979), 289–325; J. Woodford Howard, Jr., "Frank Murphy and the Sit-Down Strikes of 1937," *Labor History* 1 (spring 1960): 103–40.

18. Fine, *Sit-Down*, 145–46.

19. *Flint Auto Worker*, January 5, 1937, 2. "The Fisher Strike" was also printed in the official publication of the UAW, *United Automobile Worker*, January 22, 1937, 7. See also Lomax, Guthrie, and Seeger, *Hard Hitting Songs*, 240–41.

20. Fine, *Sit-Down*, 190–91; Levinson, *Labor on the March*, 152.

21. Fine, *Sit Down*, 145.

22. Ibid., 1-4; Bernstein, *Turbulent Years*, 529–30; Kraus, *Many and the Few*, 127–29.

23. Fine, *Sit-Down*, 4–6; Bernstein, *Turbulent Years*, 530; Kraus, *Many and the Few*, 129–31.

24. Fine, *Sit-Down*, 4–7; Kraus, *Many and the Few*, 131–34.

25. *United Automobile Worker*, January 22, 1937, 7. A handwritten copy of this song in Bud Simons Papers, Box 1, Folder "Misc. Picket Cards, Songs, etc.," ALHUA, identifies Cecil Hubel and Clarence Jobin as the strikers who composed it.

26. Copy of song in Henry Kraus Papers, Box 9, Folder 31, ALHUA.

27. Fine, *Sit-Down*, 274–78; Kraus, *Many and the Few*, 186–88, 204-6.

28. Francis O'Rourke Diary, 1936–37, entries for December 30, 1936 and January 2,1937, Small Collections O-R, ALHUA.

29. Copy of both strike songs in Simons Papers, Box 1, Folder "Misc. Picket Cards, Songs, etc."

30. Copy of song in Kraus Papers, Box 9, Folder 30.

31. Fine, *Sit-Down*, 220. Copy of song in Kraus Papers, Box 9, Folder 31.

32. The line, "To hell with G.M., Papa Sloan, and Mister Knudsen too," is from a copy of a song found in Kraus Papers, Box 9, Folder 31. *Flint Auto Worker*, January 5, 1937, 2; *United Automobile Worker*, January 22, 1937, 7.

33. Copy of song in Kraus Papers, Box 9, Folder 30, and in Simons Papers, Box 1, Folder "Misc. Picket Cards, Songs, etc." See also Lomax, Guthrie, and Seeger, *Hard Hitting Songs*, 243.

34. *Flint Auto Worker*, December 1936, 4.

35. Copy of song in Kraus Papers, Box 9, Folder 31.

36. Copy of song in Kraus Papers, Box 9, Folder 30.

37. *United Automobile Worker*, February 25, 1937, 14. A copy of "Auto Workers Jingle" in Kraus Papers, Box 9, Folder 31, identifies Jessie Lloyd as writing the lyrics.

38. Copy of song in Kraus Papers, Box 9, Folder 30, and in Simons Papers, Box 1, Folder "Misc. Picket Cards, Songs, etc." See also Lomax, Guthrie, and Seeger, *Hard Hitting Songs*, 256-57.

39. Kraus, *Many and the Few*, 103-4.

40. Ibid, 104; O'Rourke Diary, entry for December 30, 1936. See also William H. Lawrence, "There's Music Inside—And Plenty of Discipline," *Daily Worker*, January 11, 1937, 1, 3.

41. Maurice Sugar to Pete Seeger, January 25, 1947, in Sugar Papers, Box 14, Folder 24, along with a copy of the "Soup Song." See also Lomax, Guthrie, and Seeger, *Hard Hitting Songs*, 294. Well before the Flint strike, the "Soup Song" had been printed in *Rebel Song Book* (New York: Rand School Press, 1935) and *Brookwood Chautauqua Songs* (Katonah, N.Y.: Brookwood Labor Publications, n.d.). A number of the union organizers, including Educational Director Merlin Bishop, had spent time at Brookwood Labor College prior to the Flint strike. This will be discussed later in this chapter. A recording of the "Soup Song" is on Barbara Dane, *I Hate the Capitalist System* (Paredon Records P-1024, 1973); Cisco Houston, *Songs of the Open Road* (Folkways FA 2480, 1960). There is also a recording by The New Singers on compact disc on Cohen and Samuelson, *Songs for Political Action*, disc 1. For Sugar's role as an attorney for the UAW during the strike, see Johnson, *Maurice Sugar*, 191-218.

42. Sugar Papers, Box 14, Folder 11. See also Lomax, Guthrie, and Seeger, *Hard Hitting Songs*, 242.

43. Mary Heaton Vorse, "Soldiers Everywhere in Flint; Unionists Hold the Fort," in *Rebel Pen*, ed. Garrison, 179.

44. For lyrics, musical score, and historical background to "Hold the Fort" and "We Shall Not Be Moved," see Fowke and Glazer, *Songs of Work and Protest*, 36-39.

45. Kraus Papers, Box 9, Folder 31. Copy of "Collective Bargaining in Our Shops" in Simons Papers, Box 1, Folder "Misc. Picket Cards, Songs, etc." See also Lomax, Guthrie, and Seeger, *Hard Hitting Songs*, 248-49.

46. Kraus, *Many and the Few*, 143; *United Automobile Worker*, January 22, 1937, 7.

47. Fine, *Sit-Down*, 200-203; *Flint Auto Worker*, January 26, 1937, 3; *United Automobile Worker*, February 25, 1937, 11.

48. Copy of song in Joe Brown Papers, Box 14, Folder "Labor in Music," ALHUA.

49. *Flint Auto Worker*, February 6, 1937, 2.

50. Copy of song in Kraus Papers, Box 9, Folder 31.

51. *Flint Auto Worker*, January 26, 1937, 3; Vorse, *Labor's New Millions*, 76.

52. Krause Papers, Box 9, Folder 31.

53. Copy of "A Union Man" in Brown Papers, Box 14, Folder "Labor in Music." Copy of striker version of "Shipmates Stand Together" in Kraus Papers, Box 9, Folder 30.

54. Kraus, *Many and the Few*, 259.

55. Copy of song in Sugar Papers, Box 14, Folder 31.

56. "Strike Songs: Battle, Victory, Joy," *United Automobile Worker*, January 22, 1937, 7; *Flint Auto Worker*, February 6, 1937, 2.

57. Fine, *Sit-Down*, 158; Kraus, *Many and the Few*, 104.

58. *Rebel Song Book*; Kraus Papers, Box 9, Folder 31.

59. Merlin D. Bishop, interview by Jack Skeels, University of Michigan-Wayne State University Institute of Labor History and Industrial Relations, March 29, 1963, 8, 43, ALHUA. See also *Brookwood Chautauqua Songs*.

60. Denisoff, *Great Day Coming*, 32.

61. Page 15 of a typed copy of a report prepared by Merlin Bishop on "The Kelsey Hayes Sit-In Strike," in Bishop Papers, Box 1, Folder 11; Fine, *Sit-Down*, 132.

62. Vorse, *Labor's New Millions*, 76.

63. Kraus, *Many and the Few*, 103.

64. Fine, *Sit-Down*, 5-7, 132, 196-97.

65. Ibid., 5, 132, 196, 208; Kraus, *Many and the Few*, 103, 173, 181; *United Automobile Worker*, February 25, 1937, 11.

66. Fine, *Sit-Down*, 195-97.

67. Ibid., 9-10, 231, 233, 237, 246-59.

68. Ibid., 266-71; Kraus, *Many and the Few*, 189-208.

69. Kraus, *Many and the Few*, 207.

70. Vorse, *Labor's New Millions*, 77.

71. *Flint Auto Worker*, February 6, 1937, 3.

72. Fine, *Sit-Down*, 271–79. It should be noted that because the suit to evict the strikers was filed before Chevrolet No. 4 was taken, the injunction did not apply to that facility.

73. Ibid., 285–304. For John L. Lewis's role in the Flint strike negotiations, see Melvyn Dubofsky and Warren Van Tine, *John L. Lewis: A Biography* (New York: Quadrangle, 1977), 255–71; Robert H. Zieger, *John L. Lewis: Labor Leader* (Boston: Twayne, 1988), 90–92.

74. The UAWA is the United Automobile Workers of American, the same as the UAW.

75. Fine, *Sit-Down*, 190, 228. Copy of song in Kraus Papers, Box 9, Folder 31.

"Better Than a Hundred Speeches": Conclusion

1. Bishop interview, March 29, 1963, 43.

2. Pete Seeger, "Whatever Happened to Singing in the Unions?," *Sing Out!* 15 (May 1965): 28–31. For more recent comments by Seeger regarding singing in the labor movement, see Dave Elsila and Don Stillman, "Talking Union with Pete Seeger," *WorkingUSA* 1 (March-April 1998): 66–73.

3. Larkin, "Ella May's Songs," 382.

4. Quoted in the preface to Greenway, *American Folksongs of Protest*. This passage is also in John Steinbeck's foreword to Lomax, Guthrie, and Seeger, *Hard Hitting Songs*, 8.

Bibliography

Manuscript Collections

Archives of Labor History and Urban Affairs, Wayne State University, Detroit.

Merlin Bishop Papers

Joe Brown Papers

Henry Kraus Papers

Francis O'Rourke Diary, 1936-37

Bud Simons Papers

Maurice Sugar Papers

Mary Heaton Vorse Papers

Interviews

Bishop, Merlin D. Interview by Jack Skeels, March 29, 1963. University of Michigan, Wayne State University Institute of Labor History and Industrial Relations. Archives of Labor History and Urban Affairs, Detroit.

Newspapers, Periodicals, Pamphlets

Daily Worker. April 15, 1929-January 11, 1937.

Flint Auto Worker. December 1936-February 6, 1937.

Labor Defender. August 1929-November 1929.

Let's Stand Together: The Story of Ella Mae [sic] Wiggins. Charlotte, N.C.: Metrolina Chapter, National Organization of Women, 1979.

Nation 129 (July 30, 1929): 106.

New Republic 59 (July 24, 1929): 244.

United Auto Worker. January 22, 1937-February 25, 1937.

United States Government Publications

U.S. Congress. Senate. Committee on Manufacturers. *Conditions in Coal Fields in Harlan and Bell Counties, Kentucky, Hearings.* Senate Report 178, 72nd Congress, 1st session, 1932.

Songbooks

Brookwood Chautauqua Songs. Katonah, N.Y.: Brookwood Labor Publications, n.d.

I.W.W. Songs: Songs of the Workers to Fan the Flames of Discontent. 1st-35th eds. Chicago: I.W.W., 1909-76.

Rebel Song Book. New York: Rand School Press, 1935.

Bibliography

Recordings

Cohen , Ronald D., and Dave Samuelson, comps. and eds. *Songs for Political Action: Folkmusic, Topical Songs, and the American Left, 1926–1953*. Hamburg, Germany: Bear Family Records, 1996. Ten compact discs.

Dane, Barbara. *I Hate the Capitalist System*. Paredon Records P-1014, 1973. Notes by Barbara Dane and Iwrin Silber.

Greenway, John. *American Industrial Folksongs*. Riverside Records. RLP 12-607, 1956. Notes by John Greenway and Kenneth S. Goldstein.

———. *The Songs and Stories of Aunt Molly Jackson*. Folkways Records FH 5457, 1961. Songs performed by John Greenway. Stories told by Aunt Molly Jackson. Notes by John Greenway.

Gunning, Sarah Ogan. *Girl of Constant Sorrow*. Folk-Legacy Records FSA-26, 1965. Notes by Archie Green.

———. *The Silver Dagger*. Rounder Records 0051, 1976. Notes by Jim Garland and Mark Wilson.

Houston, Cisco. *Songs of the Open Road*. Folkways Records FA 2480, 1960. With notes.

Jackson, Aunt Molly. *Aunt Molly Jackson*. Library of Congress Recordings. Rounder Records 1002, 1972. With notes.

Newport Broadside: Topical Songs of the Newport Folk Festival, 1963. Vanguard Records VRS 9144, 1964. Notes by Stacey Williams.

Robinson, Earl. *Strange, Unusual Evening: A Santa Barbara Story*. United Auto Workers ER-101, 1971.

Seeger, Pete. *American Industrial Ballads*. Folkways Records FH 5251, 1956. Reissued, Smithsonian Folkways SF-40058, 1992. Notes by Irwin Silber.

———. *Songs of Struggle and Protest: 1930-1950*. Folkways Records FH 5233, 1964. Notes by Irwin Silber.

Songs and Ballads of the Anthracite Miner. Library of Congress AFS L16, 1964. Notes by George Korson.

Songs and Ballads of the Bituminous Miner. Library of Congress AFS L60, 1965. Notes by George Korson.

Songs for a Better Tomorrow. United Auto Workers, Education Department, 1963. Reissued 1986. Notes by Harry Fleischman.

They'll Never Keep Us Down: Women's Coal Mining Songs. Rounder Records 4012, 1984. Notes by Guy Carawan, Candie Carawan, and Helen Lewis.

Tucker, George, Sarah Ogan Gunning, Hazel Dickens, and Nimrod Workman. *Come All You Coal Miners*. Rounder Records 4005, 1973. With notes.

Films and Videotapes

Carawan, Guy, and Candie Carawan, eds. *Always Sing My Songs: Sarah Ogan Gunning at Highlander, 1972-1982*. New Market, Tenn.: Highlander Center for Social Research, 1983.

Goldfarb, Lyn, and Lorraine Gray. *With Babies and Banners: The Story of the Women's Emergency Brigade*. 1978.

Pickering, Mimi, prod., dir., and ed. *Dreadful Memories: The Life of Sarah Ogan Gunning*. Whitesburg, Ky.: Appalshop Films, 1988.

Bibliography

Sit Down and Fight: Walter Reuther and the Rise of the Auto Workers Union. In *The American Experience* series. PBS, 1993.

Dissertations and Theses

Grigsby, Ellen. "The Politics of Protest: Theoretical, Historical, and Literary Perspectives on Labor Conflict in Gaston County, North Carolina." Ph.D. diss., University of North Carolina at Chapel Hill, 1987.

Haessly, Lynn. " 'Mill Mother's Lament': Ella May, Working Women's Militancy, and the 1929 Gaston County Strikes." Master's thesis, University of North Carolina at Chapel Hill, 1987.

Hood, Robin. "The Loray Mill Strike." Master's thesis, University of North Carolina, 1932.

Sandler, Robert Lyle. " 'You Can Sell Your Body but Not Your Mind': A Sociolinguistic Examination of the Folklore on the Automobile Factory Assembly Line." Ph.D. diss., University of Pennsylvania, 1982.

Books

Abrahams, Roger D. *Singing the Master: The Emergence of African American Culture in the Plantation South.* New York: Pantheon Books, 1992. Reprint, New York: Penguin Books, 1993.

Adams, Frank, with Myles Horton. *Unearthing Seeds of Fire: The Idea of Highlander.* Winston-Salem, N.C.: John F. Blair, 1975.

Allen, Frederick Lewis. *Only Yesterday: An Informal History of the 1920's.* New York: Harper & Brothers, 1931. Reprint, Perennial Library, 1964.

Alloy, Evelyn. *Working Women's Music: The Songs and Struggles of Women in the Cotton Mills, Textile Plants and Needle Trades.* Somerville, Mass.: New England Free Press, 1976.

Anderson, Sherwood. *Beyond Desire.* New York: Horace Liveright, 1932.

Ayers, Edward L. *Vengeance and Justice: Crime and Punishment in the 19th-Century American South.* New York: Oxford University Press, 1984.

———. *The Promise of the New South: Life after Reconstruction.* New York: Oxford University Press, 1992.

Babson, Steve. *Building the Union: Skilled Workers and the Anglo-Gaelic Immigrants in the Rise of the UAW.* New Brunswick, N.J.: Rutgers University Press, 1991.

Baez, Joan. *And a Voice to Sing With: A Memoir.* New York: Summit Books, 1987.

Barnard, John. *Walter Reuther and the Rise of the Auto Workers.* Boston: Little, Brown, 1983.

Baron, Ava, ed. *Work Engendered: Toward a New History of American Labor.* Ithaca, N.Y.: Cornell University Press, 1991.

Batteau, Allen W. *The Invention of Appalachia.* Tucson: University of Arizona Press, 1990.

Beal, Fred E. *Proletarian Journey: New England, Gastonia, Moscow.* New York: Hillman-Curl, 1937. Reprint, Freeport, N.Y.: Books for Libraries Press, 1971.

Belden, Henry M., and Arthur Palmer Hudson, eds. *Folk Ballads from North Carolina.* Vol. 2 of *The Frank C. Brown Collection of North Carolina Folklore,* edited by Newman Ivey White. Durham, N.C.: Duke University Press, 1952-64.

———. *Folk Songs from North Carolina.* Vol. 3 of *The Frank C. Brown Collection of North Carolina Folklore,* edited by Newman Ivey White. Durham, N.C.: Duke University Press, 1952-64.

Bibliography

Benson, Carl, ed. *The Bob Dylan Companion: Four Decades of Commentary.* New York: Schirmer, 1998.

Bernstein, Irving. *The Lean Years: A History of the American Worker, 1920-1933.* Boston: Houghton Mifflin, 1960. Reprint, Baltimore: Penguin Books, 1966.

———. *Turbulent Years: A History of the American Worker, 1933-1941.* Boston: Houghton Mifflin, 1970.

———. *A Caring Society: The New Deal, the Worker, and the Great Depression.* Boston: Houghton Mifflin, 1985.

Bird, Stewart, Dan Georgakas, and Deborah Shaffer. *Solidarity Forever: An Oral History of the IWW.* Chicago: Lake View Press, 1985.

Blassingame, John W. *The Slave Community: Plantation Life in the Antebellum South.* Rev. ed. New York: Oxford University Press, 1979.

Blood-Patterson, Peter, ed. *Rise Up Singing.* Bethlehem, Pa.: Sing Out Corporation, 1988.

Botkin, B. A., ed. *Lay My Burden Down: A Folk History of Slavery.* Chicago: University of Chicago Press, 1945. Reprint, Athens: University of Georgia Press, 1989.

Brand, Oscar. *The Ballad Mongers: Rise of the Modern Folk Song.* New York: Funk and Wagnalls, 1962.

Buhle, Mary Jo, Paul Buhle, and Dan Georgakas, eds. *Encyclopedia of the American Left.* 2nd ed. New York: Oxford University Press, 1998.

Burke, Fielding [Olive Tilford Dargan]. *Call Home the Heart.* London: Longmans, 1932. Reprint, New York: Feminist Press, 1983.

Cantwell, Robert. *When We Were Good: The Folk Revival* Cambridge: Harvard University Press, 1996.

Carawan, Guy, and Candie Carawan, comps. and eds. *Sing for Freedom: The Story of the Civil Rights Movement through Its Songs.* Bethlehem, Pa.: Sing Out Corporation, 1990.

———. *Voices from the Mountains.* New York: Alfred A. Knopf, 1975. Reprint, Athens: University of Georgia Press, 1996.

Caudill, Harry M. *Night Comes to the Cumberlands: A Biography of a Depressed Area.* Boston: Little, Brown, 1963.

———. *Theirs Be the Power: The Moguls of Eastern Kentucky.* Urbana: University of Illinois Press, 1983.

Cayton, Mary Kupiec, Elliott J. Gorn, and Peter W. Williams, eds. *Encyclopedia of American Social History.* Vol. 2. New York: Charles Scribner's Sons, 1993.

Chaplin, Ralph. *Wobbly: The Rough and Tumble Story of an American Radical.* Chicago: University of Chicago Press, 1948.

Chinoy, Ely. *Automobile Workers and the American Dream.* Garden City, N.Y.: Doubleday, 1955.

Cochran, Bert. *Labor and Communism: The Conflict that Shaped American Unions.* Princeton, N.J.: Princeton University Press, 1977.

Cohen, Lizabeth. *Making a New Deal: Industrial Workers in Chicago, 1919-1939.* Cambridge: Cambridge University Press, 1990.

Cohen, Ronald D., ed. *"Wasn't That a Time!": Firsthand Accounts of the Folk Music Revival.* Metuchen, N.J.: Scarecrow Press, 1995.

Cohen, Ronald D., and Dave Samuelson, comps. and eds. *Songs for Political Action: Folkmusic,*

Bibliography

Topical Songs, and the American Left, 1926-1953. Hamburg, Germany: Bear Family Records, 1996.

Commons, John R., David J. Saposs, Helen Sumner, E. B. Mittelman, H. E. Hoagland, John B. Andrews, and Selig Perlman. *History of Labor in the United States*. 4 vols. New York: Macmillan, 1918-35. Reprint, New York: A. M. Kelley, 1966.

Condon, Mabel Green. *A History of Harlan County*. Nashville: Parthenon Press, 1962.

Dane, Barbara, and Irwin Silber, comps. and eds. *The Vietnam Songbook*. New York: The Guardian; distributed by Monthly Review Press, 1969.

Dawley, Alan. *Struggles for Justice: Social Responsibility and the Liberal State*. Cambridge: Belknap Press of Harvard University Press, 1991.

Denisoff, R. Serge. *Great Day Coming: Folk Music and the American Left*. Urbana: University of Illinois Press, 1971.

———. *Songs of Protest, War, and Peace: A Bibliography and Discography*. Santa Barbara, Calif.: American Bibliographical Center, Clio Press, 1973.

———. *Sing a Song of Social Significance*. 2nd ed. Bowling Green, Ohio: Bowling Green State University Press, 1983.

Denisoff, R. Serge, and Richard A. Peterson, eds. *The Sounds of Social Change: Studies in Popular Culture*. Chicago: Rand McNally, 1972.

De Turk, David A., and A. Poulin Jr., eds. *The American Folk Scene*. New York: Dell, 1967.

Dinnerstein, Leonard. *The Leo Frank Case*. New York: Columbia University Press, 1968.

Douglass, Frederick. *Narrative of the Life of Frederick Douglass, an American Slave*. 1845. Reprint, New York: Penguin Books, 1986.

Dubofsky, Melvyn. *We Shall Be All: A History of the Industrial Workers of the World*. New York: Quadrangle, 1969.

Dubofsky, Melvyn, and Warren Van Tine. *John L. Lewis: A Biography*. New York: Quadrangle, 1977.

Du Bois, W. E. B. *The Souls of Black Folk*. 1903. Reprint, New York: Bantam Books, 1989.

Dunaway, David King. *How Can I Keep from Singing: Pete Seeger*. New York: McGraw-Hill, 1981. Reprint, New York: Da Capo, 1990.

Dunne, William F. *Gastonia, Citadel of Class Struggle in the New South*. New York: Workers Library Publishers, 1929.

Dunson, Josh. *Freedom in the Air: Song Movements of the Sixties*. New York: International Publishers, 1965. Reprint, Westport, Conn.: Greenwood Press, 1980.

Earle, John R., Dean D. Knudsen, and Donald W. Shriver Jr. *Spindles and Spires: A Re-Study of Religion and Social Change in Gastonia*. Atlanta: John Knox Press, 1976.

Edsforth, Ronald. *Class Conflict and Cultural Consensus: The Making of a Mass Consumer Society in Flint, Michigan*. New Brunswick, N.J.: Rutgers University Press, 1987.

Elkins, Stanley. *Slavery: A Problem in American Institutional and Intellectual Life*. 2nd ed. Chicago: University of Chicago Press, 1968.

Eller, Ronald D. *Miners, Millhands, and Mountaineers: Industrialization of the Appalachian South, 1880-1930*. Knoxville: University of Tennessee Press, 1982.

Fine, Sidney. *The Automobile Under the Blue Eagle: Labor, Management, and the Automobile Manufacturing Code*. Ann Arbor: University of Michigan Press, 1963.

Bibliography

———. *Sit-Down: The General Motors Strike of 1936-1937*. Ann Arbor: University of Michigan Press, 1969.

———. *Frank Murphy: The New Deal Years*. Chicago: University of Chicago Press, 1979.

Fink, Gary M., and Merl E. Reed, eds. *Essays in Southern Labor History: Selected Papers, Southern Labor History Conference, 1976*. Westport, Conn.: Greenwood Press, 1977.

Fink, Leon. *In Search of the Working Class: Essays in American Labor History and Political Culture*. Urbana: University of Illinois Press, 1994.

Foner, Philip S. *The Industrial Workers of the World, 1905-1917*. New York: International Publishers, 1965.

———. *American Labor Songs of the Nineteenth Century*. Urbana: University of Illinois Press, 1975.

Ford, Thomas R., ed. *The Southern Appalachian Region: A Survey*. Lexington: University of Kentucky Press, 1962.

Fowke, Edith, and Joe Glazer. *Songs of Work and Protest*. New York: Dover, 1973.

Friedlander, Peter. *The Emergence of a UAW Local, 1936-1939: A Study in Class and Culture*. Pittsburgh: University of Pittsburgh Press, 1975.

Gabin, Nancy F. *Feminism in the Labor Movement: Women and the United Auto Workers, 1935-1975*. Ithaca, N.Y.: Cornell University Press, 1990.

Galenson, Walter. *The CIO Challenge to the AFL: A History of the American Labor Movement, 1935-1941*. Cambridge: Harvard University Press, 1960.

Gannes, Harry. *Kentucky Miners Fight*. N.p.: Workers International Relief, 1932.

Garland, Jim. *Welcome the Traveler Home: Jim Garland's Story of the Kentucky Mountains*. Edited by Julia S. Ardery. Lexington: University Press of Kentucky, 1983.

Garofalo, Reebee, ed. *Rockin' the Boat: Mass Music and Mass Movements*. Boston: South End Press, 1992.

Garrison, Dee. *Mary Heaton Vorse: The Life of an American Insurgent*. Philadelphia: Temple University Press, 1989.

Gartman, David. *Auto Slavery: The Labor Process in the American Automobile Industry*. New Brunswick, N.J.: Rutgers University Press, 1986.

Gaventa, John. *Power and Powerlessness: Quiescence and Rebellion in an Appalachian Valley*. Urbana: University of Illinois Press, 1980.

Genovese, Eugene D. *Roll, Jordan, Roll: The World the Slaves Made*. New York: Pantheon, 1974. Reprint, New York: Vintage Books, 1976.

Gillespie, Angus. *Folklorist of the Coal Fields: George Korson's Life and Work*. University Park: Pennsylvania State University Press, 1980.

Glazer, Tom. *Songs of Peace, Freedom and Protest*. New York: David McKay, 1970.

Green, Archie. *Only a Miner: Studies in Recorded Coal-Mining Songs*. Urbana: University of Illinois Press, 1972.

———. *Wobblies, Pile Butts, and Other Heroes: Laborlore Explorations*. Urbana: University of Illinois Press, 1993.

———, ed. *Songs about Work: Essays in Occupational Culture for Richard A. Reuss*. Bloomington: Indiana University Press, 1993.

Bibliography

Greenway, John. *American Folksongs of Protest*. Philadelphia: University of Pennsylvania Press, 1953. Reprint, New York: Octagon, 1972.

Guthrie, Woody. *Bound for Glory*. New York: E. P. Dutton, 1943. Reprint, New York: Penguin, 1983.

Gutman, Herbert G. *Work, Culture, and Society in Industrializing America*. New York: Vintage, 1977.

Halker, Clark D. *For Democracy, Workers, and God: Labor Song-Poems and Labor Protest, 1865-95*. Urbana: University of Illinois Press, 1991.

Hall, Jacquelyn Dowd, James Leloudis, Robert Korstad, Mary Murphy, Lu Ann Jones, and Christopher B. Daly. *Like a Family: The Making of a Southern Cotton Mill World*. Chapel Hill: University of North Carolina Press, 1987. Reprint, New York: W. W. Norton, 1989.

Hampton, Wayne. *Guerrilla Minstrels*. Knoxville: University of Tennessee Press, 1986.

Harap, Louis. *Social Roots of the Arts*. New York: International Publishers, 1949.

Henry, Mellinger Edward, comp. and ed. *Folk-Songs from the Southern Highlands*. New York: J. J. Augustin, 1938.

———, comp. *Songs Sung in the Southern Appalachians, Many of Them Illustrating Ballads in the Making*. London: Mitre Press, n.d.

Herring, Harriet L. *Welfare Work in Mill Villages*. Chapel Hill: University of North Carolina Press, 1929. Reprint, New York: Arno Press, 1971.

Hevener, John W. *Which Side Are You On?: The Harlan County Coal Miners, 1931-1939*. Urbana: University of Illinois Press, 1978.

Hicks, Granville, Michael Gold, Isidor Schneider, Joseph North, Paul Peters, and Alan Calmer, eds. *Proletarian Literature in the United States: An Anthology*. New York: International Publishers, 1935.

Hoffman, Claude E. *Sit-Down in Anderson: UAW Local 663, Anderson, Indiana*. Detroit: Wayne State University Press, 1968.

Howe, Irving, and B. J. Widick. *The UAW and Walter Reuther*. New York: Random House, 1949. Reprint, New York: Da Capo Press, 1973.

Jackson, Bruce, ed. *Folklore and Society: Essays in Honor of Benjamin A. Botkin*. Hatboro, Pa.: Folklore Associates, 1966. Reprint, Folcroft, Pa.: Folcroft Library Editions, 1978.

Johnson, Christopher H. *Maurice Sugar: Law, Labor, and the Left, 1912-1950*. Detroit: Wayne State University Press, 1988.

Johnson, James P. *The Politics of Soft Coal: The Bituminous Industry from World War I through the New Deal*. Urbana: University of Illinois Press, 1979.

Jones, G. C. *Growing Up Hard in Harlan County*. Lexington: University Press of Kentucky, 1985.

Kahn, Kathy. *Hillbilly Women*. Garden City, N.Y.: Doubleday, 1973.

Keeran, Roger. *The Communist Party and the Auto Workers' Unions*. Bloomington: Indiana University Press, 1980.

Kirby, Jack Temple. *Rural Worlds Lost: The American South, 1920-1960*. Baton Rouge: Louisiana State University Press, 1987.

Klehr, Harvey. *The Heyday of American Communism: The Depression Decade*. New York: Basic Books, 1984.

Klehr, Harvey, and John Earl Haynes, *The American Communist Movement: Storming Heaven Itself*. New York: Twanye, 1992.

Bibliography

Klein, Joe. *Woody Guthrie: A Life*. New York: Alfred A. Knopf, 1980.

Kornbluh, Joyce L., ed. *Rebel Voices: An I.W.W. Anthology*. Ann Arbor: University of Michigan Press, 1964.

Korson, George. *Songs and Ballads of the Anthracite Miner*. New York: Grafton Press, 1927.

———. *Minstrels of the Mine Patch: Songs and Stories of the Anthracite Industry*. Philadelphia: University of Pennsylvania Press, 1938. Reprint, Hatboro, Pa.: Folklore Associates, 1964.

———. *Coal Dust on the Fiddle: Songs and Stories of the Bituminous Industry*. Philadelphia: University of Pennsylvania Press, 1943. Reprint, Hatboro, Pa.: Folklore Associates, 1965.

Kraus, Henry. *The Many and the Few: A Chronicle of the Dynamic Auto Workers*. 2nd ed. Urbana: University of Illinois Press, 1985.

Kruchko, J. G. *The Birth of a Union Local: The History of UAW Local 674, Norwood, Ohio, 1933-1940*. Ithaca, N.Y.: New York School of Industrial and Labor Relations, Cornell University, 1972.

Lens, Sidney. *The Labor Wars: From the Molly Maguires to the Sitdowns*. Garden City, N.Y.: Doubleday, 1973.

Levine, Lawrence W. *Black Culture and Black Consciousness: Afro-American Folk Thought from Slavery to Freedom*. New York: Oxford University Press, 1977.

Levinson, Edward. *Labor on the March*. New York: University Books, 1956.

Lichtenstein, Nelson, and Stephen Meyer, eds. *On the Line: Essays in the History of Auto Work*. Urbana: University of Illinois Press, 1989.

Lieberman, Robbie. *"My Song Is My Weapon": People's Songs, American Communism, and the Politics of Culture, 1930-1950*. Urbana: University of Illinois Press, 1995.

Lomax, Alan, Woody Guthrie, and Pete Seeger, eds. *Hard Hitting Songs for Hard-Hit People*. New York: Oak Publications, 1967. Reprint, Lincoln: University of Nebraska Press, 1999.

Lomax, John A., and Alan Lomax, eds. *American Ballads and Folk Songs*. New York: Macmillan, 1934. Reprint, New York: Dover, 1994.

———, eds. *Folk Song U.S.A.: The 111 Best American Ballads*. New York: Duell, Sloan and Pearce, 1947. Reprint, New York: New American Library, 1975.

Long, Priscilla. *Where the Sun Never Shines: A History of America's Bloody Coal Industry*. New York: Paragon House, 1989.

Lumpkin, Grace. *To Make My Bread*. New York: Macauley, 1932.

Malone, Bill C. *Southern Music/American Music*. Lexington: University Press of Kentucky, 1979.

Marshall, F. Ray. *Labor in the South*. Cambridge: Harvard University Press, 1967.

McDonald, Lois. *Southern Mill Hills: A Study of Social and Economic Forces in Certain Textile Mill Villages*. New York: Alex L. Hillman, 1928.

McDonnell, John, ed. *Songs of Struggle and Protest*. Cork, Ireland: Mercier Press, 1979.

McLaurin, Melton Alonza. *Paternalism and Protest: Southern Cotton Mill Workers and Organized Labor, 1875-1905*. Westport, Conn.: Greenwood Publishing, 1971.

Meier, August, and Elliott Rudwick. *Black Detroit and the Rise of the UAW*. New York: Oxford University Press, 1979.

Miller, Marc S., ed. *Working Lives: The Southern Exposure History of Labor in the South*. New York: Pantheon, 1980.

Bibliography

Milton, David. *The Politics of U.S. Labor: From the Great Depression to the New Deal.* New York: Monthly Review Press, 1982.

Moody, J. Carroll, and Alice Kessler-Harris, eds. *Perspectives on American Labor History: The Problem of Synthesis.* DeKalb: Northern Illinois University Press, 1989.

Mortimer, Wyndham. *Organize!: My Life as a Union Man.* Edited by Leo Fenster. Boston: Beacon Press, 1971.

National Committee for the Defense of Political Prisoners. *Harlan Miners Speak: Report on Terrorism in the Kentucky Coal Fields.* New York: Harcourt, Brace, 1932. Reprint, New York: Da Capo Press, 1970.

The National Miners Union, Harlan and Bell Kentucky, 1931-32. Compilation from the *Labor Defender* and *Labor Age.* Huntington, W.Va.: Appalachian Movement Press, 1972.

Newby, I. A. *Plain Folk in the New South: Social Change and Cultural Persistence, 1880-1915.* Baton Rouge: Louisiana State University Press, 1989.

Page, Dorothy Myra. *Southern Cotton Mills and Labor.* New York: Workers Library Publishers, 1929.

———. *Gathering Storm: A Story of the Black Belt.* New York: International Publishers, 1932.

Pells, Richard H. *Radical Visions and American Dreams: Culture and Social Thought in the Depression Years.* Middletown, Conn.: Wesleyan University Press, 1973.

Perlman, Selig. *A Theory of the Labor Movement.* New York: Macmillan, 1928. Reprint, Philadelphia: Porcupine Press, 1979.

Pescatello, Ann M. *Charles Seeger: A Life in American Music.* Pittsburgh: University of Pittsburgh Press, 1992.

Peterson, Joyce Shaw. *American Automobile Workers, 1900-1933.* Albany: State University of New York Press, 1987.

Philbin, Marianne, ed. *Give Peace a Chance: Music and the Struggle for Peace.* Chicago: Chicago Review Press, 1983.

Pichaske, David. *A Generation in Motion: Popular Music and the Culture of the Sixties.* Granite Falls, Minn.: Ellis Press, 1989.

Pope, Liston. *Millhands and Preachers: A Study of Gastonia.* New Haven, Conn.: Yale University Press, 1965.

Portelli, Alessandro. *The Death of Luigi Trastulli and Other Stories: Form and Meaning in Oral History.* Albany: State University of New York Press, 1991.

Pound, Arthur. *Turning the Wheel: The Story of General Motors through Twenty-Five Years.* Garden City, N.Y.: Doubleday, Doran, 1934.

Preis, Art. *Labor's Giant Step: Twenty Years of the CIO.* New York: Pioneer Publishers, 1964.

Ragan, Robert A. *The Pioneer Cotton Mills of Gaston County, N.C.: The First Thirty.* Charlotte, N.C.: Robert A. Ragan, 1973.

Reuss, Richard A., ed. *Songs of American Labor, Industrialization, and the Urban Work Experience: A Discography.* Ann Arbor: Labor Studies Center, Institute of Labor and Industrialization, University of Michigan, 1983.

Reuss, Richard A., with JoAnne C. Reuss. *American Folk Music and Left-wing Politics, 1927-1957.* Lanham, Md.: Rowman and Littlefield, 2000.

Reuther, Victor G. *The Brothers Reuther and the Story of the UAW.* Boston: Houghton Mifflin, 1976.

Robinson, Earl, with Eric A. Gordon. *Ballad of an American: The Autobiography of Earl Robinson.* Lanham, Md.: Scarecrow Press, 1998.

Rollins, William. *The Shadow Before.* New York: Robert M. McBride, 1934.

Romalis, Shelly. *Pistol Packin' Mama: Aunt Molly Jackson and the Politics of Folksong.* Urbana: University of Illinois Press, 1999.

Rosenberg, Neil V., ed. *Transforming Tradition: Folk Music Revivals Examined.* Urbana: University of Illinois Press, 1993.

Ross, Malcolm H. *Machine Age in the Hills.* New York: Macmillan, 1933.

Salmond, John A. *Gastonia 1929: The Story of the Loray Mill Strike.* Chapel Hill: University of North Carolina Press, 1995.

Scarborough, Dorothy. *A Song Catcher in the Southern Mountains: American Folk Songs of British Ancestry.* New York: Columbia University Press, 1937. Reprint, New York: AMS Press, 1966.

Schumacher, Michael. *There But for Fortune: The Life of Phil Ochs.* New York: Hyperion, 1996.

Seeger, Pete, and Bob Reiser. *Carry It On!: A History in Song and Picture of the Working Men and Women of America.* New York: Simon and Schuster, 1985.

Shelton, Robert. *No Direction Home: The Life and Music of Bob Dylan.* New York: Beech Tree Books, 1986.

Shifflett, Crandall A. *Coal Towns: Life, Work, and Culture in Company Towns of Southern Appalachia, 1880-1969.* Knoxville: University of Tennessee Press, 1991.

Silber, Irwin, ed. *Reprints of the People's Songs Bulletin, 1946-1949.* New York: Oak Publications, 1961.

Silverman, Jerry. *The Liberated Woman's Songbook.* New York: Macmillan, 1971.

———, comp. *Songs of Protest and Civil Rights.* New York: Chelsea House, 1992.

Sloan, Alfred P., Jr. *My Years with General Motors.* Garden City, N.Y.: Doubleday, 1964.

Southern, Eileen. *The Music of Black Americans: A History.* 3rd ed. New York: W. W. Norton, 1997.

Stavis, Barrie, and Frank Harmon, eds. *The Songs of Joe Hill.* New York: Oak Publications, 1960.

Stieber, Jack. *Governing the UAW.* New York: John Wiley and Sons, 1962.

Taylor, Paul F. *Bloody Harlan: The United Mine Workers of America in Harlan County, Kentucky, 1931-1941.* Lanham, Md.: University Press of America, 1990.

Terkel, Studs. *Hard Times: An Oral History of the Great Depression.* New York: Pantheon, 1970.

Thomas, Jean. *Ballad Makin' in the Mountains of Kentucky.* New York: Henry Holt, 1939.

Thompson, Edward P. *The Making of the English Working Class.* New York: Vintage, 1966.

Tindall, George Brown. *The Emergence of the New South, 1913-1945.* Baton Rouge: Louisiana State University Press, 1967.

Tippett, Tom. *When Southern Labor Stirs.* New York: Jonathan Cape and Harrison Smith, 1931. Reprint, Huntington, W.Va.: Appalachian Movement Press, 1972.

Titler, George J. *Hell in Harlan.* Beckley, W.Va.: BJW Printers, n.d.

Tullos, Allen. *Habits of Industry: White Culture and the Transformation of the Carolina Piedmont.* Chapel Hill: University of North Carolina Press, 1989.

Vorse, Mary Heaton. *Strike!* New York: Horace Liveright, 1930. Reprint, Urbana: University of Illinois Press, 1991.

Bibliography

——. *Labor's New Millions*. New York: Modern Age Books, 1938.

——. *Rebel Pen: The Writings of Mary Heaton Vorse*. Edited by Dee Garrison. New York: Monthly Review Press, 1985.

Ware, Caroline, ed. *The Cultural Approach to History*. Port Washington, N.Y.: Kennicat Press, 1940.

Weisbord, Vera Buch. *A Radical Life*. Bloomington: Indiana University Press, 1977.

Wenner, Hilda E., and Elizabeth Freilicher. *Here's to the Women: 100 Songs for and about Women*. New York: Feminist Press, 1991.

Whisnant, David E. *All That Is Native and Fine: The Politics of Culture in an American Region*. Chapel Hill: University of North Carolina Press, 1983.

——. *Modernizing the Mountaineer: People Power and Planning in Appalachia*. Rev. ed. Knoxville: University of Tennessee Press, 1994.

Whitman, Wanda Willson. *Songs That Changed the World*. New York: Crown, 1970.

Widick, B. J., ed. *Auto Work and Its Discontents*. Baltimore: Johns Hopkins University Press, 1976.

Willens, Doris. *Lonesome Traveler: The Life of Lee Hays*. Lincoln: University of Nebraska Press, 1993.

Wolfe, Charles, and Kip Lornell. *The Life and Legend of Leadbelly*. New York: Da Capo Press, 1999.

Wright, Gavin. *Old South, New South: Revolutions in the Southern Economy since the Civil War*. New York: Basic Book, 1986. Reprint, Baton Rouge: Louisiana State University, 1996.

Wyatt-Brown, Bertram. *Southern Honor: Ethics and Behavior in the Old South*. New York: Oxford University Press, 1982.

Yellen, Samuel. *American Labor Struggles*. New York: Harcourt,Brace, 1936.

Zieger, Robert H. *American Workers, American Unions, 1920-1980*. Baltimore: Johns Hopkins University Press, 1986.

——. *John L. Lewis: Labor Leader*. Boston: Twayne, 1988.

——, ed. *Organized Labor in the Twentieth-Century South*. Knoxville: University of Tennessee Press, 1991.

Articles and Chapters

Anderson, Jay, ed. "George Korson Memorial Issue." *Keystone Folklore Quarterly* 16 (summer 1971).

Babson, Steve. "Pointing the Way: The Role of British and Irish Skilled Tradesmen in the Rise of the UAW." *Detroit in Perspective* 7 (spring 1983): 75-95.

——. "Class, Craft, and Culture: Tool and Die Makers and the Organization of the UAW." *Michigan Historical Review* 14 (spring 1988): 33-55.

Baker, Christina, and William J. Baker, "Shaking All the Corners of the Sky: The Global Response to the Gastonia Strike of 1929." *Canadian Review of American Studies* 21 (winter 1990): 321-31.

Baker, Ray Stannard. "The Revolutionary Strike." *American Magazine* (May 1912): 18-30C.

Barnicle, Mary Elizabeth. "Harry Simms: The Story behind This American Ballad." In liner notes to Pete Seeger, *Songs of Struggle and Protest: 1930-1950*. Folkways Records FH 5233, 1964, 3-4.

Bishop, Bill. "1931: The Battle of Evarts." *Southern Exposure* 4 (spring-summer 1976): 92-101.

Boryczka, Ray. "Seasons of Discontent: Auto Union Factionalism and the Motor Products Strike of 1935-1936." *Michigan History* 61 (1977): 3-32.

Bibliography

Botkin, B. A. "Folklore as a Neglected Source of Social History." In *The Cultural Approach to History*, edited by Caroline Ware, 308-15. Port Washington, N.Y.: Kennicat Press, 1940.

———. "The Folksong Revival: Cult or Culture?" In *The American Folk Scene*, edited by David A. De Turk and A. Poulin Jr., 95-100. New York: Dell, 1967.

Brazier, Richard. "The Story of the I.W.W.'s 'Little Red Songbook.'" *Labor History* 9 (winter 1968): 91-105.

Brody, David. "The Old Labor History and the New: In Search of an American Working Class." *Labor History* 20 (winter 1979): 111-26.

Bubka, Tony. "The Harlan County Coal Strike of 1931." *Labor History* 11 (winter 1970): 41-57.

Buhle, Mari Jo, and Paul Buhle. "The New Labor History at the Cultural Crossroads." *Journal of American History* 75 (June 1988): 151-57.

Coffin, Tristram. "Folksong of Social Protest: A Musical Mirage." *New York Folklore Quarterly* 14 (spring 1958): 3-10.

Dawley, Alan. "A Preface to Synthesis." *Labor History* 29 (summer 1988): 363-77.

DeNatale, Doug, and Glenn Hinson. "The Southern Textile Song Tradition Reconsidered." *Journal of Folklore Research* 28 (May-December 1991): 103-33.

Denisoff, R. Serge. "The Proletarian Renascence: The Folkness of the Ideological Folk." *Journal of American Folklore* 82 (January-March 1969): 51-65.

Draper, Theodore. "Gastonia Revisited." *Social Research* 39 (spring 1971): 3-29.

———. "Communists and Miners 1928-1933." *Dissent* 19 (spring 1972): 371-92.

Dubofsky, Melvin [Melvyn]. "Lost in a Fog: Labor Historians' Unrequited Search for a Synthesis." *Labor History* 32 (spring 1991): 295-300.

Dunaway, David King. "A Selected Bibliography: Protest Songs in the United States." *Folklore Forum* 10 (fall 1977): 8-25.

———. "Unsung Songs of Protest: The Composers Collective of New York." *New York Folklore* 5 (summer 1979): 1-19.

———. "Charles Seeger and Carl Sands: The Composers' Collective Years." *Ethnomusicology* 24 (1980): 159-68.

———. "Music and Politics in the United States." *Folk Music Journal* 5 (1987): 268-94.

Elsila, Dave, and Don Stillman. "Talking Union with Pete Seeger." *WorkingUSA* 1 (March-April 1998): 66-73.

Faires, Nora. "The Great Flint Sit-Down Strike as Theatre." *Radical History Review* 43 (January 1989): 121-35.

Faler, Paul G. "Working Class Historiography." *Radical America* 3 (March 1969): 56-68.

Filene, Benjamin. "'Our Singing Country': John and Alan Lomax, Leadbelly, and the Construction of an American Past." *American Quarterly* 43 (December 1991): 602-24.

Fine, Sidney. "The General Motors Sit-Down Strike: A Re-examination." *American Historical Review* 70 (April 1965): 691-713.

Ford, Thomas R. "The Passing of Provincialism." In *The Southern Appalachian Region: A Survey*, edited by Thomas R. Ford, 7-34. Lexington: University of Kentucky Press, 1962.

Frederickson, Mary E. "Heroines and Girl Strikers: Gender Issues and Organized Labor in the Twentieth-Century American South." In *Organized Labor in the Twentieth-Century South*, edited by Robert H. Zieger, 84-112. Knoxville: University of Tennessee Press, 1991.

Bibliography

Frederickson, Mary E., and Timothy P. Lynch. "Labor: The Great Depression to the 1990s." In *Encyclopedia of American Social History*. Vol. 2, edited by Mary Kupiec Cayton, Elliott J. Gorn, and Peter W. Williams, 1475-94. New York: Charles Scribner's Sons, 1993.

"The Gastonia Strikers' Case." *Harvard Law Review* 44 (May 1931): 1118-24.

Gillespie, Angus K. "Folklore and Labor: An Intellectual Context for the Work of George Korson." *Keystone Folklore Quarterly* 23 (fall 1979): 11-27.

Grauman, Lawrence, Jr. " 'That Little Ugly Running Sore': Some Observations on the Participation of American Writers in the Investigations of Conditions in the Harlan and Bell County, Kentucky, Coal Fields, 1931-32." *Filson Club History Quarterly* 36 (October 1962): 340-54.

Green, Archie. "The Death of Mother Jones." *Labor History* 1 (winter 1960): 68-80.

——. "A Great Rebel Passes On." *Sing Out!* 10 (December-January 1960-61): 31-32.

——. "Born on Picketlines, Textile Workers' Songs Are Woven into History." *Textile Labor* 22 (April 1961): 3-5.

——. "A Discography of American Labor Union Songs." *New York Folklore Quarterly* 17 (fall 1961): 186-93.

——. "A Discography of American Coal Miners' Songs." *Labor History* 2 (winter 1961): 101-15.

——. "American Labor Lore: Its Meanings and Uses." *Industrial Relations* 4 (February 1965): 51-69.

——. "Folksong on Records." *Western Folklore* 27 (January 1968): 68-76.

——. "George Korson and Industrial Folklore." *Keystone Folklore Quarterly* 16 (summer 1971): 53-63.

——. "Industrial Lore: A Bibliographic-Semantic Query." *Western Folklore* 37 (July 1978): 213-44.

——. "Charles Louis Seeger (1886-1979)." *Journal of American Folklore* 92 (October-December 1982): 391-99.

——. "Working with Laborlore." *Labor's Heritage* 1 (July 1989): 66-75.

——. "Labor Song: An Ambiguous Legacy." *Journal of Folklore Research* 28 (May-December 1991): 93-102.

——, spec. ed. "Aunt Molly Jackson Memorial Issue." *Kentucky Folklore Record* 7 (October 1961).

Greenway, John. "Aunt Molly Jackson and Robin Hood: A Study of Folk Re-Creation." *Journal of American Folklore* 69 (January-March 1956): 23-38.

——. "Folk Songs as Socio-Historical Documents." *Western Folklore* 9 (January 1960): 1-9.

Gunning, Sarah Ogan. "My Name Is Sarah Ogan Gunning. . . ." *Sing Out!* 25 (July-August 1976): 15-17.

Hall, Jacquelyn Dowd. "Disorderly Women: Gender and Labor Militancy in the Appalachian South." *Journal of American History* 73 (September 1986): 354-82.

Hall, Jacquelyn Dowd, Robert Korstad, and James Leloudis. "Cotton Mill People: Work, Community, and Protest in the Textile South, 1880-1940." *American Historical Review* 91 (April 1986): 245-86.

Hendrix, Bertha. "I Was in the Gastonia Strike." In *Working Lives: The Southern Exposure History of Labor in the South*, edited by Marc S. Miller, 169-72. New York: Pantheon, 1980.

Herring, Neill, and Sue Thrasher. "UAW Sit-down Strike: Atlanta, 1936." *Southern Exposure* 1 (fall-winter 1974): 63-83.

Hodges, James A. "Challenge to the New South: The Great Textile Strike in Elizabethton, Tennessee, 1929." *Tennessee Historical Quarterly* 23 (December 1964): 343-57.

Bibliography

Howard, J. Woodford, Jr. "Frank Murphy and the Sit-Down Strikes of 1937." *Labor History* 1 (spring 1960): 103-40.

Huber, Patrick. " 'Battle Songs of the Southern Class Struggle': Songs of the Gastonia Textile Strike of 1929." *Southern Cultures* 4 (summer 1998): 109-22.

Joyner, Charles W. "Up in Old Loray: Folkways of Violence in the Gastonia Strike." *North Carolina Folklore* 12 (December 1964): 20-24.

Karman, Thomas A. "The Flint Sit-Down Strike." *Michigan History* 46 (June, September 1962): 97-125, 223-50.

Kazin, Michael, Alice Kessler-Harris, David Montgomery, Bruce Nelson, and Daniel Nelson. "The Limits of Union-Centered History: Responses to Howard Kimeldorf." *Labor History* 32 (winter 1991): 104-27.

Kimeldorf, Howard. "Bringing Unions Back In (Or Why We Need a New Old Labor History)." *Labor History* 32 (winter 1991): 91-103.

Kizer, Elizabeth J. "Protest Song Lyrics as Rhetoric." *Popular Music and Society* 9 (1983): 3-11.

Knupp, Ralph E. "A Time for Every Purpose Under Heaven: Rhetorical Dimensions of Protest Music." *Southern Speech Communication Journal* 46 (summer 1981): 377-89.

Krueger, Thomas A. "American Labor Historiography, Old and New: A Review Essay." *Journal of Social History* 4 (spring 1971): 277-85.

Larkin, Margaret. "Ella May's Songs." *Nation* 129 (October 9, 1929): 382-83.

———. "The Story of Ella May." *New Masses* 5 (November 1929): 3-4.

———. "Tragedy in North Carolina." *North American Review* 208 (1929): 686-90.

Lemisch, Jesse, and John K. Alexander. "The White Oaks, Jack Tar, and the Concept of the 'Inarticulate.' " *William and Mary Quarterly* 29 (January 1972): 109-42.

Lewis, George H. "Social Class and Cultural Communication: An Analysis of Song Lyrics." *Popular Music and Society* 5 (1977): 23-30.

Lichtenstein, Nelson. "Auto Worker Militancy and the Structure of Factory Life, 1937-1955." *Journal of American History* 67 (September 1980): 335-53.

Lieberman, Robbie. "People's Songs: American Communism and the Politics of Culture." *Radical History Review* 36 (September 1986): 63-78.

Lovell, John. "The Significance of the Negro Spiritual." *Journal of Negro Education* 8 (October 1939): 634-43.

Lynch, Timothy P. " 'Sit Down! Sit Down!': Songs of the General Motors Sit-Down Strike, 1936-1937." *Michigan Historical Review* 22 (fall 1996): 1-47.

MacLean, Nancy. "The Leo Frank Case Reconsidered: Gender and Sexual Politics in the Making of Reactionary Populism." *Journal of American History* 78 (December 1991): 917-48.

Martin, Charles H. "The International Labor Defense." In *Encyclopedia of the American Left*, edited by Mary Jo Buhle, Paul Buhle, and Dan Georgakas, 368-70. 2nd ed. New York: Oxford University Press, 1998.

Miller, Lloyd. "The Sound of Protest." *Case Western Reserve Journal of Sociology* 1 (June 1967): 41-52.

Mondak, Jeffery J. "Protest Music as Political Persuasion." *Popular Music and Society* 12 (fall 1988): 25-38.

Bibliography

Montgomery, David. "To Study the People: The American Working Class." *Labor History* 21 (fall 1980): 485-512.

Nelson, Daniel. "How the UAW Grew." *Labor History* 35 (winter 1994): 5-24.

Newman, Dale. "Work and Community Life in a Southern Textile Town." *Labor History* 19 (spring 1978): 204-25.

Nolan, Dennis R., and Donald E. Jonas. "Textile Unionism in the Piedmont, 1901-1932." In *Essays in Southern Labor History: Selected Papers, Southern Labor History Conference, 1976*, edited by Gary M. Fink and Merl E. Reed, 48-79. Westport, Conn.: Greenwood Press, 1977.

Ozanne, Robert. "Trends in American Labor History." *Labor History* 21 (fall 1980): 513-21.

Raynor, Bruce. "Unionism in the Southern Textile Industry: An Overview." In *Essays in Southern Labor History: Selected Papers, Southern Labor History Conference, 1976*, edited by Gary M. Fink and Merl E. Reed, 80-99. Westport, Conn.: Greenwood Press, 1977.

Reeve, Carl. "The Great Gastonia Textile Strike." *Political Affairs* 63 (March 1984): 37-40.

Reilly, John M. "Images of Gastonia: A Revolutionary Chapter in American Social Fiction." *Georgia Review* 28 (fall 1974): 498-517.

Reuss, Richard A. "The Roots of American Left-Wing Interest in Folksong." *Labor History* 12 (spring 1971): 259-79.

———. "Folk Music and Social Conscience: The Musical Odyssey of Charles Seeger." *Western Folklore* 38 (October 1979): 221-38.

Rodnitzky, Jerome L. "The Evolution of the American Protest Song." *Journal of Popular Culture* 3 (summer 1969): 35-45.

———. "The Decline of Contemporary Protest Music." *Popular Music and Society* 1 (fall 1971): 44-50.

———. "The New Revivalism: American Protest Songs, 1945-1968." *South Atlantic Quarterly* 70 (winter 1971): 13-21.

Rosenfeld, Paul. "Folk Music and Culture Politics." *Modern Music* 17 (October-November 1939): 18-24.

Scott, Joan Wallach. "On Language, Gender, and Working-Class History." *International Labor and Working Class History* 31 (spring 1987): 1-13.

Sears, Stephen W. " 'Shut the Goddam Plant!': The Great Sit-Down Strike that Transformed American Industry." *American Heritage* 33 (April-May 1982): 49-64.

Seeger, Charles. "On Proletarian Music." *Modern Music* 11 (March-April 1934): 120-27.

———. "Folk Music as a Source of Social History." In *The Cultural Approach to History*, edited by Caroline Ware, 316-23. Port Washington, N.Y.: Kennicat Press, 1940.

Seeger, Pete. "Whatever Happened to Singing in the Unions?" *Sing Out!* 15 (May 1965): 28-31.

Stachel, Jack. "Lessons of Two Recent Strikes." *Communist* 11 (June 1932): 527-36.

Stanford, Ron. " 'Which Side Are You On?': An Interview with Florence Reece." *Sing Out!* 20 (July-August 1971): 13-15.

Stuckey, Sterling. "Through the Prism of Folklore: The Black Ethos in Slavery." *Massachusetts Review* 9 (summer 1968): 417-37.

Urgo, Joseph R. "Proletarian Literature and Feminism: The Gastonia Novels and Feminist Protest." *Minnesota Review*, n.s. 24 (spring 1985): 64-83.

Bibliography

Vorse, Mary Heaton. "Gastonia." In *Rebel Pen: The Writings of Mary Heaton Vorse*, edited by Dee Garrison, 112-27. New York: Monthly Review Press, 1985.

——. "Soldiers Everywhere in Flint; Unionists Hold the Fort." In *Rebel Pen: The Writings of Mary Heaton Vorse*, edited by Dee Garrison, 179-80. New York: Monthly Review Press, 1985.

Weisbord, Vera Buch. "Gastonia 1929: Strike at the Loray Mill." *Southern Exposure* 1 (fall-winter 1974): 185-203.

West, Kenneth B. " 'On the Line': Rank and File Reminiscences of Working Conditions and the General Motors Sit-Down Strike of 1936-37." *Michigan Historical Review* 12 (spring 1986): 57-82.

——. "Standard Cotton Products and the General Motors Sit-Down Strike: Some 'Forgotten Men' Remembered." *Michigan Historical Review* 14 (spring 1988): 57-73.

Wiley, Stephen R. "Songs of the Gastonia Textile Strike of 1929: Models of and for Southern Working-Class Women's Militancy." *North Carolina Folklore Journal* 30 (fall-winter 1982): 87-98.

Yurchenco, Henrietta. "Trouble in the Mines: A History in Song and Story by Women of Appalachia." *American Music* 9 (summer 1991): 209-24.

Zieger, Robert H. "Workers and Scholars: Recent Trends in American Labor Historiography." *Labor History* 13 (spring 1972): 245-66.

——. "Textile Workers and Historians." In *Organized Labor in the Twentieth-Century South*, edited by Robert H. Zieger, 35-59. Knoxville: University of Tennessee Press, 1991.

Index

References to illustrations appear in italics.

Index